Advance Praise for

The Declaration of Independent Filmmaking

"As inspiring as it is informative. Mark and Michael Polish have written the definitive 'how to' and 'how not to' book on independent filmmaking. Everything you always wanted to know but didn't know to ask is covered with expert knowledge and great self-deprecating humor. You must own this book."

—Bingham Ray, cofounder of October Films
and former president of United Artists

"A definitive guide to making movies outside the studio system, this book demystifies every step in the process, explaining the pros and cons of smart money versus dumb money, what you can achieve with wall paint and Styrofoam, and how to hire the best postproduction supervisor. It's thorough, well organized, and user-friendly. And even if you don't want to know the difference between Kino Flo tubes and 1200-watt HMI PARS, you'll get the total experience of making an independent film: exhausting, maddening, bankrupting, sure—but also exhilarating, inspiring, and worth every moment."

—Dawn Hudson, executive director/shill,
Film Independent (FIND)

"It comes as no surprise that Mark and Michael Polish have written such a valuable and essential book that lays out all the tools independent filmmakers need to realize their projects. These guys live in the real world: they spend their time making great movies, not talking about them. This is must reading for aspiring filmmakers everywhere."

—Len Amato, president of Spring Creek
Productions and producer of *Analyze This*

"In 1981 while on the shoot of *Once Upon a Time in America,* I was walking down a street in Italy with Sergio Leone on my right side and Federico Fellini on my left. I haven't since felt that sense of artistic wonder until Mark and Michael Polish were on either side of me on the shoot of *Northfork.*"

—James Woods

Praise for *Northfork*

"Another masterpiece: *Northfork,* by the Polish Brothers...A visionary epic set in Montana in the 1950s...A ghostly, evocative movie...After *Twin Falls Idaho,* here's more evidence that the Polish twins are the real thing."

—Roger Ebert,
Chicago Sun-Times

"A surreal and lyrical fable about loss, dreams, and the price of creating the future at the expense of the past."

—*Vanity Fair*

"Beautifully crafted."

—*USA Today*

"A magical mystery about the excavation of sacred objects and the inevitable expansion of the capitalist cosmos...Real, full-bodied moviemaking."

—*Variety*

"The Polish Brothers are at the forefront of new American cinema. They embody the true spirit of independent filmmaking."

—*MovieMaker*

"They don't make American filmmakers like the Polish Brothers anymore."
—Michael Barker,
copresident of Sony Pictures Classics

"The Polish Brothers' *Northfork* is a stunning masterpiece, an American Fellini."
—Ruth Vitale,
copresident of Paramount Classics

Praise for *Jackpot*

"Enigmatic... The acting is primo and the cinematography... is striking. The Polish Brothers have a moody, bizarrely humorous style reminiscent of David Lynch... but I think their mix of comedy and pathos works better."
—*Chicago Tribune*

"Small time has never been so sublime... Nothing's going to stop these guys."
—*The Philadelphia Inquirer*

"The Polish Brothers, who made the wonderfully atmospheric *Twin Falls Idaho,* are back in their stylistic element again."
—*The Washington Post*

Praise for *Twin Falls Idaho*

"Eerily effective... *Twin Falls Idaho* has style, gravity, and originality to spare."
—*The New York Times*

"*Twin Falls Idaho,* directed by Michael Polish, who cowrote with Mark, lulls us into a sort of vigilant trance with its sustained silences, murky lighting and languid music."

—*The Washington Post*

"In its quiet, dark, claustrophobic way, this is one of the best films of the year."

—Roger Ebert

"The brothers are as persuasive behind the camera as in front of it."

—*Los Angeles Times*

"Rarely have American independent filmmakers emerged with such a spellbinding first feature."

—New Directors/New Films: The Film Society of Lincoln Center and the Museum of Modern Art

"*Twin Falls Idaho* was the Rosetta stone of the 1999 Sundance Film Festival and one of the proudest acquisitions for Sony Pictures."

—Tom Bernard,
copresident of Sony Pictures Classics

The Declaration
of Independent Filmmaking

An Insider's Guide
to Making Movies
Outside of Hollywood

The Declaration of Independent Filmmaking

Mark Polish, Michael Polish, *and* Jonathan Sheldon

A Harvest Original

Harcourt, Inc.

Orlando Austin New York San Diego Toronto London

www.HarcourtBooks.com

Library of Congress Cataloging-in-Publication Data
Polish, Mark.
The declaration of independent filmmaking: an insider's guide to
making movies outside of Hollywood/Mark Polish, Michael Polish,
and Jonathan Sheldon.—1st Harvest ed.
p.   cm.
"A Harvest Original."
1. Motion pictures—Production and direction.   2. Independent
filmmakers.   I. Polish, Michael.   II. Sheldon, Jonathan.   III. Title.
PN1995.9.P7P57   2005
791.4302'3'023—dc22   2005008056
ISBN-13: 978-0156-02952-0   ISBN-10: 0-15-602952-9

Text set in Spectrum MT
Designed by Lydia D'moch

Printed in the United States of America

First edition
K J I H G F E D C B A

Cover photograph © the Polish Brothers, from the set of *Northfork*

Photo credits appear on page 311 and constitute a continuation of
the copyright page.

Contents

Preface   ix

Introduction: The Pipe Dream   1

1. What Makes a Film Independent?   7

2. Our First Day   15

3. Writing   27

4. Pricing Your Film   55

5. Financing Your Film   65

6. Preproduction   89

7. Casting   105

8. Production Design   123

9. Camera   143

10. Producing   161

11. Directing   175

12. Postproduction   193

13. Film Editing   203

14. Music   215

15. Sound   227

16. Independent Distribution   241

17. Welcome to Hollywood   259

Epilogue   267

Acknowledgments   271

Glossary   272

Movie Synopses   295

Index   298

Photo Credits   311

Perhaps it sounds ridiculous, but the best thing that young filmmakers should do is to get hold of a camera and some film and make a movie of any kind at all.

—Stanley Kubrick

The pledge/*Northfork*

Preface

By August 1776, nearly all fifty-six delegates to the Second Continental Congress had signed the Declaration of Independence, formally severing ties with the English monarchy of King George III. In signing, these men promised to uphold the principles Thomas Jefferson laid out in America's first document. They promised to uphold these principles at any cost.

Of the fifty-six men who signed the Declaration of Independence, the British captured and tortured five. Twelve signers' homes were burned. Seventeen lost all their property. Thomas Clark's sons were held and starved on a prison ship; when the British offered to release them in exchange for his desertion, Clark refused. Others lost their wives and children. Nine lost their lives from wounds inflicted in battle.

Our independent filmmaking experience doesn't compare to the sacrifices of our forefathers. We haven't been killed for our movies or physically tortured (though some bad reviews and hostile investor meetings have been torturous). We haven't had to live in hiding from the British army (though a few creditors on our films have tried similar tactics). The parallel is more abstract: implicit in any kind of independence from a status quo (whether the British monarchy or that other monarchy, Hollywood) is sacrifice. To make a real independent film where the filmmaker is in charge creatively, one must sacrifice personal, financial, and physical well-being.

Therefore, we name our book *The Declaration of Independent Filmmaking,* inspired by the sacrifices of the men and families who gave their lives for a society in which something purely creative like independent filmmaking can exist.

If you're seeking a book that romanticizes the adventures of moviemaking, this may not be the guide for you. This book is for those willing to forgo a visit to the dentist so they can instead buy film stock, or forgo a family vacation for the sake of having a few bucks each month to eat while they write their first screenplay.

As we've traveled for press junkets, festivals, and seminars, time and time again people ask how we made our independent films: how we raised the money, obtained the cast, found a distributor, so on and so forth. We typically give a few suggestions with anecdotes from our filmmaking experiences. While we're glad to share our independent film knowledge with those who ask, *really* explaining what goes into making an indie can't be accomplished in a short conversation. With that in mind, we wrote this book—a book that we looked for when we first thought of making a movie, but one that wasn't on the bookshelves. There wasn't even a *Chicken Soup for the Independent Filmmaker* or *Low-Budget Filmmaking for Dummies.* Thus, we wrote this book using our experiences making three indies to inform the independent film-making process. Throughout the book, we've chosen to discuss and reference our three independent films rather than speculate about how other indie films were made because we only have firsthand knowledge of our own financial and creative struggles. Still, while we've made three films, we feel there is much to learn and we don't pretend to know everything.

Whether you are a film student at an accredited university or a high school dropout with a love for movies, this book was written for anyone with a serious passion to make an independent film. We are not going to recommend or disavow film school. A higher education works well for some and for others it doesn't. Neither of us studied film in school, though one of us has a degree in fine arts. All of our indie film knowledge was learned through making films. We certainly hope our travails inspire, but at the same time you are going to have to find your own strength and path to make your movie. Getting your movie made will be an all-consuming grind, often overwhelming, but incredibly rewarding for those willing to put in the time. We have intentionally avoided writing a *Dr. Philmaking* book that prescribes quick know-it-all answers to the difficult problems you'll face while getting your first independent film made.

We have arranged this book in loose chronological order from screenplay conception to the distribution of an independent film. Certainly, this is not the only way to make an independent film or necessarily the best way, but it is a way that's worked for us. Whether you're a first-time filmmaker or simply interested in independent film production, we hope our insights and experiences making independent movies will guide you through the many adventures that lie in wait.

The Declaration
of Independent Filmmaking

Cement Slab City from the set/*Northfork*

Introduction: The Pipe Dream

We never set out to be independent filmmakers. We simply had stories that weren't being made or encouraged through the Hollywood studio system. For our first film, *Twin Falls Idaho,* we took a lot of meetings; no one in Hollywood wanted to make a film about Siamese twins by unknown first-time filmmakers with an unknown cast. On paper it doesn't sound like a very good bet. So we really became independent filmmakers by default: to make the movies we wanted to make, we had no choice but to make them independently.

Call it ambition or stupidity, but we not only set out to make one independent film but three, a trilogy. When we began this quest—moving to Los Angeles from northern California—we didn't have any family or friends connected to Hollywood. And yet, to date, we've managed to make three independent films, all of which were in the truest sense independently financed and later sold to major distributors and released around the world.

In the spring of 1997, we finished writing the first draft of our second screenplay, *Twin Falls Idaho,* and gave it to a handful of production companies. As responses started coming back to us, the difficulty in securing financing for a film about Siamese twins became very apparent. One production company was intrigued by the story of *Twin Falls Idaho* but had a laundry list of changes to go with it. And even if we implemented their notes, the production company wouldn't guarantee financing for the film.

By December 1997, after many months of getting nowhere with our *Twin Falls* screenplay, we were living in a dilapidated house in Hollywood, a teardown with peeling wallpaper, creaking floors, and rusted pipes. Having experienced the heartbreak of not getting our first screenplay, *Northfork,* off the ground and now with *Twin Falls* heading toward the same fate, our home was a perfect fit for our state of mind. Built in 1924 and fully loaded with a fur vault and massive iron safe, the house wasn't aging well even with its 1970s face-lift of aluminum windows, stucco, shag carpet, and floral wallpaper. Once upon a time, this house was probably a comfortable home for someone at the beginning of his or her career working in the newly minted town called Hollywoodland. But the house probably should have fallen when the "land" did. Time had not been kind to our hillside home; she was an aging actress, full of memories of a golden age. The plumbing was completely shot. Her arteries clogged. There was no hot water, and what cold water there was trickled meekly out of faucets constricted by layers of rust. And it seemed that Hollywood cared as little for us as it did our home. We decided to make some home repairs, and first on the list was the plumbing. We got a few estimates from Yellow Pages plumbers, who all bid the job at $5,000 or more.

We grew up helping our dad build houses. He was a pilot by trade but took providing his family's shelter literally. It was his hobby and, without a choice in the matter, became ours. Some parents see a twin birth as an unexpected mouth to feed; our father saw another free laborer to stack wood, sink nails, haul cinder block, and pull weeds. But despite our childhood of home construction, we had never tackled plumbing. By the time we were old enough to help our dad with a septic tank, we were clever enough to avoid the project altogether, not realizing then that we would end up in a house where showering was a daily dose of Chinese water torture.

Since we didn't have $5,000, we figured it was high time to learn how to plumb. We researched the materials needed, drew the floor plans, and started the laborious task of ripping out all the old galvanized steel piping. With the daily task of turning off the water main, we'd work from sunup till sundown, stopping only for the occasional meal at Dos Burritos on Hollywood Boulevard.

Here's the trick: water doesn't take electricity to get from the street to the kitchen faucet. It's all physics. It's regulated pressure coming into a line. To attain strong water pressure, the rule is to go from the street to the house and once inside to use as few ninety-degree turns as possible, reducing the pressure by turns only when absolutely needed.

After a long week of hard labor, we started to become respectable plumbers. If a prospective film investor wanted to take a meeting, we'd show up in our work boots. When a meeting seemed like a waste of time, we'd excuse ourselves, saying we had real waste to deal with at home. Instead of the film business dragging us down, we dragged ourselves down into coffin-sized spaces, sweating the pipes and soldering copper wire through cobwebs. On breaks we would look at each other covered in mud and say: "This sucks." And it did, but working on the bowels of this beat-up house was simultaneously unclogging our thinking on making our first film. After a couple of weeks of intensive plumbing repairs, as we laid foot after foot of copper pipe, maneuvering through the dirt, we finally discovered who was going to make our first independent film.

The moment of revelation came as we hovered over the kitchen sink. Turning the kitchen faucet on for the first time, a hot stream of San Fernando Valley–extorted water (see Roman Polanski's *Chinatown* for the backstory) gushed into the aluminum sink basin. It was beautiful and it was real, and we had done it for $500 and change. If we had the wherewithal to replumb an entire house, why couldn't we make our first independent film? It wasn't that plumbing made us filmmakers; it was the do-it-yourself attitude that came from making the condition we were in better.

Up to that point, all the investors we had met had put a huge price tag on making *Twin Falls Idaho*. They estimated the cost at above $5 million—way more capital than we could hope to find. Just as 90 percent of the plumbing estimates were time and labor, these proposed film budgets were inflated by the price of someone else's sweat equity and lack of ingenuity. We decided that instead of putting a price tag on our movie, we'd put a date on it. Then and there, we determined that June 1, 1998, would be the first day of principal photography. If we had only raised a few thousand dollars from friends and family, we'd make it for that and shoot the whole film in our house on weekends. At least we would have hot water.

Principal photography actually commenced on June 14, 1998, just two weeks past our target date. Once we committed ourselves to our project and began showing our conviction about its execution, a film crew jumped on board, actors wanted to participate, and even a film investor eventually signed on to finance the movie. Our enthusiasm became contagious.

The only one you can count on to get your film made is you. Left to chance and other people, your screenplay will likely collect dust and your film may never get made. So if you are attempting to make your first film, learn from our successes, and, equally, learn from our mistakes. If you hear yourself saying, "No one wants to make my movie," make sure that "no one" doesn't include you.

Where the buffalo roam/*Northfork*

1 | What Makes a Film Independent?

It's hard to say exactly what is or isn't an independent film. Most people think of financial limitations as the hallmark of an indie, but a low budget is by no means a definitive marker. If that were the case, pornography and soft-core cable movies would have to be considered independent films. Perhaps the best way to approach a definition is to define what independent film is *independent* of. Certainly, part of this is being unattached to the major **Hollywood studios,** Hollywood **micro-studios,** or **Hollywood production companies,** which ordinarily prioritize financial gain before artistic endeavor.

This should be seen for what it is. It is entirely understandable that with tens of millions of dollars on the line, profitability has to be an imperative for a studio and its film executives. To them, movies are products. To ensure

Hollywood studios:
Studios that make mostly expensive commercial films produced for mass entertainment and maximum profit. Like most big businesses, these are public companies with shareholders.

Micro-studios:
Usually a smaller film company within a larger one, charged with acquiring and sometimes producing commercially viable independents and broadly appealing foreign films.

Hollywood production companies: A separate entity or an adjunct to a studio that acquires book rights, develops screenplays, and funds film production.

profitability, studios **test-market** and edit a film accordingly, control the casting, make mandatory script changes, and demand contractual control over fundamental creative decisions that will have an impact on the essence of the film. Historically, the independent filmmakers' gospel has been to shun decisive creative interference. The films they made were, thus, divorced from the Hollywood studio system. An independent film was the way for a director to show a studio what he or she was capable of without its involvement.

Creative independence in the film world is risky because the chance of success is so remote. Of the thousands of films made each year with **private equity** (money that comes from an outside source), only a small number are accepted into the Sundance Film Festival or another major festival, and of those, even fewer get picked up for distribution. The ability to secure private equity often has more to do with the state of the economy than the quality of a screenplay. But for a first-time independent filmmaker, private equity is usually the only option to pursue. The creative upside to this is that being removed from the "hit-making" devices of Hollywood allows a young filmmaker to find his or her own voice. This is the other part of what *independent* connotes. Whatever the story, an independent film attempts to tell it in an original, visionary way. *Attempt* is the key word here, because it doesn't mean the film is brilliant or even good, but it does imply that the filmmaker is trying to express his or her vision as an artist. Of course, this is a subjective evaluation. However, we contend it is quite like the obscenity definition given by the late Supreme Court justice Potter Stewart: "You know it when you see it."

Unfortunately, this interpretive nature of independent film's definition has allowed virtually any movie that is just slightly left of center to hide in the oeuvre of independent film. Savvy Hollywood marketers now regularly label low-budget films, regardless of their artistic ambitions, as "indies." *Independent film* as a catch moniker is so broadly used nowadays that it has been reduced to the equivalent of a "fat-free" label on cheese. These "independent" studio films are directly affiliated with the Hollywood studios and were born through their devices. Not that they are all bad films, but many of them do not embody the values or the struggle of independent film.

Independent film started to become more of a brand than a movement by the mid-1990s, after several independent films crossed over into the mainstream. When Hollywood smells money, it soon invades. And why not? Hollywood saw a cheap product grossing ten, twenty, or even a hundred times its cost—and recognized a chance to turn a huge profit. Would-be commercial filmmakers saw an opportunity to show Hollywood that they didn't need big budgets to have a commercial success. Thus was the birth of what we call **cheap mainstream.** The success of cheap mainstream created a lottery-ticket market for independents where suddenly the little independent film festivals became a marketplace for selling indies to Hollywood. Independent film was no longer a small niche movement; it had become a brand. And indie success by Hollywood standards was measured by a film's

Test marketing: When a studio rents a theater, gives away tickets to a target audience, and then has the audience fill out a scorecard rating various elements from an actor's performance to the film's ending.

Cheap mainstream: A mainstream Hollywood story with universal appeal made on an independent budget.

crossover potential: whether it could eventually move from the art-house crowd to the masses.

While this book isn't intended as a history lesson on independent film, some historical perspective is worth researching. If you're interested, there are many thoroughly researched tomes chronicling the rise of New Wave cinema from Europe, through the beginning of American independent cinema, to present-day indie filmmaking. Our goal in writing this book was to illustrate a point about the realities of getting indies made in today's marketplace.

By 1997, when we were making our first film, *Twin Falls Idaho,* the indie atmosphere had wafted into the backyard of Hollywood. Even with our budget of $500,000, there was pressure from the investor and producers to make our movie more accessible, to create a film that would appeal to the malls of America. But we knew the story we wanted to tell wasn't right for a committee process of test marketing and editing. While we wanted to protect the investment, we felt we shouldn't have the kind of burden Hollywood puts on filmmakers making $20 or $30 million movies. Our first concerns were to protect our voice and vision as filmmakers, and we believed that *Twin Falls* would be a worthwhile film only if it was made without dubious compromises.

As we started to edit *Twin Falls,* there was a disagreement between the producers and us on how the film should be cut. It had to do with length and chronology. One producer suggested we start the film with a flashback and voice-over, which would have dumbed the story down for a mainstream crowd. While the producers' points could be valid from a commercial standpoint (other than the serious suggestion that we trim the film down to ninety minutes so that it could play on airplanes, which even Hollywood movies don't undertake until an airline has licensed the film), we simply disagreed.

Things became more contentious when *Twin Falls* was subjected to a private test screening, where one of the producers gave out scorecards to an invited audience so they could rate the film. Suddenly, we were being subjected to the mainstream marketing machine when that wasn't part of our original deal. Moreover, this didn't make sense for the film; the subject matter wasn't mainstream. There was no way we were going to rework this film into the standard Hollywood criteria, and, besides, we didn't have the money or resources to reshoot even if every scorecard wanted the same unanimous change. We knew that even if 80 percent of the audience didn't want one of the twins to die, we couldn't please them even if we had wanted to. Ultimately, the only thing the test screening accomplished was to make everyone involved very insecure about the choices we had made as filmmakers.

These types of conflicts are more the norm than the exception in today's independent film marketplace. Many filmmakers, after the Sundance high of screening (and for some of them selling) their movie in Park City, wake up to a nightmare of recuts and test marketing. Protecting the independence of a film doesn't stop after production is wrapped. Many independent filmmakers think that once they have **locked picture,** the war is over, that the film is creatively protected. But in reality, an indie is still vulnerable after it is sold and while the distributor is focused on selling the film.

Micro-studio

So it may be that independent film as a pure movement is now as outmoded as alternative rock was by the late 1990s. As is well documented, so-called independent studios regularly test-market their films, reedit them to audience response, and have a hand in the overall process of a film's making. Thus, while a film may be called an "indie" and credited to the sole vision of a director, a studio exec has surely left fingerprints all over the negative. Fortunately for many filmmakers, some of the executives who run the micro-studios have impeccable taste and will take a gamble on risky material. Still, many of the choices affecting the final creation of a director's and writer's vision are the businesspeople's, not the artist's.

We've been inside the micro-studios and have seen firsthand the process of how they make movies. One of their main goals is to hire bankable actors to protect their investment. It's a type of insurance policy: if all else fails, there is a built-in audience who will come out to see the movie. The logic is not hard to understand—plenty of subpar films grossed millions by riding on the coattails of a famous actor.

When we were casting our second film, *Jackpot,* we had a few talent agencies suggest some big names who were interested in the material, actors who had seen *Twin Falls* and wanted to work with us. We were flattered by some of the talent they were suggesting. If we had cast one of them, we would have certainly elevated the budget from $400,000 to at least a few million. With a bigger budget, we could have paid our actors more and had more money to shoot the film.

But we had written *Jackpot* specifically for Jon Gries and Garrett Morris, two talented actors but neither with marquee status. The choice: either make the film with the planned cast for very cheap or cast a movie star and make the picture for a sizable budget. As independent filmmakers, we opted to hire the actors who best fit the material. But if we had made *Jackpot* through a micro-studio, the execs would have insisted on having casting approval of the leads. This is why these so-called independent films coming out of the micro-studio system, while ostensibly more risky than Hollywood movies, actually share more with the Hollywood status quo than they do with the uncompromising spirit of independent filmmaking.

The distinction is important. If the *Twin Falls Idaho* screenplay had been bought by a studio and we had been allowed to make the movie for, say, $10 million, we probably would have done it, but we wouldn't have considered it an independent film. Surely, we would have been contractually bound to make some artistic compromises. We wouldn't have had the control that we had making a low-budget movie, and even that creative control was hard fought. A filmmaker's creative control works more than anything to separate an independent film from a studio film or cheap mainstream.

But the price you pay for creative freedom directing a film is having less money to make it. An art film equals danger for a sound-minded businessperson, and that's why independent films are made for as little money as possible. With the chance of success so low and the risk of losing one's investment so high, independent films are made for a fraction of what Hollywood movies cost. Now, if an indie turns out to be a great film and distributors come knocking, it's a big win for all the participants who took the gamble. An independent film investor will typically put in a set amount of money—and when the money is spent, the making of the movie is over, however imperfect it still may be.

> **San Fernando ending:** What becomes of a film after it has been test-marketed in the San Fernando Valley by a mixed crowd of supposedly average Americans. Following the screening a new ending is edited in at the studio's request. More likely than not, a sad ending becomes happy.

On the other hand, micro-studios acquiring or making independent films regularly pour more cash into the production. Numerous times a director feels a film is finished, but it's bought at a festival and treated like a first draft: reshot and then subjected to a **San Fernando ending.** A real independent film has to rise and fall on its own artistic choices and usually a meager budget. The money is spent, and what is on celluloid will inevitably be edited into your final film. That's also the beauty of it: it isn't filmmaking by committee. Independent film is an insular vision, protected from the commercial instincts of studio executives.

Through the whole process of getting *Twin Falls Idaho* made, we stayed true to the artistic thrust of the film. Whatever the film lacked, whatever flaws it still had, it was the film we wanted to make.

Mark and Michael Polish as Blake and Francis Falls/*Twin Falls Idaho*

2 | Our First Day

It's nine o'clock in the morning. We are walking to our first setup. Michele Hicks—who plays the female lead, Penny—walks beside us as our **cinematographer**, David Mullen, leads the pack. We have been on the set for an hour. The **call sheet** stated an 8:00 A.M. start time. We turn into a dim hallway. It feels like we are about to enter an arena; all the focus is about to fall on us. David gently says, "You know, this movie is riding on three unknowns"—meaning the three of us beside him. We knew David was a visualist, but he wants us to know he is also a realist. We continue our walk, climbing the stairs to the area we call our hotel. This is the bedroom set we will spend seven days shooting in, and out of the seventeen-day production schedule, Lacy Stages will house us for fourteen. There are dozens of

Call sheet: A production paper that lists the scenes to be shot that day, the call times and locations for cast and crew, and the elements required to shoot the scenes, such as props, extras, and special camera equipment. The next day's call sheet, usually the responsibility of the second assistant director, is updated throughout the day, and then given to cast and crew each night for the following day's schedule.

soundstages in Los Angeles. But none like Lacy Stages. Lacy wouldn't be considered an effective stage by most industry standards. It's more like an abandoned building. When we originally **scouted** Lacy Stages, it was known primarily for its low rents. There was a soft-core porn movie, a music video, and a low-budget film all shooting at the same time within a few feet of one another, a conveyor belt of low-budget moviemaking. And because Lacy Stages sits adjacent to the industrial part of downtown Los Angeles— a stone's throw from skid row—it feels low budget, the kind of place that would make for a perfect squat.

We wanted the story of *Twin Falls Idaho* to be situated anywhere but Los Angeles. If Siamese twins were living in L.A., they would probably be discovered quickly and immediately given their own television show. On top of this, Los Angeles has such a specific, unmistakable look—Spanish and craftsmen houses sprawling arbitrarily over the flats and the suburban sprawl of the valley, the city's skyscrapers condensed to a couple of square miles; it is a "just add water" city constructed without a plan.

Approaching the set, we meet a production assistant whose eyes are like the rest of the crew's—very concerned about the next seventeen days. She gives us our **sides** for the day.

From the set we go down to the end of the hallway and start to look at how we are going to shoot the twins coming out of the bathroom. The crew is buzzing around in a state of controlled chaos, making final adjustments. We discuss the shot with David, and he in turn tells the **gaffer** and **grips** what the first shot is going to look like.

The first person we greet on set is Andrew Coffing, our **first assistant director.** Andrew— who came to us via our former assistant director, who left after he couldn't stomach the seediness of our downtown Los Angeles location—has been working closely with the line producer to create a shooting schedule (the usual routine for a first AD). Andrew is the man to kick this movie shoot into gear, and his job is to keep it on schedule once it gets rolling. For this seventeen-day shoot, Andrew has a second assistant director, who helps him with the scheduling, and another second AD making sure the needed actors are on set.

Andrew escorts us to the bedroom set. We had been there some thirty minutes prior, mapping out the shot as filmmakers, then left for the makeup chair. We've returned as actors playing conjoined twins Blake and Francis Falls.

We have been asked numerous times: What is it like to make and act in the same film? Besides having no choice, this is like asking us what it's like being twins. We don't know any different. We have no basis for comparison. We cast ourselves in *Twin Falls Idaho* mainly because we couldn't imagine any other identical twins willing to strap themselves together in a double corset for three weeks. Making our Siamese twins look realistic required us to be painfully

Soundstages: Where movie sets are designed and built, usually a large space the size of a warehouse. Soundstages are built to prevent extraneous environmental sounds (such as freeway noise, dogs barking, traffic) from affecting the sound production. They often have open ceilings, allowing more flexible camera setups, easier lighting, and the use of movable walls or flats. Soundstages also often have built-in office space, which can be used for production offices, makeup and wardrobe space, art department space, and individual cast dressing rooms.

Sides: A reduced version of the script containing the pages of the day's shoot, enabling actors and the crew to eyeball the day's dialogue and scene setups without skimming through an entire script.

NORTHFORK

CREW CALL

8:00 AM

Check Individual Call Times on Back
No Forced Calls Without
Approval of Production Manager
Weather: Partly Sunny, No Precipitation
Little or No Wind
Sunrise: 6:00 AM   Sunset: 8:45 PM
HI: 50   LOW: 25

Polish Bros. Productions
Address
T:
F:
2nd AD: Name
Prod. Office—Phone number

Director: Michael Polish
Exec. Producer: Michel Shane
Producers: Mark Polish and Michael Polish
Line Producer: Todd King

Friday, May 10, 2002
Shooting day # 16 of 24
Production Leave: 6:30 AM
Breakfast Vans: 6:30 AM Leave
Last Van: 7:00 AM Leave
Breakfast RTS: 7:30 AM
Shooting Call: 8:30 AM
Crew Hotel: Extended Stay America
800 River Dr. South
Great Falls, MT 59405

SC#	SET	SYNOPSIS	PGS.	D/N	CAST	I/E	LOCATION
98	Homestead House–Happy bedroom	Happy sleeps	1/8	D4	6	I	Homestead House
101 pt	Homestead Bedroom/Upstairs	Gypsies help Walter up	4/8	D4	1,2,4,5,6	I	Young Ranch
36 pt	Homestead House	Irwin meets gypsies	3 3/8	D	4,5,6	I	Teton Co. Mt.
105	Homestead House	Happy opens wings	1 1/8	D4	4,5,6	I	Nearest Hospital
107	Homestead House	Happy transcribes/Flower reacts	3/8	D4	4,5,6	I	Benefis Health Care
109	Homestead House	Flower knows she has to go	1 2/8	D4	4,5,6	I	Great Falls, MT

ID	CAST	PART OF	SWF	PICK-UP	HAIR/MAKEUP	ON-SET	SCENES/NOTES
1	James Woods	Walter O'Brien	W	8:00 AM	9:00 AM	9:30 AM	101 pt
2	Mark Polish	Willis O'Brien	W	8:00 AM	9:00 AM	9:30 AM	101 pt
3	Duel Farnes	Irwin	W	1:00 PM/self-drive	2:00 PM	3:00 PM	119 pt
4	Daryl Hannah	Flower Hercules	W	per turnaround	per turnaround	per turnaround	101 pt, 36 pt, 105, 107, 109, 119 pt
5	Robin Sachs	Cup of Tea	W	per turnaround	per turnaround	per turnaround	101 pt, 36 pt, 105, 107, 109
6	Anthony Edwards	Happy	W	7:00 AM/self-drive	8:00 AM	8:30 AM	101 pt, 98, 36 pt, 105, 107, 109

ATMOSPHERE & STAND-INS	Loc./MU	SET	SPECIAL NOTES
2 stand-ins	7:30 A	7:45 A	Please be aware that weather conditions can change very quickly! Layered clothing and rain gear are advised. We will be outside so dress warmly.

SPECIAL INSTRUCTIONS

Makeup/Hair: Flower's Makeup, Irwin's Scars, Flower's Wig, Happy's Makeup, Happy's Wig, Sick Irwin

Art/Set Dressing: Antique furniture, big stray angels painting, musical instruments, Northfork painting, oil paintings, long wooden table

Grip/Electric: Scaffolding

Props: Irwin's leather case, Irwin's wings, jeweled coffee cup, large bible, leather catalog w.rice paper, music box, rifle & tranquilizers

Transpo: 1955 Ford Sedan

Special FX: Cup of Tea's teeth, Happy's Glasses and Hands

Wardrobe: Happy's suit, Irwin's costume, Flower's wardrobe, Cup of Tea's costume, Evac. Crew Suits and Fedoras

Special Equipment: Crash Pad

Additional Labor: studio teacher, SF/X supervisor

SC#	SET	SYNOPSIS	PGS.	D/N	CAST	I/E	LOCATION
		★★★★ ADVANCED SHOOTING SCHEDULE FOR MAY 11, 2002 ★★★★					
		Enjoy Your Day Off					
		★★★★ ADVANCED SHOOTING SCHEDULE FOR MAY 12, 2002 ★★★★					
7	Northfork Church	Father Harlan preaches	3/8	D 1 am	13	I/E	Northfork Church
9	Northfork Church	Hadfields drive up to church lot	2/8	D 1	3,13,20,21	E	Teton Co. Mt.
11	Northfork Church	Mr. Hadfield exits car, confronts Fr. Harlan	2/8	D 1	3,13,20,21	E	
12	Northfork Church	Mrs. Hadfield watches	1/8	D 1	3,13,20,21	E	
		★★★★ ADVANCED SHOOTING SCHEDULE FOR MAY 13, 2002 ★★★★					
montage	1955 Ford Sedan–Driving	Walter and Willis driving montage	1/8	D	1, 2	I/E	Downtown Augusta
40	Three Forks Diner	Men exit diner, Willis sees a scratch	3/8	D 2 am	1,2,9,10,11,12	E	Augusta, MT
A 40	Pillsbury Drugstore	The men see Harlan by drugstore	4/8	D 2	1,2,9,10,11,12,13	E	

UNIT PRODUCTION MANAGER	1ST ASSISTANT DIRECTOR	2ND ASSISTANT DIRECTOR
BRIGITTE MUELLER	**ANDREW COFFING**	**PETER CHRISTIAN WHITE**

| CALL SHEET | | | | | | | | | FRIDAY, MAY 10, 2002 |

"NORTHFORK"

ADVANCED SHOOTING SCHEDULE FOR MAY 11, 2002

No.	POSITION	NAME	CALL	No.	POSITION	NAME	CALL	No.	POSITION	NAME	CALL
	PRODUCTION				**HAIR/MAKEUP**				**OFFICE**		
1	DIRECTOR	MICHAEL POLISH	8:00A	1	KEY MAKEUP	BECKY COTTON	8:00A	1	LINE PRODUCER	TODD KING	O/C
1	1st AD	ANDREW COFFING	8:00A	1	KEY HAIR	ANDRE BLAISE	8:00A	1	UPM	BRIGITTE MUELLER	O/C
1	2nd AD	PETER CHRISTIAN WHITE	7:30A	1	ASST. HAIR/MU	STELLA NAZARI	8:00A	1	PROD. CORD.	JOHANNA NEMETH	UPM
1	2nd 2nd AD	COLLEEN WASSEL	7:30A					1	ASST. PROD. CORD.	LISA O'BRIEN	UPM
1	SET PA	JUAN PABLO REYES	7:30A					1	POLISH BROS ASST.	JONATHAN SHELDON	N/C
					WARDROBE			1	DIRECTORS ASST.	MAURY DUCHAMP	8:00A
1	SCRIPT SUPERV.	BETTY ANN CONARD	8:00A	1	COSTUME DES.	DANNY GLICKER	8:00A				
				1	WARD. SUPERV.	CHANDRA MOORE	8:00A				
	CAMERA			1	COSTUMER	KRISTEN WILLET	8:00A		**ACCOUNTING**		
1	DIR. OF PHOTOG	DAVID MULLEN	8:00A					1	ACCOUNTANT	BARBARA LONG	N/C
1	1st ASST.CAMERA	KEITH EISBERG	8:00A					1	CLERK	SCOTT HERRICK	N/C
1	2nd ASST.CAMERA	MARY STANKIEWICZ	8:00A		**ART**						
1	LOADER	SAL ALVAREZ	8:00A	1	PROD. DES.	ICHELLE SPITZIG	O/C		**LOCATIONS**		
1	2nd UNIT DIR.	ADAM REHMEIER	8:00A	1	CO-PROD. DES.	BRANDEE DELLARINGA	O/C				
1	2nd UNIT DP	JEFF GUZIAK	8:00A	1	ART DIRECTOR	DAVID STORM	O/C	1	MANAGER	RJ BURNS	O/C
1	2nd UNIT 1st AC	MARCUS LOPEZ	8:00A	1	SET DECORATOR	ERIN SMITH	PER I.S.				
1	VIDEOGRAPHER	MATT POLISH	8:00A	1	COORDINATOR	ROB MORTON	O/C		SECURITY	PER LOCATIONS	
1	STILL PHOTOG.	ANDRE BLAISE	O/C	1	SET DRESSER	RYER BALKA	PER I.S.		POLICE	PER LOCATIONS	
									FIRE SAFETY	PER LOCATIONS	
				1	PROPMASTER	CHAD BRAHNAM	8:00A		**POST PRODUCTION**		
				1	ASST. PROPS	SAM DEBREE	8:00A				
	ELECTRIC				**CONSTRUCTION**			1	EDITOR	LEO TROMBETTA	N/C
1	GAFFER	JP GABRIEL	8:00A	1	FOREMAN	DEL POLISH	O/C	1	ASST. EDITOR	JASON TUCKER	N/C
1	BEST BOY ELECTRIC	KRIST HAGER	8:00A	1	SCENIC	ROBYN RIVERS	PER I.S.				
1	ELECTRICIAN	CHRISTOPHER SMITH	8:00A	1	SCENIC	LANCE BAKER	PER I.S.		**SPECIAL EFFECTS**		
1	ELECTRICIAN	JULIA NIELSON	8:00A	1	SCENIC	JILL FORSYTH	PER I.S.	1	SPFX	GARY TUNNICLIFFE	8:00A
								1	SPX	MIKE REGAN	8:15A
								1	WEAPONS	TORRENCE HALL	N/C
	GRIP				**TRANSPORTATION**				**MEALS**		
1	KEY GRIP	BRIAN BRANTON	8:00A	1	COORDINATOR	MITCHELL BERGMAN	O/C				
1	BEST BOY GRIP	JASON McKNIGHT	8:00A	1	CAPTAIN	CHARLES GATSON	7:30A	1	CATERER	GOURMET GIRLS	
1	DOLLY GRIP	JOSH COHEN	8:00A	1	CAMERA TRUCK	BRET BERGMAN	MITCH	1	CHEF	TRUDY WALDO	
1	GRIP	RANDAL GRIMM	8:00A	1	PICT. CAR CORD.	FLEET FACKLAND	MITCH	1	CHEF	SYLVIA ROSTRON	
				1	PICT. CAR WRAN.	DWAYNE BOYER	MITCH	1	HELPER	JIM ROSTRON	
				1	HONEYWAGON#1	JEFF RENFRO	MITCH				
	SOUND			1	VAN DRIVER	CHRISTINE SCHUMAN	MITCH	1	CRAFT SERVICE	CURT AYERS	8:00A
1	SOUND MIXER	MATT NICOLAY	8:00A								
1	BOOM	MONROE CUMMINGS	8:00A						**ADDITIONAL PERSONNEL**		
1	UTILITY	ELI KAUFMAN	8:00A					1	MEDIC	DAEL NELSON	8:00A
								1	STUDIO TEACHER	RANDI GRAVES	
38	WALKIE-TALKIES							1	UTILITY STAND-IN	JUSTIN FATZ	8:00A
								1	UTILITY STAND-IN	IDA	8:00A
								1	CASTING	TINA BUCKINGHAM	O/C

ADDITIONAL NOTES

A massage therapist is available on Saturday to any crew member who would like to make an appointment. She will be available every Saturday (our day off) to soothe your battered body. Do yourself a favor and schedule an appointment as soon as possible, her book is filling up fast!

JIMMY WOODS QUOTE OF THE DAY

"You're not a visual person. That's why you're in the camera department."
—Jimmy Woods to Camera Department

"Would you like to try a Glicker?"
—Michael Polish, regarding Danny Glicker's new cookie creation

Gaffer: The chief electrician who works with the director of photography to execute the lighting of each scene.

Scouting and tech scouting: When the key crew, from director of photography to set designer, visit different locations to determine the ideal places to shoot the movie. Filming logistics (what special equipment will be needed because of location parameters), possible rental costs, and overall limits and benefits of a proposed location are discussed.

Recans: Film stock that has been opened, not used, and repackaged at a discount.

close together. While writing the screenplay, we studied different kinds of conjoined-twin fusions and decided that Blake and Francis would have a fused torso and share a middle leg. We drew a diagram of how we wanted the twins to be presented—having two arms and three legs—and researched what could be achieved visually. The easiest scenario involved employing CGI (computer-generated imagery). This idea was immediately dismissed, however, due to our limited $500,000 budget: the budget, all in, wouldn't pay for the necessary effects. So, instead, we spent time in front of a mirror, side by side, angling our bodies to hide our inner arms. What the camera didn't see would allow us to play the part. One of us had to stand slightly behind the other, making a leg disappear. This created the illusion we needed but only from the front; if we contorted just so, we could make the visual work. Walking in tandem was a whole other matter.

We are about to roll our first few feet of **raw film stock.** We're happy to say "raw"—as in new—because we had a disagreement with a producer some twenty-four hours before who had wanted us to use **recans.** But the money saved (about two grand) was hardly worth the risk of possibly damaged film. The cost to reshoot a scene, which we'd have to do if the recycled film was damaged, would be immeasurable. The cost includes not just labor and additional stage rentals but also the fact that we might never replicate the magic of the original take. When trying to cut costs, don't cut your intelligence.

The other reason we refused to accept cheap recans was that we had spent the previous week testing our stocks for an elaborate and unique processing and printing technique. It would have been insane to switch stocks after all that preparation.

We stand in our corset, dressed in full costume, which was tailor-made for Siamese twins (a truly double-breasted suit), ready for the first

Focus puller: The first assistant cameraman, who is responsible for adjusting the focus during the shot.

Rack focus: The changing of focus within a shot from one subject to another.

setup. This will show the twins in their everyday routine coming out of their bathroom. After lengthy discussions on how best to present what people could certainly perceive as a grotesque image, we have chosen to present the twins in a way that will distract the viewer from their freakish appearance: a tailored suit and tie, short-cropped hair.

We position ourselves behind the door. The camera sits in the opposite corner of the room, and behind it an anxious crew tends to last-minute details. The costume designer approaches us and thrusts a few more safety pins into the hidden pant leg to keep it out of the camera's sights. The **first assistant cameraman** (AC), who is also the **focus puller** on this shoot, gets his marks to **rack focus** while the **second assistant cameraman** secures the camera into position. Because we have a small crew, the second AC is also responsible for loading the **negative film** into the **magazines.**

Camera duties vary depending on the budget of a movie. There are movies where the **director of photography** (DP) doesn't operate the camera but has a **camera operator** on his team. For a studio picture, every crew member has a specific set of tasks that, in theory, should allow the production to move forward without delay. Such luxuries rarely exist in low-budget filmmaking. An indie's budget requires each member of the crew to do more than one job. You're not asking your cameraman to do makeup, but he or she may have to help light the scene, change the lenses, or do any of those extra things usually left to an assistant.

David (our DP) signals to us that the camera is nearly ready as the second assistant cameraman prepares the **slate** by writing in the scene number and take number.

Andrew, our first AD, is waiting for the makeup artist and costume designer to vanish off the set so we can make this shot happen. Up until now, the first hours of production have been smooth; the hotel set generally looks nice; the green paint is a bit darker than we imagined, but it's a minor point and now is not the time to discuss color swatches—it would be like a boxer in the ring not being happy with the color of his shorts. Now is time for the twins to convincingly walk out of the bathroom.

The AC holds the slate before we shoot a scene/*Northfork*

Prior to this three-legged stunt, the only other time we tried a tripod trek was as kids, when we'd enter into the potato sack race on the Fourth of July. Being brothers was the strength; being twins was the added advantage—putting our legs in a sack and hopping in a race is what we were born to do. The design for the Siamese twins was something a bit more complex. It required us to wrap ourselves together, to become one body, to move as one. But what to do with that extra leg when we walked? We tried to think in terms of an amputee and how, in the past, makeshift replacements worked as missing limbs. If we used a thin stick for a leg, it would be easier to hide. We needed a peg leg. To create this, we took an old professional-sized football and chopped it in half, and then grabbed a broomstick and cut it to size. The football fit nicely over a bent kneecap and the broomstick held enough weight. We felt like a double-headed Captain Bligh. When we took our first practice walk in our house, witnessed by a few friends, our first unstable step was met by the ground—we fell hard. With more practice we were able to grunt our way to believability. Learning to balance one of our legs on a stilt tucked discreetly behind our backs took weeks of practice, but it was the breakthrough that proved we could make our movie without special effects.

Slate: A hinged piece of wood, the size of a clipboard, struck together before a take to create a loud "clap" sound. The slate (sometimes referred to as the clapper or sticks) creates a visual and aural marker used later to match picture and sound.

Action: Two things must happen before you hear the almighty command. First, the camera has to have speed (the film has to run through the camera at the rate of twenty-four frames per second, unless beforehand you have decided to vary the speed for slow motion, etc.). Second, once the camera has speed, the sound needs to be at the same rate so that the picture and sound synchronize. If either element falls out of sync, you will have a dubbed foreign film on your hands: the actors' mouths won't match their dialogue.

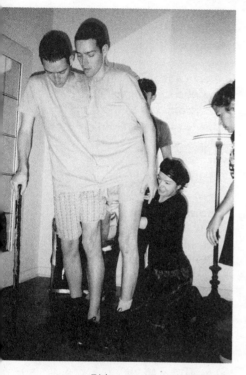

Trick or treat! Trying to hide Michael's leg/*Twin Falls Idaho*

All the departments are now ready. We are waiting for Andrew to call the word **"action"** (we have given him this responsibility while we are acting). The camera and sound are steadily at speed when the second AC goes in front of the camera to hold up the slate, clicking the sticks together. Our AD Andrew calls out, "Roll sound." Our sound mixer speaks into his recorder, "Scene seventeen, take one." As his recorder continues to roll, he calls out, "Sound speed." This means audio is now being recorded and is running at proper speed. "Sound speed" is also the cue for the assistant cameraman to start rolling film. Once the camera is running at twenty-four frames per second (this usually takes a second or two), we are ready to start. We grip each other at the waist, taking our first step on film together, teetering on the peg leg. It is one small step for us as Siamese twins and a giant step for us as filmmakers. Every muscle in our bodies is focused on keeping the peg leg stable. We use a cane to stabilize the effort, but the stick feels like a toothpick holding a weight-bearing wall. The twins really must look as if they have been conjoined for twenty-five years: a marriage of the flesh.

The pressure to nail the first shot has been compounded by years of trying to make this movie happen: the research, the rewrites, the agony of financing. We have a budget and a number of days to shoot, in this case $500,000 and seventeen days. Time and money are the two major limitations that face a first-time filmmaker, and usually every problem that arises in production comes from having either too little money or too little time, or too little of both as money commonly buys more time. If bad weather arises and you need to shoot another day, money buys that extra day. Without money, your sunny-day exterior shot has become your rainy-day exterior shot. Anytime you are knocked off your shooting schedule, you will spend more money.

One more step and we've crossed from the bathroom into our green bedroom. We've nearly made it through the first walking scene. Sheer will keeps us moving forward until we are at the edge of the room. Penny sits on a bed applying her makeup with her back to us as she witnesses Siamese twins for the first time through the reflection of her compact mirror. She turns around

> **Best boys:** Best boys are department liaisons. The best boys of each department work together. This is the case for art, production, grip, electric, and camera. The "seconds"—second assistant director, second AC, best boy grip, best boy electric, and art department coordinator—all coordinate and liaison with each other. The department heads for makeup, costume, locations, and others usually liaison for themselves.

to face us, visibly taken aback by our conjoinment, as the scene ends. The crew members share Penny's amazement at seeing us conjoined for the first time.

Although the scene has come together well, we still feel nervous about the many more steps these twins will have to take. We know we are walking a fine line between realism and a B movie titled *My Boyfriend Is a Siamese Twin.* But this line is ours to walk—and it is the line that all true independent filmmakers must walk when making their movies: an independent film succeeds or fails on the choices of its creators. There isn't a backup plan—a safety net—for independents. There isn't a band of executives approving your every move. The creative decisions are made by the filmmakers; the film's destiny is in the hands of its creators.

The Stallings Family/*Northfork*

3 | Writing

To our minds, writing the screenplay, whether for an independent or a Hollywood film, is the toughest part of the filmmaking process. A screenplay is your blueprint, your game plan, the map that gives you confidence and gives you direction throughout the journey of making your movie. An independent screenplay's success is determined by the dedication and perseverance to finding that highly rewarding place called *originality*. For an indie, originality should be the main ingredient since that is how an unknown screenplay can rise to the top of the heap. Original voices are what independent films should be about, and that starts with the screenplay. For a screenplay to be original, it doesn't necessarily mean its form and premise are breathtakingly new. The form of your screenplay should support the story.

Since nearly every conceivable premise has been expanded on in one way or another, your particular passion for the premise, your subtle take on it, will be the foundation of your screenplay's originality.

Along those lines, it is worth mentioning that there is a decent chance that the general premise of your screenplay, which you came up with all by yourself, is someone else's general premise, too. There is always a threat that your script will become outmoded by happenstance. However, if you truly are making an independent film, where your unique take on the subject matter is going to be fully expounded, a premise's general scope is not nearly as critical as it would be in a multimillion-dollar Hollywood picture, where a film needs to be able to be condensed into a one-sentence catchphrase.

While we were gearing up to write *Twin Falls Idaho,* we heard through the grapevine of two other projects that were currently being written about Siamese twins. Rather than rethink our story out of fear of the unknown, we kept expanding our seed concept just as we had before. We knew that the film we were going to make wasn't about Siamese twins, quintessentially. It wasn't going to be a biopic about the life of Chang and Eng Bunker. If that were the case, perhaps rethinking the relevance of our picture would have been in order. Unless your film's premise is wholly similar to someone else's finished screenplay, you should stay with the initial idea that inspired you to begin with, trusting that your own voice will differentiate your work.

The Ancient Art of Ty-Ping

There's one question you should answer before you write your first screenplay. Why am I undertaking this long, at times unavoidably painful, journey? When you commit yourself to becoming a screenwriter, you commit to a work life of solitary confinement. As a writer, you're checking yourself into your own personal prison, punching a keyboard rather than license plates.

Not that a writer's life isn't gratifying—you'll occasionally wander out to the yard, look up into the sky, and ponder your own existence. But screenwriting, truth be told, is a selfish enterprise. You may be seduced by the new world you're creating and suddenly your significant other isn't as significant. Getting your script written will take most of yourself away from everything else. All you have is you. And you can't flirt with becoming a screenwriter. You need to fully commit yourself to the long hours of dredging. That's why it is worth a little self-evaluation before you check yourself in.

It's not necessarily a bad thing to want accolades and a large paycheck, both of which come later, if they come at all for a screenwriter; however, at your essence, you ought to keep an intrinsic creative drive that supersedes those desires because superficial fuel won't last. You should want to share something deep in yourself, a side of your soul that you feel is worthy of someone else's consideration. Perhaps you'll be more comfortable working within the commercial restraints of mainstream entertainment. And that's okay; it certainly makes gauging a career a lot easier. Regardless, you need to know where you are coming from before you begin to write. Be honest with yourself, because you can't lie to the page. It will always win the staring contest.

A week myth: The bookshelves are lined with books by authors proclaiming that a great screenplay can be written in six to eight weeks. Some even profess an interval of as little as a month. That's only twenty-eight days if you start writing in February. The reality, though, is that there is no shortcut to researching and then writing a great script. If you rush, you might possibly get something that resembles a first draft, but it is doubtful it will be something you'll want to share with the outside world. A screenplay shouldn't be seen as a get-rich-quick scheme. One of the hardest battles you'll have to fight is getting people connected to the industry to read your material. You want your screenplay to be in the best shape possible.

"What if?" It's a small but loaded question. It's the best question to ask yourself when sitting down to start thinking of a story. "What if?" is the key that will open the door to all the possibilities for your story.

After taking a good long look at your motivations for writing a screenplay, you'll be able to better answer the question of what sort of film you ought to write.

Immaculate Conception

When we began thinking of writing our first feature film, we really didn't know where to start. Our film education took place sitting on a couch in Rocklin, a suburb of Sacramento, watching—via cable television—a wide variety of maverick films made in the 1970s and 1980s. Due to its lack of content, cable television would air a movie ten to fifteen times a month. Through repeated viewings, we could watch and learn what we loved about certain movies. Back then we didn't have a notion that we were going to be filmmakers. The films that caught our attention were stylistically all over the map, from Sergio Leone's *Once Upon a Time in America* to Steven Spielberg's *Jaws*. What we did find in all the movies we enjoyed was an original story that finely rendered an alternate world. Our interest was a mix of both tourism and escapism, as we traveled to an apocryphal future with *Mad Max* or the alien unknown with *Close Encounters*. The stories could be dressed up in anything, but at their core they were intriguing and unpredictable. They had us suspending our disbelief, but not our intelligence. It was this exaltation of invention that shaped our storytelling sensibilities. These imaginative films replaced the wonderment we had for Santa Claus with a new mythology of flawed heroes, foreign landscapes, and strange encounters.

So where does one begin? Well, the first thing we did was read a couple of screenwriting books, suggested by friends in the industry. They laid out the basic architecture of screenwriting. These books gave a recipe. The ingredients and how to mix them up were explained in detail and were pretty easy to follow. We could see how the recipe had been applied to many successful movies. The more we read, though, the more we felt the straitjacket getting tighter. We refused to believe that by page 10 "the reader" had to understand "the mission" of "the protagonist" or all was lost. The way we saw it, our imaginations were free-range and these books were barbwire restricting our creativity from wandering. We put the screen-writing books down and began to write from our gut, thinking many a karaoke singer can do a bang-on impression of Bob Dylan, but how many have developed their own voice and their own material?

Our first screenplay idea was really just a visual image of wings that had been cut off an angel. We flipped this image around in our heads for a while; these wings, we thought, what if these could be bought and displayed in the same fashion a hunter would display the head of a buffalo or an elk. A literary agent had seen the short

Pitching: When you tell someone verbally about the basics and highlights of your screenplay, you are "pitching" your script. A successful pitch is a colorful summation of the key plot points and characters that make up the story. A good pitch is often the key reason a screenplay will sell or a young writer will secure representation from a well-established literary agent. To communicate your proposed film's creative and financial worth is a very important element in getting any movie made. You should be able to tell your story persuasively, with a natural enthusiasm.

film we made and told us to call him when we had a completed script. Well, we didn't have a script, but we had an idea. We told him we were thinking of writing a script about angel wings being cut off, as if to taxidermy them, with a plot about salesmen going door to door selling them to the towns-folk as a religious token. We could tell he was struck by the strangeness of it, and he openly encouraged us to complete the screenplay—which we hadn't begun. In a way, we had just "**pitched**" our screenplay idea, and the positive response felt better than getting money. It was fuel for us to head back to our apartment, where we'd begin picking through our memories and pecking at the keys.

Although we had only some abstract images, we knew we wanted our film to be set in northern Montana. We felt that's where the buffalo had roamed. Why not a herd of angels? The theme of angels started us looking into their biblical background, and while there we began to notice that most religions had a flood that held great moral value. Our grandfather was a builder in this part of the country on the Hungry Horse Dam constructed in Montana in the 1940s and 1950s—a horse was abandoned there during the harsh winter, and when the workers returned the next spring, they named the dam after its emaciated state—and we had seen this dam up close as children and were taken with its awesome cement face and deafening mechanized whirl. On guided tours, black-and-white photos hung in the interior of the dam. They told the story of the land and lives that the lake covered. We began looking at the dam as a massive headstone. Our aim was to incorporate our angel-wing concept with the dam and its surrounding community. For a working title, we kept going back and forth between three names: *Southfork, Middlefork,* and *Northfork,* all rivers nearby. We eventually decided on *Northfork* because the prefix, *north,* fit well with the angelic theme we were developing. We felt we had reached the point where the kaleidoscope of ideas surrounding *Northfork,* though vague and just formed, made us want to explore the story further. This was a good indication that our initial spark, angel wings, was a gust of real creativity—enough, perhaps, to fill the sails of an entire screenplay.

Budget Cuts

The one major difference between writing a commercial screenplay and an independent screenplay is the budget. We read several books and heard from many people saying don't write with a budget in mind. That is not the right mind-set when writing an independent screenplay. Budget consideration should be at the forefront—especially if you already have an idea of what the budget will be. Our first draft of *Twin Falls Idaho* was written without a budget in mind; it included locations in South America, locomotives, and epic travel sequences. That first draft would have been an expensive movie to make, requiring a studio's

Cut it out: When faced with budget cuts, look for the heart of your story—what keeps the story beating, what keeps the story alive. If your main character is the heart of your story and isn't present in a scene, it's likely the scene can be cut.

participation. Once we got our initial feedback from our first draft, we knew we would never get a multimillion-dollar budget. So we started to design the story around having $500,000 or less. We removed the costly locations and expensive toys from the story. What was left was a screenplay that had minimal locations but still had a strong central story. We figured that five great-looking sets would be better than twenty-five mediocre ones. Yes, we lost some potentially beautiful wide-open scenes in foreign places, but what we gained from our limitations was priceless. What we didn't realize when we began condensing our story was that we were gaining an intense sense of claustrophobia. Blake and Francis were conjoined and now locked together in a hotel room—heightening their physical deformity.

With three intertwining stories, *Northfork* is a large cast on an epic landscape. We designed the screenplay to have the look and feel of a huge and expansive movie on the surface, but the heart of *Northfork* is actually small in size. It has two main locations: the orphanage and the gypsy house. Between them is a father and son driving through the mountainous landscape that is Montana. This space gives the two storylines some breathing room and makes *Northfork* epic in scope without the expense.

Council

...ollywood demands condensable, star-driven plotlines written in a ...ied-and-true manner, independent screenwriters are free to write obscure stories and tell them in unconventional ways. An independent writer's approach, then, to theme and structure is bound only by his or her artistic preferences. Though, generally, a successful writer's *style* will naturally complement the scope and scheme of the story. This is one measure of a well-conceived independent script: if the script is telling a unique story, does the writer's *style* reinforce it?

Learning how the great screenwriters differ in style is best apprehended by reading their works. It is easy to obtain them by either purchasing them online or going locally to a film-oriented bookstore. Even major bookstores such as Barnes & Noble and Borders now carry script collections, featuring several or all of the screenplays written by a celebrated screenwriter, many of them independent. After you finish reading a screenplay, watch the film. If a scene confounds you while reading, watch how the director interpreted it. The writer's style, the synthesis of structure and story, is then obviated on the page by what's on-screen. By studying from the masters of the craft, you will learn how to maneuver through a screenplay's landscape and have access to a vocabulary to cull from while writing. But integrate, don't imitate. The origin and essence of the story and the way in which you tell it needs to come from you. Whether you write a masterpiece right off the bat or pound out seven drafts of your first screenplay, staying true to your own artistic inclinations is the only way to realize something meaningful.

And don't get frustrated if your style takes a few drafts to truly present itself. First-time writers are often deceived because screenplays are shorter and, thus, appear easier to write than a novel or a biography. Word for word they are certainly sparser than most books. What is often misunderstood is that a screenwriter works within a landscape of confinement, similar to a poet writing in metrical verse. Although the dialogue is free-form and the scene length indeterminate, in a successful script—independent and studio alike—there is a constant rendering of detail, which deftly eliminates all but the absolute essentials.

An independent film may be about anything or anyone and may come from anywhere. This is part of the pleasure of independent screenwriting: the plot and its characters are as wide as the writer's imagination. While many indies tell stories that Hollywood would term *edgy,* having a violent theme or a sexually explicit one doesn't by itself qualify a film concept as independent. Actually, the opposite is often true: contriving street credibility and pandering to some independent expectation is contrary to the whole point of making an independent film. Telling a G rated children's story with wit and captivating visuals would make an excellent independent film and would be comically subversive against the backdrop of bad low-budget horror movies permeating today's independent film festivals.

Whatever it is you plan on telling, cull from the best and worst your life has had to offer, finding those particular yet universal threads. If your subject matter is slow and cerebral, you will have to imbue it with enough commonality to merit its making. When we decided one of the twins would die toward the end of *Twin Falls Idaho,* we knew the death would have to feel like the loss felt by any closely linked siblings. The twins' conjoinment needed to become a metaphor for death, love, family—the crux all people live under. The point being, an independent film idea may be unique and still universal.

Talk and type: To get your screenplay moving forward, try sitting at your computer and just typing as you talk. Don't stop. Don't edit. Not for punctuation, not for grammar. Those corrections can easily be made later. You don't want to interrupt your flow. Let it continue. Your scenes, your dialogue, even your scene descriptions will have your personal style because you didn't edit yourself.

Character revelations:
Sometimes the smallest of details, the subtlest of proclivities, will make a character in a screenplay become three-dimensional. Be on the lookout for real-life human tics that you can appropriate for use in your screenplay. When you see someone do something that captures your eye—maybe it's chronic nail biting or a constant flip of the hair—jot down what you have witnessed. Subtle behaviors and habits often speak volumes about an individual, and in a screenplay they can add depth and meaning to a character without the need for dialogue.

A Character Piece

At one of our first jobs while in high school, we worked the late shift at a cardboard factory, hauling cutout carrying cases for beer and wine coolers. Terri, a girl with a classic mullet, ran the forklift; she would tear off a piece of a cardboard box of choice and munch on it as she worked. It was her *thing*. A box muncher. You do the math. One's character is in the details. Independent films, restrained by their small budgets, rely on colorfully written characters. Since explosions are few and special effects fewer, character development is usually where the fireworks reside. It is impossible to define what personality traits make one character more memorable than another or which dialogue conventions work well and which do not. However, there is, if nothing else, in winning independent films (and the better Hollywood films, too) a specificity to detail both in dialogue and manner provided by the writer—and then later expanded on by the director and actors.

Early in the development of *Twin Falls Idaho*, we were watching a documentary on the history of foghorns. There was an old weathered seaman who had worked the same ship for thirty years, and he knew the rhythm of the ship's horn so well that when he spoke, he would anticipate the horn's blare. We loved the seaman's odd relationship to the horn and quickly sketched his interaction with it in a notebook. As we developed *Twin Falls Idaho* further, with the twins living in an old hotel with a resident elevator man named

D'Walt, the foghorn idea immediately found its home. Our elevator man, similarly old and experienced in his job, would speak around the dinging of the floor bells as the elevator continued on its repetitive path. Had we waited until the next day or week to jot down the inspiration from the documentary, we probably would have lost its essence.

While you develop your characters, also think about what you may be able to communicate by inference, by omission. Sometimes it is what isn't revealed that makes a character memorable and imaginative. Not showing Norman Bates commit the grisly murder in the shower of Hitchcock's *Psycho* gave the scene its unforgettable tension. Not showing the shark in *Jaws,* up until the final confrontation, gave the film its teeth, as it were. In *Twin Falls,* a simple glimpse of the twins' fused torso was all that was needed to convince the viewer. The chalkboard quote we always abide by is, "Freedom is embracing your limitations." By not only embracing but creating limitations for your characters, you will enhance the overall effect of your film.

Scribbles: We try to write down a descriptive experience as close to its occurrence as possible. The initial spark caught by overhearing or seeing someone or something dulls as the week drags on. Since most screenplays, even independents, are rewritten several times, capturing a character's essence in the first draft is always preferred. This facilitates an easier rewrite, with the character's nuances already on the page.

re:Search

One of the best ways to flush out the contours of a potential screenplay is research. No matter how compelling your premise may be, the seed concept may take you only through the first ten pages or so. Educating yourself on your premise is the easiest way to develop it into a full-length script. As you study the background of your subject matter, the mood and sway of your future screenplay should start to reveal themselves. As you develop your

The black hole: The Internet, cyberspace—it's a black hole for aspiring screenwriters. It's a great tool for instant research and fact finding but can easily become a time waster for researching that will not benefit your story. And with instant messaging and e-mails, it's all too tempting to divert your attention and energy away from creative writing to the instant gratification of personal correspondence.

independent film concept further, the heart of the story you are about to write, through your research, should start to challenge your presumptions of the story line. In a sense, the initial screenplay idea begins to write and rewrite itself by the addition and subtraction of new information. The boundaries you will negotiate once you start writing begin to congeal, and the once-limitless premise becomes a finite, albeit rough, overview.

We began researching *Northfork* by watching a PBS documentary on the building of the Hoover Dam. This really helped us understand the magnitude of earth and water involved in a massive dam project and awakened in us the cinematic possibilities of capturing its architecture. While reading a book on American dams built between the 1930s and the 1950s, our initial concept of angel wings and salesmen began to merge into one story of a small soon-to-be-flooded town. Our salesman, we thought, would be hired to evacuate the holdout residents moments before water submerges their town's history. Through further research, we discovered that the first *Life* magazine cover was of Fort Peck Dam in Montana. It was a wide shot of its enormous cement spillway, the image a stunning monument to a fully industrialized America. The Fort Peck photo reinforced our enthusiasm for the story both visually and historically. A book on angel wings told of an old parable in which God gave each of his angels a choice to leave with him for heaven or to remain on earth. The angels who chose to stay behind lost their wings as a consequence. We found this was a powerful metaphor for humankind as a grouping of wingless angels. We began to envision an orphanage and a dying orphan boy searching for his wings, searching for his way out of his earthly confinement. All our research had now laid the foundation for our story.

Research can help you get to the truth of your story. The whole point of doing the background work is to find where the truth in your story resides. During the initial stages of developing the *Twin Falls Idaho* story, we kept trying to get inside the head of conjoined twins. We wanted to know what that would feel like. We could relate to being twins, to the closeness that twins feel, but not to the fusion of flesh. We kept feeling we would want to be ripped apart. We even thought of a humorous take on a divorce court proceeding between the conjoined twins. In 1996, the time of our research, the Internet and even the libraries we visited didn't have much in the way of information on Siamese twins. They were perceived to be somewhat of a sideshow spectacle. Then, lo and behold, on a "special" *Oprah,* conjoined girls took the stage. They were as innocent and as frightened as baby birds. It was that *Oprah* that gave us the single most important element to realizing Blake and Francis Falls. The conjoined girls nestled their heads into one another and would whisper back and forth. They were carrying on their own intimate conversation. As the interview progressed they finally opened up a bit, saying the one most important element that would send shockwaves all the way through our draft. These girls didn't want to be separated. They were fine with being conjoined. And the more we researched other conjoined twins, the more we found this to be almost universally true.

Story Structure

First-time filmmakers, in their exuberance to tell an original story, sometimes make the mistake of structural self-indulgence in the name of artistic freedom. By virtue of the film's *independent* status, the viewer is asked to excuse slipshod anachronisms and audio and visual incongruities. One of the artistic luxuries in developing an independent film's structure is it need not be beholden to an immovable genre, whereas a broad romantic comedy would never, in substance, stray from its whimsical, nostalgic timbre. In an independent film, the creator can explore an evolving landscape of divergent emotions. However, changing the tone of your film midstream must be purposeful. If your film starts out as a black-and-white murder mystery and then, halfway through, becomes a Technicolor musical, you should find an ingenious way to make the two halves a meaningful, unified whole. A successful independent screenplay uses structural shifts as well-conceived thematic devices. It's similar to a jazz soloist effortlessly weaving in and out of the tonal center of a composition. While any child can make atonal music, only a serious musician can create meaningful harmony from dissonance. Your aim while researching your independent film—however avant-garde your stylistic approach begs to be—is to justify your choices.

In *Northfork,* a boy named Irwin is dying. He's one of the central characters in the film. The issue we had to resolve structurally was that from a cinematic perspective death is listless and bedridden. Since we wanted to create action with the boy and empathy for his failing health, we knew we would have to use either flashbacks or dream sequences. Those were the only two options we had as defined by the structure of the story we wanted to tell. Similarly, to enhance the story's overall tone in *Twin Falls Idaho,* we kept the structure linear and chronological. At the story's center is the freakish pallor of two people literally connected, and yet our aim was to create an intimate emotional connection with the viewer. Had we jumped back and forth out of the present story, we would have lost an intimacy we were committed to creating. The bottom line is that structural choices should support the story.

Getting with the Program

We had started writing our first screenplay: the following weeks were grueling. The learning curve was steep and we were starving. Our original idea needed an original story put into a proper script format, of which we were just learning. The electric typewriter we had wasn't cutting it. Trying to do the margins for characters and dialogue was frustrating and tedious. What we didn't have was a computer, something that would help us process our thoughts rather than slow them down. We had read about some software programs that would automatically format for screenwriters' needs. So we bought the cheapest Power Macintosh available. After that, we needed the program that would auto-set the guidelines so we could stick to the writing. As we were strapped for cash, we searched the L.A. *Recycler* and found someone selling a popular screenwriting software for less than half of what it was selling for at retail. You'll travel to some pretty strange places to find things that will facilitate your dreams. This place was one of them.

We went through Greek pearly gates to the midcentury subdivision called Mount Olympus up to a Hollywood Hills house. At the entrance to the walkway was an overly designed wrought-iron gate. The guy who placed the ad for the software led us inside through a door and then inexplicably through another two doors. Into deep darkness, we walked inside, across a shag-carpeted living room and into a garage. We passed by all these different roommates doing their own things. We figured anything they were selling must be illegal.

This garage had been converted into an office, carpeted for a thirty-by-thirty-foot room, but you could still feel the cement garage floor underneath it. The guy who placed the ad explained that screenwriting software allows its users to make two backup copies. He then told us he had successfully hacked it. By duplicating his entire hard drive, he could run off as many

Technology trap: Technology can be a great seductress. But the latest screenwriting program, story-extracting software, or high-speed personal computer isn't going to do the hard work of creating a compelling story. Time is better spent honing your talents than upgrading your technology.

copies as he desired. He then started talking about writing and filmmaking; he showed us a pamphlet on how to literally sell stock in your movie. It appeared way too complicated, but the notion stayed with us. (We ended up applying a similar method when financing *Jackpot.*)

With our hacked software successfully installed on our hard drive, we were ready to sit down and do what you can't buy: write. We talked about our ideas surrounding the angel wings. We tossed back and forth scenes that interested us. We weren't overly concerned with structure or plot; we just created scenes and then started linking them together. The screenwriting software immediately allowed us to focus on crafting a story rather than worrying about margins.

Elements of a Screenplay
The Scene

The most fundamental element of a screenplay is a **scene.** A screenplay is a series of scenes that combine to tell a cohesive story. A scene reveals a small part of your overall story and is typically a slice of time moving chronologically within itself. Writing a cohesive screenplay is like building an enormous jigsaw puzzle with one critical addition: before the assembly can begin, you actually have to handcraft each piece. The crafting of each puzzle piece can be thought of as the writing of each scene. Just as in a puzzle, if one piece of your screenplay changes, all its surroundings must be refitted.

Novel approach: Unlike in a novel, description in screenplay should either be readily visible to the camera or be able to be captured by the camera through the action of an actor. If a description won't be seen on the screen, it should be removed from the scene.

Scene Heading

In a screenplay, the beginning of a scene is marked by a **scene heading.** The scene's location and whether it is day or night will be written in capital letters, informing the reader of a new scene and its basic setting. Here's a scene heading from scene 3 of *Northfork:*

```
EXT. LAKE NORTHFORK—DAY.
```

Here the scene heading clearly and concisely tells the reader the shot is an exterior shot (EXT.) of Lake Northfork during the day. Quite often a scene heading coincides with a change in location. However, a scene change is not always a signifier of a location change. Particularly in independent screenplays, where locations are often less transitive, scenes may be divided by emotional breaks in the story line. Regardless of surroundings, scenes should naturally end in the way a well-constructed sentence effectively closes on its period.

Scene Description

Within each scene, a writer must include the necessary visual information to transport the page to the eventual screen. A **scene description** almost always follows a scene heading. Writers vary on how much information they choose to incorporate. Many screenplays are dialogue driven and use stage directions sparingly. Our scripts, on the other hand, are very explicit in their art direction. Here is the scene description that follows the former scene heading shown above, again from scene 3 in *Northfork:*

```
Reappearing is the ash-colored coffin. It continues
to peacefully drift on the lake, disturbing Walter's
train of thought.
```

The reason we use detailed scene descriptions is that we want everyone on the crew—in particular the costume designer, the director of photography, the set designer, and the makeup artist—to know very specifically what we are going for.

.

Character and Dialogue

Two key components within a scene (which all actors depend on) are character and **dialogue.** The following is scene 47 from *Jackpot*, where Sunny Holiday's manager, Les, is giving a pep talk to Sunny on the wisdom of his beleaguered karaoke tour:

> LES
>
> Patience, Sunny. There is a journey to the pot of gold, man, okay. There are ten of you every square mile in L.A. All fighting for something that they won't get, right. Sleeping in a car doesn't guarantee you'll become a star. Now, you act like I haven't been there. I've seen it. They will chew you up in a month and spit you out so fast. What I'm talking about is the groundwork that no new artist wants to do. We're making fans, Sunny, who will feel like they discovered you. The power of discovery, that is an advantage, man, that no new artist should overlook.

In all screenplays, the character is the *who* of who is speaking, and the dialogue is the *what* of what is being said. The character speaking above is Les. Notice how his name is written in capital letters, formatted in the center of the page, with his dialogue immediately following, likewise page centered.

Sunny Holiday scopes Tangerine at the Milk Bar/*Jackpot*

Scenes are constructed in a purposeful way to make the characters and their lines the most easily recognizable and readable text on the page.

Camera Directions

A scene will occasionally have some basic camera direction written into it. This is usually when the camera move is essential to the scene. For example, a scene in which a newspaper is shown in close-up revealing a plot point would be written in capital letters as CLOSE ON NEWSPAPER.

"PAN LEFT," "ZOOM IN," "ZOOM OUT," "DOLLY RIGHT," "CRANE DOWN"—these types of camera directions are up to the writer's discretion. The rule of thumb is that a camera direction should be used only when it is essential to the comprehension of the scene. We rarely write camera directions because we use storyboards from the perspective of the camera lens for each shot before we shoot our films.

Transitions

The last major screenplay element that resides within a scene is called a **transition,** marking the scene's end. A transition describes what type of cut will be used to segue to the following scene and is written in capital letters and centered page right. There are only a few prescribed ways to transport from scene to scene. The most common transition is the **cut,** sometimes referred to as the **hard cut,** where the next scene immediately follows the previous scene without hesitation. The trend today is to not notate a straight cut on the page; rather, a new scene heading is the indicator that a new scene has arrived. If the straight cut is extreme from, say, morning to evening, a hard cut is often marked as such:

CUT TO:

Less frequently used transitions include the **dissolve,** which slowly fades out one scene while the next scene fades in, creating a momentary overlap.

There is the **fade-out,** where a scene fades to black (or any color, but usually black) before the next scene enters the frame. There is also the **fade-in,** where the next scene fades in from (typically) black, slowly overtaking the screen. And lastly, there is the **match cut,** a hard cut that connects one scene with the next scene through a visual reference point.

While writing *Northfork,* we used a variety of transitions for specific purposes. We used a dissolve each time our sick orphan, Irwin, would slip into a dream sequence. The dissolve sets the visual tone of entering an altered state. We employed many match cuts between the three sets of salesmen hired to evacuate the holdout residents of Northfork. For example, as one set of salesmen opened their case of commemorative angel wings, we'd cut to another scene with a different set of salesmen similarly framed in the shot, opening their case of angel wings.

Acts

A large section of a screenplay is invisibly divided into a sequence of scenes that is termed an **act.** Stage plays, such as Shakespeare's, use acts to visually delineate the overall story into several major sections. A screenplay, unlike a stage play, does not mark an act's beginning or ending on the page. Rather, an act is a theoretical division screenwriters use to better comprehend and articulate their story. Yet, assuredly, it is part of most screenwriters' vocabulary because it readily defines a major turning point in the sweep of a story. Films written in the standard model of the Hollywood studio system are broken down into three acts. Act I is the setup, Act II is the conflict, and Act III is the climax and resolution. Interestingly, an infinite number of stories can be told rather persuasively in this manner. Three acts follow a perfectly linear progression: beginning, middle, to end, while resolving the central conflict resolutely.

An independent film screenplay may or may not abide by the Hollywood three-act standard model. Federico Fellini's *8½,* if we can term the Italian masterpiece independent, could easily be divided into 8½ acts or more de-pending on where one chooses to divide the enjambment of story, while Billy Bob Thornton's *Sling Blade* is a perfectly concise three-act film.

The Protagonist

Many screenplays have a central character called a **protagonist.** A protagonist is the center of the story's solar system to which all other characters and their subplots revolve. What makes independent films' relationship to a protagonist different to that of Hollywood's is the abstract way in which multiple protag-onists may relate to one another. An independent film has the choice of using several leads, telling separate stories, which indirectly relate to one another while rarely sharing screen time. More often than not, a Hollywood screen-play will use a single protagonist to make the telling and selling of the script easier, with one famous actor as the linchpin to the whole proposed film.

As you write your independent screenplay, the role of a protagonist or protagonists may change and morph as you further define your story. While writing *Twin Falls Idaho,* we initially tried having both twins, Blake and Francis Falls, as equal leads. When we were approaching the midway point of our first draft, something was amiss emotionally. As we wrangled with our story, we decided to make one of the twins become the sole protagonist. Thus, Blake became the authoritative voice for their struggle, while Francis suf-fered silently with a dependent illness. This required rewriting many scenes to capture the new dynamic. In *Northfork* we wanted the opposite effect. We mindfully divided up the scenes between all the leads to create a larger pic-ture of the community of Northfork and in true independent fashion kept several leads from ever meeting each other on-screen.

In a commercial Hollywood screenplay, the protagonist's likability, as it would be perceived by a mainstream crowd, must almost always be overtly obvious for the script to be **green-lit** into a movie. The lead character must either be a good person from the get-go or, through the story's progression, come to terms with his or her inherent flaws. An independent film, on the other hand, has much more leeway to feature a centrally flawed lead character who doesn't necessarily have to evolve morally. In *Jackpot,* our protagonist, Sunny Holiday, leaves his wife and child for a broken dream. Every choice Sunny makes along the way lacks moral fortitude: he cheats on his wife; he doesn't pay child support; and finally, at the film's close, he makes no effort to reconcile with his abandoned family. Throughout the movie, Sunny sinks deeper and deeper into his questionable life choices. While we felt Sunny would resonate somewhat with an average audience—we've met a town full of Sunnys—we also knew that without some sort of heartfelt redemption at the end of the film, his likability would be in question. But that was the story we wanted to tell. We had to accept the fact that Sunny wouldn't be loved by all. He would have his detractors. If we had chosen to bring Sunny home, had him give up his dream and live happily ever after with his wife and baby girl, it would have satisfied more people. The point is, for an independent screenplay, you have the choice to make your characters, and most important your protagonist, as morally flawed as you feel your story dictates. We feel *Jackpot* succeeded as an indie because Sunny's story is a truthful one; life usually doesn't have a San Fernando ending. If we had conformed Sunny to a Hollywood mentality, we would have been lying to the audience. Sometimes telling a harsh truth costs you your character's commercial appeal.

Character Arc

In a screenplay, a key character's emotional evolution is termed a **character arc,** whether your screenplay employs a true protagonist or is an ensemble piece featuring several leads of equal importance. This can be simply conceived of as the distance from point A of your story's premise to point B of your story's resolution that a character has traveled emotionally. The scenes and more broadly the acts surrounding them are the architecture in which characters emotionally evolve.

In *Twin Falls Idaho* we had three main characters, in *Jackpot* there were two leads, and in our ensemble piece, *Northfork,* there were fifteen key cast members. A larger cast is a tricky independent screenplay to write. The writer must strike a balance between each character's arc and giving the piece some sense of unification. A larger cast also means a larger budget. So for your first screenplay, try to keep your cast of characters as compact as possible.

However many characters you end up writing, each one, however minor, should be a valuable component to the story.

Rewriting

When you have your first draft done, it is time to share your work with the outside world to see whether a second draft is soon in order. Contact a few people you have personal relationships with and ask them to read and critique your screenplay. It's best to find film-savvy people who want you to do well in life. A frustrated screenwriter may not be the best choice. Likewise, choosing your best friend or immediate family member may not illicit an objective analysis. You want people to read your script who have read scripts before. You want advice from people who understand the basic parameters of scriptwriting. An actor is often a great repository of advice. If he or she isn't interested in your characters, that may be something to seriously consider when you write your second draft.

Someone reading your story and telling you what they didn't get is crucial to helping you as a writer, as a communicator. As you wrestle with your first effort, with its subtlety and heavy-handedness, feedback can sometimes be really hard to take. When you've spent so long cooking your first screenplay, eating your own words hurts.

After finishing our first draft of *Northfork,* we were eager and excited to receive feedback. The first person we gave it to was our agent, Paul Schwartzman. The next morning he called us. Immediately we thought he must have loved it. He kindly invited us over for dinner to discuss his thoughts. We drove over to his house confident we had written something really special and original. After we ate dinner, we sat around the table and got the lashing of a lifetime. Paul proceeded to go over every single word, one by one, asking us what each one meant. It was brutal. Every thirty or so pages, we would ask him if he liked the script. He wouldn't answer us; he just kept deconstructing it—word by word. By the end of our meeting, we were exhausted. All of our words didn't amount to much. Through the lashing, we couldn't fully support why we wrote what we did. As we were leaving, we asked, "Do you at least think it has potential?"

Paul smiled. "Do you think I would have done this for the last three hours if I didn't?"

Driving home, we couldn't help but feel like failures. *Northfork* was the first feature we had written. We had spent a good part of the year writing it, and now we felt like we just sucked. Because we did. At home we continued to sink into self-doubt. Looking back, this was the turning point. We could shut down and never write again, or we could rise to the challenge and turn

ATTN: Detail: What kind of chair is your character sitting in? What color are the walls in his or her bedroom? What is the make and model of the car your character drives? These details sound minor, but, for example, people make different judgments about a person who drives a Pinto than about a person who drives a Porsche. You instantly sense one's personality by such things as the car one chooses to drive. All too often we read screenplays missing key details that would help define the characters and their lives. Make sure your screenplay isn't missing the color and texture that brings your make-believe world alive for the reader.

our meaningless words into words that mattered. The next morning we began doing just that.

When we sent out the first draft of *Twin Falls Idaho,* we had learned quite a lot from the mistakes we made writing *Northfork.* Overall, our feedback from the first draft of *Twin Falls* was much more positive than for *Northfork's.* But still there were plenty of comments to consider. Many readers came back to us saying they wanted more dialogue between the twins. Although we never actually increased what was said between Blake and Francis, we detailed more fully in the second draft the emotional connection between the brothers. We took the comments we had received and used them in a way that we felt enhanced the readability of the screenplay without sacrificing the pace of the story.

The way to avoid the first-draft blues is to sift through the various critiques with the same acuity you used to write your screenplay. We give serious weight only to comments that come with an intellect behind them. Did the reader offer suggestions to resolve his or her perceived flaw in our story? If so, do the suggestions resonate with us? When a reader analyzes our screenplay, we then analyze the reader's analysis. In this way, we stay in control of our story, incorporating the helpful insights of others while discarding the rest.

While your first draft is circulating and you're slowly receiving feedback from various sources, take a break from your screenplay for a few weeks. Give yourself a small window of time to become inspired again. When you have enough comments to start your second draft, look first at the areas of collective criticism. If multiple people are critiquing the same character or set of scenes, those areas most likely need to be rewritten. Of the three independent films we have made, we wrote four full drafts of each screenplay before we actually shot the film.

Rewrites are a slower, more precise process than a first draft's concentrated effort. When we start a new draft, we go back to the heart of the story and strip away as much extraneous information as we can. On the third draft of *Twin Falls Idaho,* we cut nearly thirty pages of several opening scenes explaining the twins' background. It took us two full drafts to come to terms with losing our beginning. If we had given up and accepted our second draft as the best and final effort, the film would have never been financed.

Fort Peck, Montana, the setting for the dam town/*Northfork*

4 | Pricing Your Film

How did you finance your film?" That is the question we are most often asked when we speak at colleges, film festivals, or film seminars, and its answer is the most important knowledge we can share with anyone trying to make a movie. Money is what starts and stops a production. It controls everything a filmmaker does. And yet the question most beginning filmmakers forget to ask of themselves is, "How much will my movie cost to make?" Usually they don't have an answer, or they will say, "Under $2 million," or, "It's an independent film, so it's not going to cost very much." But whether it's $10,000 or $10 million, it's almost always a figure they couldn't personally afford. An average-priced low-budget movie, like *Twin Falls Idaho,* costs $500,000 to make. Even a super-low-budget movie will likely cost at least $20,000, and most investors would rather put their money into real estate than into six reels of celluloid.

So how much is that six reels of film going to cost you, and who is going to pick up the bill? Well, at this stage in the development of your film, you need to answer a few big questions of your production:

- Where are you going to shoot your movie?
- Are you going to build sets?
- How much film will you need to shoot?
- What format will you use (35 mm, 16 mm, video)?
- Can you get a discount on camera and lighting equipment?

Everything needs to be explored and priced. You should be considering all the elements in your screenplay, especially those that may make it cost-prohibitive. Are there too many location moves? Countless independent films fall prey to overzealous set changes. A film spanning three continents is fantastic to envision, but not if it means never seeing your movie made.

As we mentioned previously, we were faced with this dilemma in the early drafts of *Twin Falls Idaho.* Originally, the story was epic in scope, having locations in several countries. The twins were well traveled. But as we began to examine the true cost of the screenplay, the location moves were one of the most expensive elements in the budget. So we had to decide whether this film was about twins or travel. Was the travel a necessary element in the movie we wanted to make? We decided we could still make the movie we wanted without the expensive location moves. Once we removed the location shifts, the budget was reduced by two-thirds. We had a similar struggle over location with *Northfork,* but in *Northfork*'s case the location was essential. It was a period piece set in Montana, and there was no way to cut the location budget. *Northfork* ended up being four times more expensive than our other two previous films, and the location costs were one of the reasons why.

Make it your job to know the real cost of making your movie. This job is known as line producing in the business. A **line producer** knows the nuts and bolts of striking deals and hiring for a film production. With the help of a **production manager,** a line producer breaks down the screenplay and then organizes the budget, calculating the proposed cost. Experienced line producers who work in independent film know how to make films for scant money because they are familiar with the terrain; they know where to spend, where to skimp, and who to talk to for deals. Line producing can require just as much creativity as writing and directing. On some indies, the duties of the line producer are shared by the production manager and the filmmaker/producer. That is why getting to know the true cost of your movie is so worth pursuing. It is often the essential part of a filmmaker's job.

When we had finished the first draft of *Twin Falls Idaho,* we had our script read and ruminated on by several micro-studios and other "indie" production companies. The comment we kept hearing was that our script was too expensive to make and too perverse to justify a multimillion-dollar budget. This **script coverage** reinforced our reasons for wanting to make *Twin Falls* independently. One of the readers said

Line producer: After the producer, the line producer is the most important business and logistics person on the set. He or she basically runs the shoot, including making sure all guild contracts are filed and overseeing the production manager and accountant to ensure the film doesn't exceed budget. Hiring an experienced line producer who can foresee inevitable snares in the production schedule and budget estimates is always well advised.

Production manager: The production manager manages the budget, hires the crew, and actively supports the needs of the film (also known as the unit production manager or UPM).

Script coverage: At film studios, big and small, people are hired solely to read scripts and write critiques of them. The higher-ups are too busy to read a pile of scripts weekly, so they employ people to weed out the unworthy. If a screenplay doesn't condense conveniently for the reader, a script may be dismissed regardless of its potential.

our movie was very dark. Another reader said he found the screenplay too disturbing. The readers couldn't get behind an expensive film about Siamese twins. The more feedback we received, the less likely we felt *Twin Falls Idaho* would ever get made.

The screenplay of *Twin Falls Idaho* was priced by the studios at a minimum budget of $5 million, largely because of the expectation of the visual effects needed for Blake and Francis to look truly conjoined. **CGI (computer-generated imagery)** seemed to be the only creative solution the studios had for the conjoined twins. The expenses quickly mount when a central character is digitally manipulated. This was the misperceived paradox within *Twin Falls Idaho:* If the film was made for cheap, it would make the twins look phony and, therefore, wasn't worth the gamble; if it was made for a digital-effects-heavy budget, it would have the necessary look, but the risk would be too high to lure in an investor.

Instinctively, we knew there must be an inexpensive yet visually captivating way to shoot our conjoined twins. We'd sit notebook in hand, contemplating the technical difficulties, questioning the true costs of production. We began to think of the optical illusions inherent in a two-dimensional surface such as a painting. We thought about camera angles and careful lighting techniques that might create the appearance of fully three-dimensional Siamese twins. With our cinematographer, David Mullen, we started storyboarding the script: where we would drop light, how we would maneuver realistically within each scene's depth of field.

Once we were able to fully visualize the twins, we turned our gaze toward pricing out some of the other major production expenses. We called up Fujifilm and Kodak and got quotes on film stock: Fuji was notably cheaper. We called up Panavision, spoke with a product manager, and sent over a *Twin Falls* screenplay. After the manager read it, we were invited in for a meeting. We ended up with a camera package including a few Primo lenses (the best and most expensive) for a price way below studio cost. The more we researched the price of making *Twin Falls,* the lower the budget fell. Rather than relying on a studio executive to price the line items on our budget, we took the meetings with film development labs, camera houses, equipment rentals—all of the major costs associated with production. And the film we were told couldn't be made for less than a few million dollars was suddenly doable for a fraction of the cost.

CGI (computer-generated imagery): Very expensive, time-consuming digital animation wherein each pixel in the affected area of the scene is redrawn to create stunning visual imagery. A filmmaker can literally paint his celluloid canvas with whatever he or she imagines.

If you are in the same place we were, pushing a screenplay that you really don't know the cost of, you can't expect an investor to take your project seriously. Not knowing the cost of your film stops you from allaying an investor's fears. You need to answer the big questions of production, such as location, cast, camera rental, lighting rental, catering, film and lab costs, and any special effects. Don't be afraid to go after the high-end expensive equipment, materials, and development labs used by Hollywood. Often these companies will work with independent filmmakers, offering incentives in hopes of a long, fruitful mercantile relationship. So be clever and crafty as you work out ways to bring your screenplay to life. The good news is all the preliminary work you do **preproducing** your film will help you make a better picture on a tighter budget. Remember, your goal is not to simply secure financing, but to make the money you end up raising go into the right areas of production, where its value shows up on the big screen.

Designing a Screenplay Presentation

An effective way to answer the questions of production is to create a screenplay presentation that visually explains the complexities of a story through artwork and photography. A screenplay package is a great sales tool. The artwork and photographs serve as an adjunct to the screenplay, lingering in a prospective investor's mind as the screenplay is being read. The presentation should be the bridge between your art and the investor, showcasing what is artistically possible for a relatively small amount of money. What you choose to present to the investor is a question your screenplay can answer. You want to bring the most challenging elements to the forefront. For us, this was the conjoined twins: how were they going to be represented in our movie? Investors have to be comfortable with your story, and it's your job to help guide them through your vision. Since independent filmmaking is about taking the alternative routes to make your movie, your search for financing may be unconventional. Anytime you search for money, such as a loan, the person or bank requires you to have good credit and be a reputable person. As a filmmaker, what credits do you have? And if it's your first time, what do you have to show that makes someone invest in you?

For *Twin Falls Idaho,* we made twenty-five black, bound, fabric-covered folders, which we kept at hand for investor meetings, containing pictures, artwork, biographical information, and the screenplay. We felt that no matter how visually oriented readers were, they could not comprehend the conjoinment of the twins without actually seeing them (see the picture on page 14). The twins were the movie, so if readers couldn't visualize their conjoinment, then no matter how well the story was written, it didn't really matter.

Inside the folder, along with the script, was an old-fashioned four-by-five black-and-white photograph of the twins shot with a 1920s hood-and-flash camera. We also included several pencil sketches of the twins in various scenes in keeping with the mood of the photography, followed by basic biographies of the key crew members who had already committed. The

Hand in wooden hand—Irwin and Happy/*Northfork*

screenplay and its artwork, photographs, and crew biographies were neatly assembled and bow-tied together with felt string, creating the look of an ornate Victorian novel. All the supplies we used, from the paper stock to the cardboard folders, were found at a large art supply store, Pearl Arts & Crafts, and an office supply store, Staples. Many stores scattered about the United States in most major cities will have these supplies.

While the screenplay (except for a dramatic picture of the twins conjoined) was intentionally like any screenplay—standard white copy paper, all text, three-hole-punched, with brass brads through the top and bottom holes—the accompanying photos, drawings, and bios were on a very fine linen paper. The result was a script that, on the one hand, was flanked by convincing visual representations of its story and, on the other, when removed from its folder, conformed to the minimalist standards of a professional screenplay. The dual effect was powerful enough that even prospective investors who did not want to finance our film would request to hold on to the packaging.

We created the *Twin Falls Idaho* screenplay presentation by hand, and it was a laborious task. Fortunately, we had briefly worked at a print shop and learned enough about typography and drafting to make our presentation look professional. But you need not have any print experience to create a great presentation. If you own a computer, consumer design software such as Adobe Photoshop, Desktop Publishing, Quark, and Adobe Illustrator is incredibly sophisticated, not too difficult to learn, and capable of producing exquisite presentations. If you are not computer-savvy or feel overwhelmed, partner up with someone who can help. Graphic art students are always looking for ways to build their portfolios; many of them are specialists in one or more of the design programs and most likely own them as well as a scanner. If you actively seek out help and invest the time in creating memorable imagery, there is absolutely no reason why your screenplay presentation should be anything less than an inspired accompaniment to your script.

Even today we continue to make screenplay presentations for every project we're considering.

Walter and Willis deliver a sign from God/*Northfork*

5 | Financing Your Film

If you have an original, well-written screenplay, it's a good bet someone somewhere on the face of this planet has the adventurous spirit and the money (or part of it) to bankroll your film. This should, however, give you little encouragement to while away your hours, because finding the right investor and motivating him or her to read your script is a full-time enterprise. You're going to be chasing money all over and possibly into some pretty dark places. You are searching for an exceptional person willing to take a big chance. So where does a filmmaker find an investor? Think of anyone directly or indirectly in your purview who may have a vested interest in your story being told. We have had three different types of financing. In the case of *Twin Falls Idaho,* because the investor had twin siblings, it enhanced our prospects. You should think as broadly as you can while also talking with your friends, family, acquaintances, former classmates—anyone and everyone who might be able to help you find a benefactor. To have some connection with an investor is always positive: it allows you to have an introduction that would not come via a blind letter to a stranger.

What you can count on as you begin to take meetings, as you challenge yourself to find that one person or several people willing to gamble on your art, is rejection. But remember, you are not alone. Everyone worth their salt in the independent film world has faced rejection because challenging films are the hardest to get made. John Cassavetes, an independent maverick who helped create the independent film movement, took acting gigs in movies in order to fund his own unique films. Struggling to find money is part of the territory when it comes to making indies. The thing to remember is that finding an investor is a process. One potential investor pursued though ending in failure will often lead to multiple new investor contacts. If someone is impressed with you, even if he or she will not put up the equity, he or she may know someone who will; people with money communicate with other successful, wealthy people.

There are numerous reasons an investor will pass on an independent film, many of which have nothing to do with the quality of the screenplay. We met an executive financier whose sole goal was to exploit the freakish nature of Siamese twins. We met one investor who wanted to fund a film for no other reason than to cast himself.

Despite the hoops and headaches of pursuing investors, there are still plenty of people who manage to get their films funded. Without exception, the filmmakers we know who have managed to make a movie have one thing in common: they refused to give up in the face of daunting odds. They positioned and repositioned themselves for that one opportunity, and when it came knocking, they were ready for it. They were willing to sacrifice an income and a normal family life for their shot at making an independent film. To successfully pursue their dream, they had to make its pursuit a way of life. Of our thirty or so *Twin Falls* investor meetings, only one of them led us to a person with the money and the will to take a gamble on our screenplay.

In the Neighborhood

Before *Twin Falls Idaho* was even written, we tried to find independent funding for our first screenplay, *Northfork.* We had just finished shooting a short film called *Bajo del Perro,* which chronicles a boxing match between neighborhood kids, and were showing it at a festival sponsored by the Directors Guild of America in Hollywood. We had shot *Bajo* on 16 mm for three grand; the festival committee liked our film enough to give us an unexpected $5,000 grant. At the time it seemed like a large windfall, and we left feeling fairly confident we would get our first feature made.

We lived a few blocks away from the Directors Guild and were walking home after the screening with our short film in a canister. An actor we recognized, Jon Gries, walked by us and simply asked, "What's in your can?" Up until that point, Jon thought we were anything but filmmakers, because he had only ever seen us walking our dog. We told him it was our short film, and he was genuinely interested, pointing to his house nearby, saying, "Drop me off a copy; I'd love to check it out." We wouldn't have had this encounter if we had stayed in our hometown—and that's something to think about. You want to surround yourself with people in your city who are making films. Obviously, Hollywood is full of them. Your chances of meeting the right person drastically increase when the whole city is doing what you want to do.

Jon Gries was the first person we met who was making a living working in Hollywood. We remembered him as the character Lazlo, the introvert living in Val Kilmer's closet in *Real Genius*. We duped a VHS copy of our short film and put it in his mailbox. We didn't hear from him for several days, but when we did, he said he liked the short and asked us what we planned on doing next and if we had a script finished. We told him about *Northfork* and dropped off the screenplay on his front doorstep.

The next day we drove up to San Francisco to show our short film at a festival. We called Jon from a roadside pay phone hoping he'd read *Northfork*.

"Did you read it; did you like it?"

"It is really ambitious for a first movie," he said, "but I like it. It is original, although I think it needs another draft. I like the poetic, surreal elements. It's very brave. You just write from the gut."

Inspired that Jon Gries might help us find some financing for *Northfork,* we wrote another draft and really crafted it into a more readable script. Jon had begun acting in a movie called *Casualties*. He introduced us to one of the producers on the film, Rena Ronson. Rena worked for a production company (now defunct) called Transatlantic and had read *Northfork* at Jon's prompting. She told us that while she thought the screenplay showed promise, it was too big of a movie for first-time filmmakers to make. She put a large price tag on it since the location was Montana. Deflated, we could feel the meeting coming to a close, when she asked, "What else do you got?"

"Well," we told her, "we're just starting to write a screenplay about Siamese twins."

She gave us one of those looks that only someone who can change your destiny can give you, and then said, "If you write that movie, I'll make it."

That was all the encouragement we needed. If this meeting was going to materialize, we needed material. We locked ourselves in our house for six weeks, baking the *Twin Falls Idaho* screenplay. We started in November 1996, and by mid-December we got our first taste of how Hollywood really works. From the beginning of December, when the ski vacations start, to the beginning of

Angel homestead, jacked up and split to move/*Northfork*

February, when the Sundance Film Festival closes, nearly no one is looking to read a new script by off-the-map filmmakers. What we began to understand were the rhythms of Hollywood: the festivals, the holidays, the weekends. Those are no-fly-zones for first-time filmmakers. We found out the hard way that it is best to get your script out well before a holiday, and if you know a major film festival is soon to happen, prior to its commencement.

Weeks went by and finally we got a call from Rena. "Well, it's definitely a first draft," she said, "but I love the relationship with the twins." She had some basic notes, some scenes she thought could be better flushed out, but overall she was encouraging about the prospect of making it. Thus, we began to rework our first draft. It is always a thin line between incorporating investors' and producers' notes for the betterment of the piece and making changes solely in the hopes of getting your film financed. In the case of *Twin Falls,* Rena's notes were reasonable and in most cases were welcomed pointers on a first draft. We had it in our minds that if we could nail the next draft, she would help us make our movie.

We had recently become friends with an experienced agent who asked us a troubling question one afternoon.

"Did she **option** your script?"

"Option?" we said.

"Did she pay you some money for the exclusive right to make your movie?"

"No," we said.

Well, we didn't have an option—we now knew that—but we still had a young executive who believed in what we were trying to do. We dropped the second draft off on Rena's front porch. She called a few days later to tell us how much improved the script was and that she was going to pitch it to Transatlantic. About a week later we got a strong dose of reality. Transatlantic passed on our screenplay. It was too "freaky" for their tastes. Rena was still super-enthusiastic about getting our movie made. But the problem remained: nobody else was. This was a big lesson for us on how a commitment in Hollywood is the same as being married in Hollywood: there really is no such thing as commitment. In Hollywood, artists and business-people are trying to turn creativity into a livelihood, and, unfortunately, even a low-budget independent film, with few exceptions, will cost hundreds of thousands of dollars. So while Rena wanted to make *Twin Falls Idaho,* she still had to convince someone else to spend the money, which also meant that saying "I'll make your movie" was more an intention than an actuality. Remember, a verbal commitment is very different than a written agreement signed off on by both parties. And even then a contract can be broken; nothing is 100 percent. So many ideas are batted around in Hollywood in conversation that you couldn't possibly try to enforce casual commitments.

Option: When someone in Hollywood with power and money is red-hot enthusiastic about turning your screenplay into a movie, even if a rewrite is in order, they will pay to secure an interest in your project. That is what an option is: *x* amount of dollars paid to you for the exclusive rights to your screenplay for *y* period of time. The amount and period vary depending on the financial standing of the person or company optioning the material, the perceived commercial viability of the project, and the talent of the lawyer or agent negotiating the deal.

We called Rena, telling her how frustrated we were with the situation. "Look," she said, "I'm frustrated, too—in fact, I'm leaving Transatlantic so I can have more freedom to do things like produce your movie. We'll get it made; just be patient."

Three weeks later Rena left Transatlantic for a higher position at another production company called Lakeshore. In her new work contract, she clearly stated her intention of finding financing for *Twin Falls Idaho*. It wasn't a binding commitment from Lakeshore, but it showed us how serious Rena was about seeing our movie get made.

After a few months when nothing materialized at Lakeshore, we started losing faith, looking elsewhere, meeting other producers and other production companies. Our short film, which had been so well received, meant nothing to Hollywood; it wasn't even a bleep on its radar. We were just two young guys from out of town hustling a feature screenplay like everybody else.

Frustrated, we looked to our friend Paul Torok, an energetic go-getter fresh out of USC film school who wanted to be a film producer, who began making calls on our behalf and currying favors from friends in the entertainment business. A few weeks into preproducing *Twin Falls Idaho,* we got a call from him. Paul told us that yesterday he'd gone to Cirque du Soleil and won an Acura Sport in their raffle.

We drove out to the car dealership with Paul and walked onto the Acura sales floor with much fanfare and confetti. Paul posed and gave the car salesmen that much-needed publicity picture in their new car. Two blocks away, we sold Paul's new fully loaded Acura—leather seats, power everything, killer stereo—for twenty-four grand, opened a bank account, and began intensifying preparations for shooting *Twin Falls Idaho.* It was exactly what we needed—and fitting for a film about perceived circus freaks.

Within a few weeks, because we had been continuously researching and planning, we had most of the logistics of production figured out: a competent film crew lined up, clothes and props designed for the twins, our house reconfigured as a movie set, and $24,000 in the bank to make our movie. All in all, we were in surprisingly good shape to produce what we hoped would be a great super-low-budget indie. Yet there still were some other investment opportunities we had been pursuing. On the edge of Beverly Hills, in a sterile white office building, we met with a **foreign film sales agent** who was convinced that if we would agree to cast a popular B-movie actress as Penny, he could raise nearly a million dollars by preselling the *Twin Falls* territorial rights to Europe.

We sat in the sales agent's office and voiced our concerns. "She isn't right for the part," we said.

"I hear what you're saying, but this will get your movie made."

After weighing the pros and cons, we reluctantly agreed to offer her the part. Two days later she turned down the role. Again in his office, we were pleased and thought we could now move on to other prospects.

"You both now need to write a personal letter to her, stating how much you love her work, how she would be perfect for the part; it may sway her decision."

Foreign sales agent: A person who sells domestic films to foreign distributors for release in foreign territories around the world. If a film sells in a foreign territory, an advance will be paid by the foreign distributor to the sales agent, who takes a cut (usually between 20 and 30 percent plus recoupment of expenses), and the remainder goes to the filmmaker and/or producer. It is unlikely any further monies will come in after the advance from a foreign territory because the reporting of foreign box office receipts are very hard to track.

"Write her a love letter?" We were stunned.

"Is there a problem?" the investor said in all seriousness. And with that, the two of us got up and left, content to make *Twin Falls* on our own terms.

Meanwhile, Rena continued to pursue other contacts while we were busy preparing to shoot. We got an optimistic call from her six weeks before we were set to start. This would be the final meeting we would take before making *Twin Falls Idaho* on the twenty-four grand Paul had received from selling

Foreign presales:
Foreign presales (or
"preselling foreign," as
it is often called) is a
term referring to the
acquisition of a film,
prior to its completion,
by a foreign distributor
for exhibition in a
foreign territory or
territories. Often some
or all of the foreign
rights to an independent
film are sold in advance
to help finance the film.
The sales agent will
want to leverage the
star power of the cast
against the film's
proposed budget. If
the gamble seems
worthwhile, a foreign
sales agent may directly
or indirectly put up the
equity in return for a
percentage of the
money raised (anywhere
from 15 to 30 percent)
plus back-end profit
participation.

his car. We had a meeting with Paul, and we discussed the possibility of the new investor. We knew we would be giving up a lot, but before we said no, we took the meeting.

Sitting in an office across the street from the La Brea Tar Pits, we met Joyce Schweickert. She was a very easygoing, down-to-earth person who loved art, theater, and particularly movies. Her attraction to our screenplay was enhanced by personal experience: Joyce's two younger sisters were identical twins. Exhausted from the past year of dead-end meetings, we dug deep and found the fuel to give it our all. We went through every detail, from our investor packet to our pictures. With every piece of preparation we showed her, the more she was filled with enthusiasm. All our preparation was now paying off.

"I'm certain you can make a great film. I just hope it isn't too freaky for everybody else," she said with a tone that made us believe she just may want to finance the film.

She continued: "But if you can make a completed film for half a million dollars, I'll put up the money."

"Not a problem," we said enthusiastically. We shook hands and thanked Joyce for her belief in our film and left with *Twin Falls Idaho* on its way to being fully funded. We did in the end give up a lot in the way of the actual deal—producers' credits, back-end participation, etc.—but what we gained as filmmakers was well worth the sacrifice to get our first film made.

Do-it-Yourself

After *Twin Falls Idaho* had been shot, sold, and released by Sony Pictures Classics, we received several offers to make studio films. The prospect of working with a comfortable budget and big-name talent was exciting, not to mention a nice payday. But we just weren't thrilled with the scripts. Our interest in making a film comes from the material, whether self-written or not. This distinction in motivation is one of the big elements we believe distinguishes an independent filmmaking career from a standard Hollywood one. Regardless of how enticing all the other elements may be, if the writing does not speak to us, we will pass on a lucrative project.

But we had good news at the time; we had found another investor for our next independent film, *Northfork*. *Twin Falls Idaho* had made an impression in France, receiving a top honor at the Deauville Film Festival. Canal+, the biggest French media company, had a subsidiary film-finance wing that wanted to fund our next picture. We hashed out a broad-strokes deal, over a series of late-night transcontinental phone calls, where Canal+ would invest $2 million making *Northfork*. Having failed previously at financing *Northfork*, we saw the French film fund as a welcome opportunity for us to make this rather epic independent film on our own terms.

With the *Twin Falls* press tour coming to an end, our sights were set on making *Northfork*. We flew up to Montana to do further location scouting while we waited for Business Affairs at Canal+ to draft the terms of the finance deal. The winter weather was drawing near, making the whole preproduction process rather urgent because the film's visuals were designed around a frosted Montana. We had a maximum of six weeks of prep before shooting had to start. Most of the

Business Affairs: The department within a film studio overseeing, managing, and executing the financial and legal issues of filmmaking. Also found at talent agencies.

key crew members from *Twin Falls Idaho* were quickly rehired and at once started assembling their teams.

We had some momentum going: *Twin Falls Idaho* had received a massive amount of press, and the reviews were, on the whole, very strong. It seemed logical to us in some humanistic way, since we had proved our mettle making *Twin Falls,* that our next picture should be a kinder, gentler process.

Two days home from scouting the Montana outback, we received a crushing fax from the French folks who had promised to invest in our film. In an apologetic paragraph, we learned that Canal+ was being bought by another media behemoth and, cursorily, the independent film—finance wing was to be dismantled. *Northfork* had officially lost its financing, and with the weather soon to change, all hope of making *Northfork* that coming spring was lost.

The production in full swing/*Northfork*

Rather than throw in the towel, bemoaning the unpredictable turns of independent film financing, we redoubled our efforts into making another movie. We knew *Jackpot* could be shot for much cheaper than *Northfork,* and it was essentially ready to go, having already been written and even cast, with Jon Gries and Garrett Morris as its leads. We could shoot it for south of a hundred grand and raise the rest of the financing for postproduction and song licensing (sure to be hefty in a music-laden film) once we had wrapped principal photography. We even had the main location, the 1971 Galaxy, convalescing on the street by our house.

Brainstorming with our lawyer, we came up with a finance strategy for *Jackpot* that allowed for smaller investments from multiple investors, similar to a private company selling futures of its business. We proposed selling shares of *Jackpot* for $25,000 each, with a total of sixteen shares for the full budget of the film, $400,000. Each share would give an investor a slice of the film's potential earnings for a relatively small investment risk. We wrote a list of people who may want to invest: friends, family, and people we had recently met while promoting *Twin Falls Idaho.* We petitioned them first, calling each one personally and explaining how it was we hoped to finance *Jackpot.* Within a week, we had four investors committed.

With $100,000 in the bank, we had enough money to safely shoot *Jackpot* (which consequently was the first feature film shot and released on **24P high-definition video,** followed soon after by George Lucas's *Star Wars: Episode II*). As we geared up to shoot, more investors jumped on board. By the time we actually started rolling film (or to be digitally accurate, zeros and ones), we had over $200,000 in the bank. We were able to capitalize on the momentum of *Twin Falls Idaho* despite a very disappointing false start with *Northfork* because we refused to give up. *Jackpot* was shot in fifteen days on the road, mostly on Victory Boulevard (Los Angeles), and was released in

Blue Sky law: Don't let people who cannot afford the risk invest in your film. This prevents people from overextending and bankrupting themselves. The Securities and Exchange Commission (SEC) has issued a money-raising rule called Regulation D, which governs private money raising. Each state also has its own so-called Blue Sky laws, which are similar to Reg D. Reg D divides the money-raising process into two basic categories: (1) Raising money from rich people, and (2) raising money from nonrich people. Rich people are called accredited investors under these laws; they must have a $1 million net worth or a regular income of more than $200,000. A rule of thumb used by lawyers is that any one investment should not comprise more than 10 percent of an investor's

theaters by Sony Pictures Classics nine months later.

The LLC and the LP

For super-low-budget films, the filmmaker usually "just makes it," and as such owns the film individually. However, when a filmmaker obtains money from other people, the usual practice is to form some type of business entity to carry out making and marketing the film. Prior to the mid-1990s, the typical business entity was the limited partnership, or LP. The defining feature of an LP is that the investors in the LP do not have personal liability regarding the film beyond the amount of money they invest. (Imagine the opposite: a filmmaker asking you for your unlimited-balance credit card to make a movie.) In the 1990s most states authorized a new form of business entity, almost identical to the LP, called the limited liability company, or LLC. The major difference between the LLC and the LP is that the person who manages the LLC has no personal liability for the LLC's debts: you're not personally responsible to pay back the debt or have an investor come after your personal assets (home, car, savings), whereas in an LP, the person managing the LP has unlimited personal liability for the LP's debts. (In the "old days" of the LP, the managing person [called the general partner, or GP] would incorporate him- or herself in order to avoid this unlimited liability; thus, each project required the costs of maintaining two legal structures.) The LLC has, since the late 1990s, become the typical business entity for filmmaking, given its flexibility and lower organizational costs. The old GP of the limited partnership has been replaced by the manager or managing member of the LLC. Investors in the LLC are called members and are not responsible for the liabilities of the LLC.

LLCs are easy to form. You file a certificate with the state, enter into an agreement among the members (like the old bylaws of a corporation), and get issued a taxpayer ID number. You should form the LLC when you are ready to accept money from an investor. This is also the time to bring on an accountant and/or an attorney to handle the corporate and accounting details. Most of the time these professional services require payment; if you're lucky enough, you can work out a deal with an accountant and lawyer to provide their services at a price that works for your budget.

If you are going to raise money from anyone other than close friends and/or family, then state

net worth. If an investor is not accredited, then the laws are super-protective of the investor. You have many specific obligations to such investors, in form and substance. In short, you have the obligation to explain the entire investment to them, in writing. If what you give them is unclear, or misleading, the investors can sue you (personally) for their money back, claiming that you failed to satisfy all of the requirements. The law does not prevent non-accredited investors from investing in deals, but the many burdens placed on the company when accepting funds from nonaccredited investors are rarely worth the risks, cost, and hassle. That is why private investors are almost always limited to rich people, and family members.

and federal securities laws regulate the process. Suffice it to say, an attorney and accountant are necessary at such a juncture.

Recouped: A general term used when a film has done enough box office to pay back its entire budget, and sometimes also thought to include the repayment of a distributor's advance. Broadly speaking, when a film reaches the point where it is recouped, it is now considered profitable and a portion of future box office, video and DVD sales, and network and cable rights will go to the filmmaker and/or producer. The term is also used when an investor has received all of his or her money back from a film investment. If an investor is said to be "recouped," it does not mean that the film itself has become profitable, only that the investor has been paid back.

What investment terms do you give investors? A common starting place for single-film productions is that from any monies received from exploitation of the film, the investors will receive 100 percent of such monies until they have gotten their investment back, or **recouped.** Thereafter, investors will continue to receive 100 percent until they have been paid a certain level of profit, for example, 5 or maybe 25 percent (a preferred return). After the investors have recouped and received their preferred return, further proceeds are split fifty-fifty between the investors and the filmmaker team. Many permutations of this simple equation exist, and the foregoing should not be read as standard or chiseled in stone. Rather, it is a common starting point in analyzing single-film production deal structures.

Bank Loans

For a first-time independent filmmaker, acquiring a bank loan as means to finance a film is highly unlikely. Banks have no interest in the merits of a screenplay or the tenacity of a filmmaker; they are solely concerned with a film's "value" as it relates to a guaranteed return. In short, an independent filmmaker will need to have a distribution deal in place, a contract that states how much a distributor will pay when the film is completed, in most cases to garner a bank loan.

If a **negative pickup** deal or distribution guarantee is in place (this will likely occur only with a stellar cast and a reputable filmmaker and/or producer), a bank loan may be a way to finance or to finish financing a film. The issue then becomes how much the bank loan is going to cost the production. The bank will want interest on whatever money it puts up and sometimes profit participation in the film itself. We received a bank loan during the postproduction of *Northfork,* after we had received a negative pickup deal from Paramount Classics. The deal from Paramount was what secured the loan. In retrospect, the money we spent on the bank loan really hurt *Northfork*'s bottom line. To carry us through the expenses of postproduction, we had to later repay a substantial amount extra in fees and interest to the bank. We would have been much better off financially had we found another way to raise the postproduction funds. On the other hand, we got to finish our film and make *Northfork* without studio or producer interference. So, though we lost in profitability, at least we maintained our creative control. If you're considering a bank loan, weigh the pros and cons carefully. We can tell you from personal experience that it is frustrating to put everything you have into making a film, only to finish it in worse financial shape than when you started.

Dumb Money vs. Smart Money

Despite our success securing financing for *Twin Falls Idaho* and *Jackpot, Northfork* ended up being a financing nightmare and, truth be told, was never really financed until the film was shot and sold to a distributor, our credit cards maxed out with tens of thousands of dollars in debt, and our Los Angeles home signed away as a loan security.

The fiasco began when we wanted to relieve ourselves of the executive producer's duties. We hired enthusiastic executive producers with a very sharp lawyer. We were under the impression that since these executives were financing preproduction along with us, they would perform their duties and finance the production under our signed agreement. Warning: All filmmakers should be wary of signing a producer's agreement with an outside producer that does not implicitly demand quantifiable performance from him or her. The deal we ended up signing used language that required us to credit executive producers, and their companies, and even peripheral associates, even though they provided very little in the way of funding.

The trouble in finding financing for *Northfork* was compounded by a major change afoot in the independent film world: the independent film marketplace—particularly the foreign sales side, which had previously paid a premium for a well-known cast—had softened considerably. Had we made *Northfork* with the same cast and sought financing five years earlier, the budget would have almost certainly been met in any number of scenarios. But the times, we found, had changed: the dot-coms had gone bust, the stock market had fallen, and financially successful "independent films" had become more and more just clever marketing slogans for Hollywood-funded pictures.

As the grim reality of *Northfork*'s unfinanced start date approached, our usually sporadic migraine headaches had become a constant morning wake-up call. We had a meeting set in Orange County—situated forty-five miles outside of Los Angeles—to meet with a so-called artistically inclined, wealthy widow whose deceased husband built the landscape of flip-flop floor plans, also known as tract housing. The meeting, set up by our executive producers, sounded like a slam dunk: our potential investor, we were assured, loved *Twin Falls Idaho,* was very interested in filmmaking—having just started a script-writing class at her local community college—and also happened to have $50 million to play with.

When we arrived at her estate, we found our hopeful fairy godmother surrounded by her very serious and very skeptical older sister and brother-in-law. The older sister commanded the conversation and dismissively described her younger sister as an impulsive do-gooder who wanted to get into the film business. We surmised our potential investor was the only one in her family with the deep pockets, and her sister was there to make sure she didn't lose her savings on shooting an "art film" in rural Montana. After half an hour of fresh lemonade and a grocery list of reasons why not to invest in our independent film, we turned directly to the mansion matriarch and asked her what she thought of our screenplay.

"Well," she said, "I have yet to read it, but I plan on having my screenwriting professor give it a go and tell me if it's any good."

We craned our heads out to the sloping lawn as gardeners shaped hedges into rhinoceroses and things. We sat quietly thinking to ourselves that after two independent films made from self-raised financing, which were released theatrically and generally well received, our third film should be much simpler to fund—it only got tougher. And yet here we were an hour out of town with an investor who had not even taken the time to read our script. We could have been patient and probably convinced her that we would do her investment right. But **dumb money** will cost you more in the long run. Investors who don't know what they are doing will eventually find someone who does—namely, a lawyer—and they will overcompensate for their lack of knowledge with a lovely lawsuit.

Still, after nearly a year of searching, our executive producers had procured no substantial financing. Every few months we were told a new deal was on the table, but its parties and parameters would not be revealed until we signed off on an exclusive deal with them. We were so focused on putting the crew together and finishing a third draft of *Northfork,* we lost sight of the plain fact that our financing wasn't coming together and there was no money to make the movie. Unlike our last two films, *Northfork* was budgeted at well over a million dollars, and its cost could not be lowered due to the expense of shooting on location in Montana, which was an intractable element of the story. To make matters worse, we had an unbelievable cast committed—James Woods, Daryl Hannah, Anthony Edwards—and a stellar film crew was beginning to gear up, rejecting other job offers, counting on our word that this movie was going forward.

Finally, a week before *Northfork's* shoot date, our executive producers found a real lead, an investment banker out of Texas. We'll call him J.R. He had a maverick spirit and a passion for movies. The investor was sent a script with a list of our committed cast. He was very interested in exploring a financial participation. It was decided that our executive producers, our lawyer, and the two of us would fly to Dallas to meet with J.R. All of us would sit down in the same room and formalize a finance deal.

We met inside J.R.'s forty-fourth-floor office suite with an inspiring view of downtown Dallas. Our executive producers started the meeting by saying they had several deals on the table and that this possibility was but one of many opportunities they had set up for *Northfork.* Since our film was set for production in one week, we felt it was high time to show whatever cards we collectively had and try to structure a last-ditch finance deal. Our executive producers, however, infuriated our Texas investor by refusing to tell him these other deals. The meeting ended with a huff from everyone in the room, and we went back to our hotel all too aware that *Northfork,* once again, was coming to a screeching halt.

An hour passed while sitting on a comforter and watching reruns of *Dallas* on television when we decided to take matters into our own hands. J.R. was **smart money**; he wanted to know that we were going to be smart with his. Smart money can be expensive, too, because the investor knows what he or she is doing. They understand the risk versus the reward. But the terms are laid out on the table for all parties to see. We picked up the phone and called J.R. directly. He invited us to come meet him alone in a local bar to try and see if we could salvage the deal. We threw on our jackets and jumped in a cab. We found him drinking at a rear table.

"We are going to drink and talk and drink and talk some more until we get this thing worked out," he said.

"Sure," we replied, and settled into the brown leather chairs. A waiter soon showed up with all sorts of vodka concoctions: red ones, green ones, sex on this, love on that, and a dozen iced Stolichnaya vodka shots.

"Listen, your executive producers are assholes—I don't trust them. The point is, I like you guys and you know I'm from Texas and we shoot straight here, you know what I mean?"

"Yeah," we said.

"The thing of it is, I've never made a movie—I mean put money in a movie—because it is crazy business, just plain dumb, like riding a bronco bareback; you're bound to take it in the nuts—you know what I mean?"

"Yeah," we said.

"But you guys know the game, you've done it before, and you've got a great cast, and I like you guys and I figure if I'm gonna take it in the nuts, at least Daryl Hannah might be around to nurse me back to health, right?"

"Sure," we said, as our investor thrust a shot glass in each of our directions.

"Here's to *Northfork*." He raised the shot as we followed.

We drank and winced and nodded affirmatively.

"Call your son-of-a-bitch lawyer and tell him to get down here. Let's try hashing this out right now."

Paul Mayersohn, our lawyer, showed up half an hour later looking sober and sort of like a son of a bitch. Paul had been our lawyer since *Twin Falls Idaho* and like us would do just about anything to get a movie made. J.R. flagged the waiter, and our lawyer was delivered a bevy of vodka drinks. We were glad to see Paul realized the gravity of the situation and was willing to take a hangover if it meant closing this deal.

We talked shop until 2:00 A.M. J.R. wasn't coming around because of our contractual agreement with the executive producers. He had made up his mind and no matter how drunk he got, he was just not going to do business with our executive producers. We even offered to fire them—but in actuality we couldn't. Another main sticking point was an **exit strategy,** basically how was he going to get his investment returned. All savvy investors want to be the first in and the first to get money out. We couldn't offer a timeline that made J.R. comfortable. We had to finally call it a night while Paul decided to stay. He was going toe to toe with J.R. to get a deal done—even if it meant he would need a liver transplant when he returned to Los Angeles. The next morning we woke up hungover with the hope that Paul had closed a deal. We checked his room and he had not checked in. Somehow he had managed to walk across town and check into another hotel. As we arrived at his hotel, we knocked on his door. The door slowly crept open and standing there in his boxers with two nicotine patches on each arm was Paul. He was so hungover he could barely muster the words, "We have no deal."

"Really?" we said. With the way he looked, he had to have closed a deal.

"J.R. wants to see us to have breakfast. We may be able to do something then, but I don't think so." Although we felt we had one more shot, Paul was right: we didn't close a deal after a three-hour breakfast meeting. We were exhausted and then some. But J.R. had one more offer…a lift to the airport. Nice.

The ride was long, we were leaving disappointed, and there was nothing more we could say. We needed to be in Montana in a few hours to start production. J.R. parked his SUV and handed us a business card. On the back he had written his American Express number and expiration date. He told us the card had a $100,000 credit line. We smiled. It was clear that J.R. didn't want to get involved openly. We figured he saw too many liabilities with these executive producers. He looked at us and said, "Just charge it."

Independent crane shot/*Northfork*

6 | **Preproduction**

atching the daredevil Evel Knievel prepare for his Caesars Palace jump reminds us how preproduction feels—the long wait for the action to happen. We don't want to see all of his practice runs up the ramp, or the tuning and rechecking of his motorcycle. We want to see this guy fly over the fountains. And maybe then we will witness a historic feat or perhaps worse—Evel Knievel eating shit. The unknown is the exciting part of the event: The action. The drama. No matter how prepared you think you are for making a movie, you aren't prepared enough. There is no way of foretelling what will happen after preproduction. When Evel Knievel crash-landed that outrageously long jump to the other side of the Caesars Palace fountains, he broke a hundred bones. His motorcycle was totaled—so was he. He paid a

A Chevy pancaked the costume designer's car/*Northfork*

heavy price for his ambition, but it wasn't as if he just ran up the ramp without a plan. When he took off—in his mind—he was prepared.

Having been through three productions, the Evel Knievel analogy is about as close as it gets. Prepare for everything as thoroughly as you can and be mentally prepared for that which you cannot foresee or control. Your lead actress may fall ill; a snowstorm may ruin your exterior shot; your wardrobe vehicle may flip over, trapping two of your costumers inside (it happened to us). Preproduction, in essence, is survival training for the film shoot. And if you manage to make the movie you intended—whether you break a few bones or not—you accomplished the goal of preproduction.

The span of time before you shoot (usually around six weeks for an independent film) when all the logistics are thought through and organized is **preproduction.** While you may have been planning and researching the fundamentals of making your movie since you completed writing your screenplay, actual preproduction commences only when a few key variables are in place. Typically, preproduction begins when your line producer and production manager have been hired and some financing is secured, with the expectation that the rest is on its way. Really, preproduction shouldn't start until the film is fully financed. However, in the indie world, sometimes starting the film—partially financed—is what gets the rest of the film financed. It's a risky move and should be undertaken only with extreme caution. Once preproduction is truly under way, the film is going to be made, period. If there is no money to make your film, preproduction might hobble along for a few weeks but will soon come to a screeching halt.

Once you have financing, the first person hired is most often the line producer. He or she is in charge of planning and then running the business and logistics side of the shoot. This includes making sure all guild contracts are filed and overseeing the budget. You want to hire an experienced line producer who can foresee inevitable snares in the production schedule and budget estimates. The other key player in organizing preproduction is the **unit production manager** (often referred to as the production manager), whose responsibilities include creating the budget, hiring the crew, and actively supporting the needs of the film. The unit production manager will work closely with, and essentially oversee, the **production coordinator.** On independents, particularly those made for under $500,000, a line producer may also take on the responsibilities of the production manager (or vice versa), which lowers costs but increases the workload for the person overseeing both posts. While the line producer and/or the unit production manager have no direct say in the creative

Unit production manager: Often referred to as the production manager or UPM, this person ensures that the cast, crew, and equipment make it to the set each day and handles the day-to-day cash flow of the production. Sometimes the UPM works with the first assistant director to break down the script and to create a preliminary shooting schedule. Other duties include negotiating equipment rental, overseeing locations, and hiring the crew. During preproduction the UPM works from an office; during production the UPM splits his or her time between the production office and the set, depending on the needs of the day. If an experienced line producer isn't hired, the UPM likely will be on the set, making sure everything goes as smoothly as possible.

decisions being made, when they handle their responsibilities competently,

Production coordinator: There aren't many desk jobs on an independent film shoot, but the production coordinator is one of them. The production coordinator works hand-in-hand with the production manager to make sure all of the administrative details are being executed. If a shot in the film requires a dolly or a crane, the production coordinator will be the one on the phone negotiating the deal. Production coordinators often come to the job with a ready list of contacts for the crew, tech department, and craft service. The job is a sort of catchall to handle the needs of the production manager.

they greatly enhance the creative process, freeing up the filmmaker to focus on artistic quandaries rather than financial or technical ones.

There is definitely an indirect effect on the creative process from the line producer and the production manager. Putting the most money into what will show up on screen is really their jobs' mission statement. Balancing camera packs against catering bills may not sound artistic, but the balancing act may make the difference between a good film and a great film, or even a bad film and one that is decent.

Once you've chosen the line producer and/or production manager, you will actively prepare for the shoot. Whatever organizational skills you possess will certainly be useful as you and an ever-growing team of crew members grapple with a mountain of tasks. The following is a basic list arranged in chronological order—though many tasks will overlap—of what needs to be accomplished in preproduction.

1. Creating the budget
2. Hiring the crew
3. Casting the film
4. Choosing locations
5. Breaking down the shooting script
6. Creating the shooting schedule and production boards
7. Securing locations

8. Contracting with vendors for stage rentals
9. Negotiating key equipment deals with vendors
10. Constructing any needed sets
11. Acquiring props
12. Choosing, designing, and manufacturing wardrobe
13. Camera tests for any special effects or specialized development techniques
14. Makeup tests for actors

THE BUDGET | The production manager, often in concert with the line producer, culls through the script and will usually come in with a first-draft budget that represents a reasonable estimation of overall costs. Throughout preproduction, the budget is refined as new information about production requirements becomes available. Later in preproduction, when the script is fully broken down, a much more specific budget will be generated. A standard film budget, Hollywood and independent alike, is divided between **above-the-line costs,** which refers to the creative team (usually the writer, director, actors, and producer), and **below-the-line costs,** which refers to essentially everything else—such as goods and services, including the production staff salaries. This dividing line, which visually cuts the budget into halves, has been established so you can easily eyeball creative expenses versus technical ones.

THE CREW | This is your army, and the outcome of the battle ahead will be determined by the quality of these people and the conditions you provide for them. You need to have a real feel for the kind of project you're about to embark upon with all its physical and financial limitations. Typically, an independent film's tight budget will make a large crew prohibitive. But keep in mind, for a quality film to be shot, a small crew will mean more work for everyone

Motley crew: When Henry Miles set up the first film exchange program in 1902, allowing exhibitors to rent films as an alternative to buying them, the demand for new films increased dramatically. The rush was on to create a factory-like methodology for making movies. The studio system, formed in the early 1900s, began to define and title every facet of film production. The real point of interest from a modern independent filmmaker's perspective are the job descriptions, which, when understood, make communicating on the set much easier.

involved, with many people doubling up on job responsibilities. Like a fine balancing act, your crew size needs to conform comfortably to the needs of production and the constraints of your finances. Weigh each crew decision carefully and when the budget demands, hire a team member who can tackle more than one slot on the roster. During the production of all three films, both the hairstylist and makeup artist also worked as still photographers.

It helps if your crew members have a background in the kind of movie you're attempting to make. Every film bends in a certain genre direction, and finding a key crew member who has already demonstrated an understanding in this form is a handy prerequisite to enlisting his or her service. The cinematographer of our three movies, David Mullen, had shot numerous low-budget features before we worked with him. While he had never shot a piece like *Twin Falls Idaho*, he had the experience we needed.

The crew you can secure is usually predicated by the size of your budget, but don't let your tight dollar demands impede you from reaching out to those people you consider the most qualified. Often talented people will take on an independent film to diversify their portfolios. Even if you don't get your first choice, the top people in their field know talented up-and-comers. We asked well-known costume designer Milena Canonero (*Barry Lyndon, Titus, Dick Tracy*) if she would do the costuming for *Northfork*. She was busy on *Solaris*, but she said she knew a young costume designer whose work she admired:

Daniel Glicker. We met with Danny the next week, and it was an obvious match.

This brings up another important point: if you haven't worked with an individual before, don't be seduced solely by his or her screen credits. That's only part of the story. Talk with other filmmakers or crew members who have worked with him or her.

As the filmmaker, you will probably be most concerned with hiring the director of photography, the costume designer, and the **production designer.** These are the big three creative departments on a set. The line producer and the production manager will often oversee the hiring of the rest of the crew. They will have already worked with many of the people they will suggest to you. It is very important that your potential crew person is comfortable working on a lower budget and shorter production schedule than he or she may have previously.

Production designer: In a strict sense, the production designer is the head of the art department and oversees the overall visual design of the film from set design and costuming to make-up and hair. However, on an independent, the PD, if the production is fortunate enough to have one, is mostly concerned with the design and decoration of the locations and sets.

Equipment decisions will have an impact on the size and needed expertise of your crew. This is why it is worth considering early on what important gear decisions lie ahead, such choices ranging from the battery of lighting equipment to the far-ranging effects of certain camera mounts. During the *Northfork* shoot, we had a one-ton truck full of all our lighting equipment, allowing us a good deal of flexibility but also demanding several people for setup and breakdown of the equipment, as opposed to *Jackpot,* where we basically had a utility van with the bare lighting necessities. This gave us less control but made our small crew mobile.

While there is no strict figure on how much each crew member is to be paid on an indie, each member will be paid significantly less if your shoot is nonunion. The line producer and production manager will be charged with

The crew takes advice from the Almighty and begins to load the ark/*Northfork*

negotiating crew rates. The most notable union in its influence and domain is the **IATSE** (International Alliance of Theatrical Stage Employees). The organization represents most of the better-known artisans in the film industry. The IA, as it is better known, has a studio mentality and can inflict an injurious control upon your project. Its rigidity can make the going very tough. Fortunately, over the years, conditions have improved in the adversarial relationship between independent film productions and the IA management. Today the IA has separate agreements for low-budget films with rates based on the size of the budget. But your line producer and production manager will need to do their homework in investigating union rates and researching the costs for health and welfare benefits. Most indie films—as all three of ours have been—function outside the parameters of the costly IATSE jurisdiction.

In addition to the IATSE, your line producer and production manager will have to chart an agreement with other labor representatives, such as the **International Brotherhood of Teamsters.** They, along with IATSE, monitor independent films on a regular basis and try to enforce union wages wherever budgets permit. Other unions to consider: the Writers Guild of America (WGA), if the writer is a member, and the Directors Guild of America, if the director is a member. This is a daunting rung in your ladder of preproduction events, and you would be well advised to pick up a copy of the *Brooks Standard Rate Book* to begin research on the current rates and contract information for all the guilds and unions.

In the hiring process, it's up to your line producer, production manager, and you to determine the status of your crew members. Are they to be represented as employees or will they be independent contractors? You'll need to weigh the advantages and disadvantages of these two approaches.

If all this technical information makes you feel overwhelmed, fear not, your line producer and production manager should be well versed on how to plot the best course. Their knowledge will be supplemented by a film attorney and a film accountant. The filmmaker isn't expected to know the details of every crew contract or union requirement. But because it is your film and you are ultimately responsible, it is wise to learn as much as you can. Don't be too timid to ask questions or discuss your concerns.

Transportation coordinator: A transportation coordinator rents shuttles and vans, finds classic automobiles, hauls trailers for the cast—anything and everything on wheels is the transportation coordinator's responsibility. A small independent film may or may not employ a transportation coordinator, depending on the demands of the shoot.

Location manager: A location manager's responsibilities include scouting a site, talking to its owner, and coming up with the rental bid. During the shoot, the location manager is responsible for arranging crew parking, making maps to locations, acting as a liaison between the property owner and production company, securing all necessary government permits, and dealing with any neighbors who may be affected by the shooting of the film.

Accountant: While the producers and the production manager are intimately involved with the budget of the film, the accountant is the only one hired who is singularly concerned with bookkeeping. The accountant is rarely on set. His or her job is to clearly track production spending. The producer and filmmaker usually control how the budget is appropriated, while the accountant is responsible for showing how and when the money was spent. A careless accountant can put the whole shoot in jeopardy by creating a muddled financial picture, scaring the investor(s).

Once you've contracted your crew, getting the most out of them for the least amount of money will depend on your time-management skills. There are ways to cut costs without jeopardizing the creative possibilities of the project. Develop a schedule that limits your crew to the specific needs of each day. For instance, when a scene is daytime exterior and it doesn't require much in the way of lighting, you can give the extra electricians the day off. It is common practice to schedule only certain people to work on certain days or even specific hours. And, finally, be good to your crew. No matter what the budget, keep them well fed—with a reasonable turnaround time. They are there for you, and you should respect their efforts on your behalf. If a crew sees how deeply you believe in your project, they will feel the same way. Making an indie is an emotional roller coaster, and you'll need to inspire a crew to work hard for little money.

The SAG Independent Contracts

SAG (Screen Actors Guild) has worked closely with independent filmmakers. SAG has a user-friendly website with a link to the independent contracts: sagindie.org. Currently, SAG offers five different contracts that cover the indie spectrum depending on the budgetary constraints of a picture.

Student Film Agreement: For students enrolled in film school. Performers may defer 100% of their salaries.

Experimental Film Agreement: Total budget of less than $75,000.
Limited Exhibition Agreement: Total budget of less than $200,000.
Modified Low-Budget Agreement: Total budget of less than $500,000.
Low-Budget Agreement: Total budget of less than $2,000,000.

When a production signs one of these contracts, SAG is granted a lien on the film and its members will always be in first position to recoup compensation when their performers have been paid on a deferment.

Preproduction Duties

BREAKING DOWN THE SCRIPT | Using a scheduling program such as Movie Magic, the AD divides the script's contents into what are termed "breakdown sheets." These sheets organize all the various requirements in the script, assigning to each scene a number and listing its required components. The goal of **breaking down a script** is to show its physical properties so each member of the crew can easily see what is required of him or her on a given day during the shoot. Breaking down a script into its various components is the way in which you can schedule your film. The various components comprise the daily scheduler, which is called a Day Out of Days report:

- Location: Tells where a scene is set.
- Scene numbers: Every scene in a script is numbered chronologically.
- Int. or Ext.: Defines whether the scene is inside or outside.
- Time of day: Tells whether it is day or night, sunset or sunrise (called the "magic hour" for the beauty of the lighting).
- Scene description: Explains what details are in the shot, such as furniture, key props, and characters' costumes.

- Approximate shooting time: Estimates how long the scene will take to film.
- Cast: Tells who is needed on set.
- Extras: Tells what sort of background actors are needed.
- Props: Gives any additional information about objects needed on set.

The end result of properly breaking down a script is a film completely organized on both **breakdown sheets** and **production boards.** This allows everyone from all facets of the production to understand what is expected of them and allows you to understand the real cost and complexities of the shoot on any given day.

Whoever breaks down the script—usually the first assistant director—begins by underlining all pertinent information in the script. After a go-through is completed, the next step is to transfer the information onto the breakdown sheets. The most common way to do this is to use a software program such as Movie Magic Scheduling. This can be purchased at a host of film-oriented supply stores or online. Once the breakdown sheets are completely filled in, the information is transferred to production board strips. We've provided a blank breakdown sheet that you are welcome to use as a template.

SCHEDULE | Once you hire your assistant director, he or she will begin **calendaring** the entire film. Every scene will be numbered with a

Food for thought:
Crewing up an independent film is about finding talented people willing to work the extra hours for little or no pay. One way to bolster crew morale is to supply at least one or two really good cooked meals a day. Thus, choosing a caterer is actually an important consideration. Make sure your production manager checks the prospective caterer's references and speaks with someone from the caterer's last production. Also, ask to sample some of a caterer's cooking. If a caterer really wants the job, they will gladly supply a sample of their cuisine.

Cinematographer M. David Mullen and first AC/*Northfork*

date, approximate duration, and a location with an address and a contact person.

PRODUCTION BOARDS | Once the first assistant director has transferred the key script information onto breakdown sheets, he'll transfer the breakdown sheets onto paper strips called production boards. Each scene to be shot, with its essential information, is represented by a movable "strip" so that the shooting schedule can be easily changed around and adjusted as needed. This allows the cast and crew to see the big picture of shooting day-by-day, week-by-week. Production boards are usually generated with a software program such as the aforementioned Movie Magic Scheduling. When fully assembled, they show the entire shooting sequence.

Scene # ____	**Breakdown Sheet**	Date: ____

Scene # ____
Script Page ____
Page Count ____

Date: ____
Bkdown Page # ____
Int/Ext: ____
Day/Night: ____

Scene Description: _____

Setting: _____

Location: _____

Sequence: _____ Script Day: _____

Cast Members	Extras	Props
Sf/x Makeup	**Costumes**	**Vehicles/Transpo**
Set Dressing	**Makeup**	**Special Equipment**

Additional Labor

Notes

Production Board–GLASGOW, MONTANA

dam spillway area

Sc.						
Sc.	18, 22, 23	EXT	IN 1955 FORD SEDAN/NORTHFORK DAM WILLIS APPROACHES WALTER; READS LETTER. OTHERS EXIT	Day	1- 2/8 pgs.	1, 2, 9, 10, 11, 12
Sc.	24	EXT	NORTHFORK DAM THE SIX MEN MEET & GREET	Day	4/8 pgs.	1, 2, 9, 10, 11, 12
Sc.	A4	INT	IN 1955 FORD SEDAN/NORTHFORK DAM YOUNG WALTER & GIRL FROLIC IN BACKSEAT	Day	1/8 pgs.	1

-- END OF DAY 1 -- Mon, Apr 22, 2002 -- 1- 7/8 pgs.

Sc.						
Sc.	6	EXT	NORTHFORK DAM MAYOR ADDRESSES CROWD, CAKE IS CUT	Day	6/8 pgs.	26
Sc.	86	EXT	NORTHFORK DAM WALTER & WILLIS MEET MARVIN & MATT	Day	3/8 pgs.	1, 2, 9, 10
Sc.	A24	EXT	NORTHFORK DAM THE MEN ENTER THE DAM	Day	2/8 pgs.	1, 2, 9, 10, 11, 12

mini-move to spillway/admin office

Sc.						
Sc.	B24	EXT	NORTHFORK DAM CREW'S POV OF MAYOR	Day	1/8 pgs.	26
Sc.	26	INT	ADMINISTRATION OFFICE RUDOLPH GOES OVER AGENDA	Day	7/8 pgs.	1, 2, 9, 10, 11, 12
Sc.	57	INT	ADMINISTRATION OFFICE RUDOLPH LECTURES HIS STUDENTS	Day	4/8 pgs.	1, 2, 9, 10, 11, 12

-- END OF DAY 2 -- Tues, Apr 23, 2002 -- 2- 7/8 pgs.

Sc.						
Sc.	28, montage	EXT	IN 1955 FORD SEDAN - FORMER NEIGHBORHOOD W & W CRUISE VACANT NEIGHBORHOOD	Day	1 pgs.	1, 2
Sc.	46	EXT	IN MARVIN FORD - YOUNG RESIDENCE FORD PEOPLE, CHEVY PEOPLE	Day	1 pgs.	9, 10
Sc.	52	EXT	YOUNG RESIDENCE MARVIN GETS LEATHER CASE FROM TRUNK	Day	1/8 pgs.	9, 10

-- END OF DAY 3 -- Wed, Apr 24, 2002 -- 2- 1/8 pgs.

Sc.						
Sc.	47	EXT	IN EDDIE FORD - JIGGER RESIDENCE JIGGER FIRES ON EDDIE & ARNOLD	Day	6/8 pgs.	11, 12, 23
Sc.	53	EXT	IN EDDIE FORD - JIGGER RESIDENCE EDDIE DUCKS AS JIGGER FIRES	Day	1/8 pgs.	11, 12
Sc.	58	EXT	JIGGER'S RESIDENCE EDDIE AND ARNOLD DUCK SHOTS	Day	1/8 pgs.	11, 12, 23

company move to diner

Nick Nolte in pew/*Northfork*

7 | Casting

"If I ask you for money on behalf of my client, then my actor doesn't like your script."

—Hollywood agent

After financing your film, casting your film is the second emotional roller coaster you'll have to ride. Add to the drama that your film may be **cast-contingent,** where the financing is predicated on a bankable cast. This is why our most asked question beyond "How did you finance your film?" is "How did you attain a cast with the likes of Nick Nolte, James Woods, and Daryl Hannah?" To say it was solely the screenplay that attracted them would be only half the story. All of our cast members have had unique paths to the parts they came to play in our films. Some parts were easy to cast, some more difficult. All were a lesson, giving us insight into the casting of movies.

There are just as many different routes to cast a film as there are to finance it. There's the obvious front-door approach, going straight to the agent who represents your desired actor. Then there's the back door, where you meet an actor through a friend or an associate. We've gone through the front and back doors to contact the right actor, even through a few bedroom windows. The most important thing is getting the actor you feel is right for the part.

We've learned that every film will have its own specific needs and casting hurdles. *Northfork,* for example, needed a famous enough cast to justify the near $2 million budget. We had to find actors that would attract potential investors. We couldn't shoot *Northfork* in Montana for half a million dollars like, say, we had filmed *Twin Falls Idaho,* which we cast with a whole different mind-set.

Hope and Prayers

Father Harlan, a self-proclaimed sinner for fifty of his sixty years. He carries the hope of North-fork on his slender frame. As written in our screenplay, Father Harlan's role was as important off-screen as it was on-screen. Father Harlan was the role that was going to anchor the film and hopefully get it financed. Everyone who read the screenplay pointed to Father Harlan as the coveted role. The role was the heart of the screenplay; we needed an actor who had weight, a heavy— someone with depth and history. We wanted an American actor, a legend, or someone with legendary talent. We knew that the perfect actor existed; we had ideas of who could play Father Harlan, beginning with Paul Newman. We realized getting him to commit was a long shot, but why the hell not try? At the time, Newman wasn't acting much. So we thought there was a chance he may consider the role. It was a dream that lasted a minute and then we woke up. Newman's agent told us he wasn't available.

Our next choice was Gregory Peck. Another actor who didn't need another job. We've admired his performances for years. We knew it was another long shot, but again, why not try? Our goal was to find an actor whom we grew up watching and admiring, someone who might not be around too much longer. Unfortunately, Gregory was too ill to consider traveling, not to mention that Montana's extreme weather conditions required an actor in good health. We continued our search for Father Harlan but came up empty. We then turned our attentions to the part of Walter O'Brien, another lead character, who was the head of the Northfork Evacuation Committee. Being a younger part than Father Harlan, we figured the role of Walter would be easier to cast. We still needed some kind of name for the part to help secure our budget. We weren't a cast-contingent production—we didn't yet have the financing, so how could we be?—but we knew later when we went to sell the film that name actors would help our esoteric Montana epic appeal to distributors.

Breaking In: An Actor's Worth

What else do you do in Hollywood on a Friday night than break in to a foreign film finance company? It was 10:30 P.M. and the janitors were starting to clean up. We had a key but didn't even need it because the door was wide open. The janitors were making the rounds. We were with a foreign financier who had interest in *Twin Falls Idaho*. Our goal tonight was to figure out what a particular actress's value was in foreign territories. The financier had previously funded a film with the company we were now breaking in to.

We turned on the reception lights, revealing framed posters of films we had never heard of, released in some far-off place, a galaxy away from Hollywood. Many of the films were straight-to-video productions; some were dubbed from foreign languages. This company had made a lot of money in the 1980s during the VHS boom when product was in demand. It was quantity versus quality. Back then if you had a film with any sort of name actor in it, you could count on a nice payday from video sales alone.

The financier quickly headed to a large metal filing cabinet while the two of us picked through papers on desks. The financier pulled out a couple of files that contained lists of actors' names, the films they were in, and how much the film sold for in each foreign territory. What we saw in black-and-white was that an actress we were considering was worth $250,000 to $500,000 in the foreign marketplace. The financier jotted the stats down on a piece of paper and we split, leaving the door wide open.

Independent films have adopted the '80s video mentality of using a star to sell the film. The star often determines the budget—it's the nature of the film business: the star, more so than story, attracts an audience.

Casting Director

We have never actually had a **casting director.** We feel we are the best judges when it comes to casting our films. Most productions hire a casting director to evaluate and sift through the huge mountain of talent that is out there. Most casting directors have a pulse on who is up-and-coming or know where there is some hidden talent waiting to be discovered. Casting directors can alleviate a huge workload and present whom they think is right for your parts.

Typically, a casting director sits with the director, and they come up with a list of actors and actresses whom they feel best complement the roles. After they complete the list from the most desired to the more re-alistic, it's then up to the casting director to contact the actors' representatives—either an agent or a manager. Depending on the level of the actor, some agents won't even allow their clients to read your script without a **written offer.**

We hadn't experienced the formal offer process until *Northfork.* While casting the role of Cup of Tea, we originally offered the part to Gary Oldman but had to wait numerous weeks to get an answer; he eventually declined due to his schedule. We made several more offers to a handful of actors, but with a shooting schedule looming, we were running out of time. We had reached a place in our career where we could make an offer to nearly anyone, but there was no guarantee we'd get our first few choices. And although we imposed time restrictions—usually a week to ten days—we now had less than twenty-four hours before Cup of Tea was to shoot in Montana. We realized we were being unrealistic about whom we could attain for the role. We wanted an actor to complement Nick Nolte and James Woods. The size of the role to us read bigger than it really was. Getting a big name to play a small part up in Montana was proving impossible. We learned that playing the waiting game is not a wise choice when a shoot date is imminent; it only frustrates other departments and prevents them from doing their preparatory work. We finally found our Cup of Tea in actor Robin Sachs through special effects supervisor Gary Tunnicliffe in Montana. It was the night before the shoot and our costumer, Danny Glicker, was scrambling to fit him until two in the morning. Danny knew the territory

Written offer: A written offer consists of the name of the role you are offering to the actor, how much you are willing to pay for the actor's time, and a general start date and approximate time commitment. You can include how long the actor has to respond to the offer. Since this is a formal offer, you cannot petition other actors for the same part until you have a response. You can, however, have other actors read the part, but you cannot offer them the role. It is wise to put a time limit on how long an actor has to respond to the offer because agents and actors are notorious for taking their time. Making formal offers to actors is time-consuming and can really hold up the casting process.

that comes with independent film, but this type of stress can be prevented. Don't let Hollywood, its system and its ways, control yours. Don't allow your control on the casting process to be indefinitely delayed by procedure. Always keep a tight hold.

Michele Hicks plays Penny/*Twin Falls Idaho*

Casting: Our First Film

We went into *Twin Falls Idaho* with the mind-set that we would find the best actors we could get for the parts. Not the best name actors, but actors with the best acting ability. Having never made a film before, we knew on paper we didn't look like a promising investment. We were first-time actors, writers, and directors. Add a $500,000 budget and a seventeen-day shoot, and you have a recipe for disaster. Now what experienced actor with brains would want to jump on that train wreck? We knew no actor or actresses on the A list would risk doing a film that looked like a B movie (none of the A list even read the script with a tagline about Siamese twins and a hooker).

We didn't go fishing for talent at the big three talent agencies, which at the time were CAA, ICM, and William Morris. The producers sent the screenplay around in hopes of getting a bite, but we knew there wasn't any bait to attract the A list—just a hook that no one wanted to get caught swallowing. As we predicted, we didn't even get a nibble.

So we knew that we had to be resourceful when it came to casting. We cast ourselves as the twins and our neighbor friend Jon Gries as the exploitative lawyer Jay Harrison. Through Jon Gries we got to Garrett Morris and offered him the role of Hey Zeus. Meeting Patrick Bauchau, whom we wanted to play Doctor Miles, was another connection through Jon. Meeting Patrick was easy, but getting him to commit was like getting the French to commit to war. It was a long and lengthy process of in-depth talks about everything except moviemaking.

Patrick had a beautiful sloping garden, and when he wasn't acting, you could drive by and find him planting or pruning. We would spend many late afternoons sipping tea and learning the one thing we had none of—patience. We wanted him to commit, but we didn't want to force him. We didn't even know if he liked the script. We rarely even talked about his character, Miles. But the more we sat with Patrick not discussing our film, the more we developed the character Miles around Patrick the person, from Patrick's worldly views to his pruned accent. The meetings were very beneficial. He and his character were fusing together like our Siamese twins.

While our hearts were set on casting Patrick, the casting conflict came out of nowhere when we finally got the funds to shoot the film. The financiers and the appointed producers wanted some name actors on board, or, as we like to say, they wanted to pull some insurance policies in case our film was a disaster. They could hope to at least sell the film with a name actor attached. One of the roles the producers thought could attract some name talent was Miles. At this point, we had already been courting Patrick for over three months; we didn't have a commitment, but we had faith that in the end Patrick Bauchau was going to play the role. Since we failed to attract name actresses to the part of Penny, we thought that the financiers and the producers realized that the only star was going to be the story and that *it* was what we needed to bank on. Our thinking was to surround the star with solid actors of whatever recognizability. In previous years there were quite a few independent films that used the "story as the star" strategy and had success.

Then again, we empathized with our investor: the $500,000 wasn't ours and it needed some kind of fail-safe protection. So we had to pull back from trying to acquire Patrick while the producers offered the role to several famous actors of their choosing. We were frustrated. What message were we now sending to Patrick? A few days passed and Patrick left for his house in

France. Who knew if he would return to do our movie. The producers finally came around, but at that point it was hard to get in touch with Patrick. We sent word to everyone that Patrick had the part and that his days to work were such and such. A week passed and we began shooting the movie. The morning of his first day, Patrick waltzed in, just off the plane from France. He was ready for the role of Miles. Little did we know then that this practice in "faith" was a rehearsal for what was going to take place in the casting of *Northfork.*

The Gamble

We had already successfully cast two films, but it was our third, *Northfork,* that would prove the most difficult. There were a couple dozen roles to fill, but not a couple dozen actors we had friendships with to fill them. We can only compare our casting office (our personal office reconfigured) to the Dallas Cowboys war room on draft day. With Jonathan Sheldon (our assistant at the time), we listed all the characters in *Northfork* and correlated desired actors' names to the parts using our brick office wall as a giant bulletin board. We listed actors from most desirable to most available, allowing us to eyeball our casting progress.

Scheduling actors is another kind of creative talent. When you're attaining talent for minimal money, that typically buys you a minimal amount of their time. With our focus turned from trying to cast Father Harlan to the role of Walter O'Brien, we searched for an actor in his fifties. We submitted the *North-fork* screenplay to all the major agencies. We waited to see who would respond to the material. Chris Andrews from ICM called and suggested his client James Woods for the role of Walter. Every agency large or small has an agent with a pulse on the independent world. Chris Andrews understood the indie game: no money but, perhaps, a good career film for his client to make. The idea of Woods immediately clicked because physically as Walter he matched up well with the person we had in mind to play opposite him, Mark Polish (or as one of us likes to call him, me). We thought of capturing an older Jimmy Woods, older than he had played in the past (except for the octogenarian in *Ghosts of Mississippi*), really pushing him into a reflective part.

We had a phone conversation with James and invited him to one of our screenings of *Jackpot*. When the screening ended, James walked out and said he was very interested in working with us in the role of Walter O'Brien. That was the good news. The bad news was an impending Screen Actors Guild strike. If we didn't get the rest of the film cast and shot by July, there was a good chance we wouldn't be able to cast any union actors. Hollywood was in a mad dash to get projects cast and shot so that if a strike occurred, their shelves would be filled with movies they could release until the strike was resolved. Both sides, SAG and the studios, were predicting a long-fought battle.

The strike was averted when a compromise was reached on royalties, taking off some time pressure. *Northfork* wasn't ready yet to move into production, and we wanted to avoid pressuring ourselves into making it prematurely. Our financing wasn't in place. James went to another project and we closed up shop. Another low point. We lost James Woods to another movie. The other actors we were considering started taking jobs. Then we got offered acting parts in Neil Jordan's *The Good Thief.* So we traveled to Nice, France, to act in a film starring Nick Nolte. When we got on set, Nick was instantly friendly and put us both at ease. Matt Tromans, Nick's British-born assistant and confidant, was equally gregarious. Matt was very bright and you could see why Nick had him around. One night before going to dinner, Matt went into Nick's hotel suite, which allowed us to take a peek at his room; when we looked in, it was covered with pages of handwritten research he had done for his character, pinned up all over the walls. It was as if he were writing his own movie on the history and life experiences of his character. It was a sight we'd never forget.

At night after the shooting day was wrapped, Nick, Matt, and a few of us would head to a dark wood-stained bar and have a drink. Usually we'd talk about film—and Nick Nolte, being a true supporter of the independents, would give us all a lesson on independent filmmaking. As it turned out, while we were in France, *Jackpot* was playing at the Seattle International Film Festival as was a film Nick starred in, Alan Rudolph's *Investigating Sex.*

We were all sitting, enjoying ourselves, when the two of us got a call from our dad saying *Jackpot* had won an award at the festival, the New American Cinema Award. Nick was very congratulatory and supportive, and the whole experience felt hyper-real being in the South of France and having a celebratory toast with Nick Nolte. As the shoot in Nice wound down, Nick took us aside one night and said, "You know, when we get back to the States, let's do something together. Do you have a part for me in that next one you're doing?"

"Yeah, of course," we said.

Back in L.A., we worked feverishly to get what we hoped would be a final draft of *Northfork* complete. We were thinking Nick could play Walter, who is essentially the lead; Nick had a salesman's haircut at the time, and it seemed like a good fit. Our main focus was getting the script polished. We knew Nick's schedule would start to fill, so we wanted to squeeze in there and see what he thought of the part. A few weeks later, we had a draft we were fairly happy with. So we brought the script over to his house and took a tour of his beautiful Malibu compound. We discussed the script with Nick, and he told us about his younger days of selling Bibles and sleeping in cemeteries. Those details reinforced our thoughts of Nick playing Walter. Matt Tromans was enthusiastic and was going to read the script that night. He asked us what character we thought Nick would be right for. We said we were leaning toward Nick playing Walter, but we would be happy if Nick played a grave digger. A few days later Matt called and said he loved the script. He had one suggestion. Nick should play Father Harlan. Matt, being close with Nick, knew what he would gravitate toward. Nick had done a salesman role in the past, and Matt thought Father Harlan would be an interesting change. We hadn't cast Father Harlan at that point. We mulled it over for about half a second and agreed. Nick then read the script and was immediately drawn to the role of Father Harlan, a preacher who takes care of an ill orphan. His mother had recently passed away and he felt that he had played the role of a caretaker in real life. With Nick Nolte committed, we finally had our Father Harlan in place.

Casting: The Breakdown

Whether or not you employ a casting director, when you start to cast your film, the first thing you need to do is break down your script. What we mean is separating the roles. If you don't feel comfortable doing this, someone else can do it for you. There is a service appropriately titled the **breakdown service.** This is a legitimate casting service, and they want to know that you are also serious—meaning that your project is actually going into production or is close to it. The breakdown service we used was upset with us when we had to send *Northfork* through their service twice (a year and a half apart). Talent agencies pay a fee to subscribe to their service, and they don't want to list roles that aren't actually going to happen. It's a waste of time for everyone.

Once your cast breakdown is out to the industry, be prepared for a flood of submissions and for your phone ringing off the hook. Even if you request that no phone calls be made, agents and managers will call in hopes of getting their client in for an **audition.** We allow everyone to submit their clients. We had boxes upon boxes of **headshots** during our casting process. You just never know whose headshot you're going to come across. Actors and actresses you'd never think of end up being submitted. While it's time-consuming, we have found solid talent like Rick Overton, who was in *Jackpot* and *Northfork.* He was someone who was well-known and loved among the comedy circuit, but we never knew he existed.

The Angels—behind Cup of Tea are Flower Hercules, Happy, and Cod/*Northfork*

You need to develop a casting strategy that reflects the creative needs of your film. Is it the kind of ensemble piece where a wide swath of auditions is required to fulfill your roster of talent? Or is it a more intimate piece where selective interviews would be the best way to secure the services of your key cast members?

Auditioning

For most, the critical courtroom for deciding on your actors is the casting session. You've made your determination on whether this event is going to be a broad, open casting environment or a more intimate, selective auditioning process. First and foremost is creating a favorable working atmosphere for the actors. Careful explanation of the characters to your prospective cast is absolutely essential. This event is both a working relationship and chemistry lesson between the director and each actor who auditions. Script pages are handed out and discussed, and at the appropriate moment, a reading of these pages is performed. If a particular actor strikes a chord during a performance, have another scene ready that offers a different dramatic challenge in your screenplay. Remember your film's range and dramatic objectives, and construct an auditioning process that will illuminate the different emotions that are crucial to the key of the performance.

Videotaping these sessions may be helpful to you. You may complete the reading with a certain evaluation of the talent in front of you, but a subsequent review of these readings with your producer will allow an open exchange of each actor's strengths and weaknesses. Don't assume that by hosting a series of auditions your search for cast members is complete. Consider yourself a bit of a detective in search of clues. Solving the mystery of assembling your special cast may take you to many a small theater, where the sudden glimpse of a certain actor may resonate with your specific needs.

Meeting

When a filmmaker takes a general meeting at a talent agency, a stack of actor headshots accompanied with brief bios on the back are the usual door prize. After a filmmaker has chosen a few candidates for a given part, there will be a reading for the filmmaker and likely the producers. This is where we diverge dramatically from the Hollywood casting procedure: we never have an actor read for us. We don't believe in it. We make casting choices based on the conversations we have had with the actors. We want to hear how an actor responds to the script. Reading, for us, is just a cruel elimination process. Our goal isn't to eliminate anyone. We just want to find a great person to play the part.

We're fortunate to have relationships with some gifted thespians. We couldn't imagine putting Anthony Edwards through an audition so he could show us what we already know. But even with unknown actors, we prefer not to have them read. Instead, we will ask an actor we know and trust for his or her insights, or on some occasions we'll hire an unknown on a hunch. We hired one guy—must have been twenty-one—who sent us a letter explaining his passion for acting and how he liked *Twin Falls.* We choose from our gut, rather than by committee. The best casting advice we can give you is this: cast the part naturally, the way you wrote the script. You are not necessarily looking for a great actor—you are looking for an actor who will be great in your part. Many times we've looked at an actor, thinking this guy's got a great performance in him, only we don't have the part for him. And then we have to pass on him because there is no sense forcing a good actor into the wrong part. There's also little sense in casting a high-profile actor who needs to reinvent himself. In recent years independent films have become what we call acting rehab, where an actor has to detox from all the Hollywood big-budget bullshit and get down to some solid acting.

The Return of Jimmy

Almost a year had passed. The strike didn't happen. We had Nick doing the role of Father Harlan, and we were on the search for a Walter. Chris Andrews invited us to an Academy Awards party. This would be the ideal casting situation. We could meet talent that we'd otherwise never be able to even reach. There we ran into James Woods. He asked if we had shot our movie in Montana. We said we hadn't yet but were going in a month. "Great, why don't you invite me up there?" he said jokingly. We took his mobile number and arranged to have a meeting with him on Monday at the Chateau Marmont. Just like we do with investors, we brought all and any reference material for James to look at. James has a great love for still photography. So the pictures of Montana's barren plains hit him where it counts. He was inspired. We told him we were planning on shooting during the end of winter in northern Montana. "That's cold," Jimmy said. "What's the budget?"

"Well," we said hesitantly, "when we get the money, it will be the minimum: low-budget SAG scale."

"Damn," Jimmy said, "that's *really* cold."

Despite his trepidations, James was firmly on board. He quickly got on his mobile and starting recruiting other talent. Within minutes he had Marshall Bell committed as Mr. Stalling and Graham Beckel as Marvin—two roles that needed to be filled.

Nick of Time

It's one thing to hook a big talent like Nick Nolte; it's another story trying to reel him in. The easiest way to put it is Nick is on his own time. We knew Nick wanted to play the part of Father Harlan, but he couldn't commit. Legally or personally. With *Northfork* we were up against the 500-pound un-jolly green giant they called *Hulk.* Nick Nolte was contractually obligated to fulfill the role of the Hulk's father, and the part of Father Harlan was conflicting. They were two trains on the same track, heading for one another. Up to the final moment, not too many people on either production knew Nick's involvement with *Northfork.* It was quickly becoming a myth that Nick was going to show up and play the father. We had already changed the schedule twice to accommodate him, and we couldn't push it back any further. We needed him and we only had six days left to shoot. The problems were exacerbated by Nick Nolte's unbelievably dense schedule with *Hulk.* Matt Tromans, Nick's assistant, was very helpful and kept us in the loop with what was going on, but the reality was looking grim. Nick was tired, overworked, and who knows what else. We were waiting and waiting for Nick to call, to commit to a firm timeline. Most everyone around us had given up hope. The history of independent film is filled with great actors who were almost in movies. We knew Nick liked the script and wanted to do the part, but a $100 million action movie is a hard thing to sneak away from.

We had reached the breaking pointing waiting for Nick Nolte and were in full crisis mode financially: who was going to play Father Harlan and how were we going to pay for this movie? Matt had arranged a meeting with Nick so we could discuss the part of Father Harlan. On the way up to Malibu, the meeting was canceled. We pulled into a Denny's off the 101 and ate some kind of Slam. We were as close to Nick as we could get. We didn't say much to each other as we ate. We just quietly prayed for his deliverance. Driving home, we remembered a conversation with Matt Tromans in the South of France. He had said Nick responds to personal letters and believes that the humanity people still have left is in letter writing. Struck with the recollection, we composed a straight-up-from-the-heart letter stating how much his participation in *Northfork* would mean to us. "If we could have just a few days of your time, it would mean a lifetime to us" was one of the lines, and we meant every word of it. We faxed the letter to Nick that night, and the next morning we left on a plane to Montana.

When Nick agreed to work out his schedule to be in *Northfork,* we were elated. He said, "I'm gonna do it, I don't know how, but I'll get up there. And let's just keep this between us, not the agents and everybody." That was fine with us, and we started working around *Hulk.* We got his sizes from *Hulk*'s costume designer, his shooting schedule from Matt. We had it fairly well mapped out that Nick would be in and out of Montana in six days at the beginning of *Northfork*'s shoot.

When we got to Montana and started the first day of shooting with James Woods, everything was great except we had only enough money for a few days of shooting—that's a month short—and Nick's schedule on *Hulk* had changed, forcing us to move his scenes to the end of our shooting schedule. The production staff scrambled to work out the logistics; the assistant director, Andy Coffing, twenty-four hours out of an appendectomy, was tirelessly rescheduling the days. And since our deal with Nick was a secret, we couldn't complain to his agent or manager; we had to accept it. We would have midnight conversations with Nick's assistant, trying to get the schedule worked out. Nick had white hair and a beard and wasn't permitted to change it. "No problem," we said. "Let's just get him up here."

All the while, James Woods was being incredibly patient. James would sneak off somewhere in the Montana mountains where he could find cell phone reception and help us cast some remaining parts and even called a few buddies to see about financing the film (although they never panned out). We ended up giving him an executive producer's credit for his unyielding support. Our focus (when we weren't shooting the movie) was redirected at getting Nick Nolte up here, but apparently he was fatigued from the long hours on *Hulk*. As the *Northfork* shoot wore on, the production team thought there was no way in hell Nick was ever going to show up.

We were getting scared, too. The money we had been lent was nearly gone, and without Nick Nolte in the picture, the budget would be hard to recoup. Not to mention, we did not have a backup. Matt Tromans called the day before we needed Nick to shoot. His voice was weary. "The only way we are going to get Nick up there in time is by a fucking jet. He is exhausted and in no shape to travel. He needs rest. A few days at least." We hung up the phone and immediately began ringing personal jet companies that would take American Express. Jonathan located one in Van Nuys, California. The ticket would be around ten grand. We didn't have a choice. We called Matt back and asked if he could get Nick on the plane that evening. We had Jonathan meet them both at the airport and practically lock the door. When we got the message on our mobile phone that the plane was in the air with Nick Nolte on board, we thought, *Finally*.

Moving on up/*Northfork*

8 | **Production Design**

Whether or not an independent film has a full-fledged **production designer,** the job of production design is an inescapable part of a movie's making. Everything from choosing the texture of wallpaper to the construction of movie sets falls under the domain of production design. Simply put, **production design** is the visualization and then the physical representation of what is written in a screenplay. A thorough production design turns each scene into a visual scheme that when filmed will showcase architecture, color, spatiality, textures, and all the tangible elements making up a shot's composition. We all know by now that when making an independent, time and money are not on the filmmaker's side. Certainly, most independent films lack the funds for substantive builds, but, truth be told, poor production

Art director: Because production design is so integral to a film's aesthetic success, an art director is hired. An adjunct to the production designer, an art director helps the PD's vision to be realized.

Set designer: On an indie, the set designer is helping the production manager in whatever way he or she can. On a Hollywood film, a set designer is essentially an architect dealing with the specifics of a big build. For your independent purposes, finding a set decorator who can integrate with your PD is all that matters. When the production designer has conferred with the filmmaker and a general sense of how the sets will look is established, a set designer will draft the general architectural plans for the builds at the PD's request.

design is most likely due to a lack of ingenuity more than a lack of money. The filmmaker needs to explicitly express the flickerings he or she sees on the page to the production designer, the art director, the costume designer, or even to makeup and hair. If not, the result is a hodge-podge of incompatible colors, textures, and symbolism, as each department does its own thing. The bottom line: it's ultimately the responsibility of the filmmaker to make sure he or she can shoot a great-looking film.

If your film cannot afford an experienced production designer, as none of ours could, you'll have to research much of the look to authenticate the story yourself. The enormous studio builds—where an art department the size of an army brigade works around football field–sized spaces inventing, constructing, painting, and then decorating a movie's universe—are not possible for most independent films. Rather, independent production design is about out-thinking the budget and outsmarting the financial limitations. It may be worth your while to hire an ambitious novice. Consider hiring a set designer who wants to double as a production designer or an art student with an architectural background who will work for cheap. We've tried both approaches, and while we had to do much of the design ourselves, having someone function as the production designer made the art department work more cohesively.

Color/Paint

Paint is cheap, and yet it can be the basis for a film having a highly stylized, expensive look. Your **four-wall drama** doesn't have to be a four-white-walls drama. Paint is your ally in the battle to make your independent film visual. It's the most fundamental way to visually convey emotion, to emphasize mood, to highlight the subtext of a film. Since film is, at its source, a visual medium, its color spectrum—spanning the three primary colors of light, blue, red, and green, and their infinite offspring—is film's fundamental communiqué. A screenplay that has been visually rendered by a production designer or an ambitious filmmaker will have a specific color palette attached to it. A color palette sets the tonality of shade and saturation as it relates to story and specifically character, unifying the film in a broad visual way. Many independent filmmakers, though, spend little time contemplating the vocabulary of color, and thus will chalk up their films' incongruous look to

Set decorator: Reporting directly to the production designer, the set decorator is in charge of dressing the sets with whatever is necessary to make the scene visually pleasing. Everything that should reside in each scene—including floor mats, lampshades, framed pictures, flowers, and furniture—is the set decorator's job to note after reading the screenplay.

Prop master: The prop master reads the script and breaks down all the needed props. The prop master and the set decorator have very different jobs: the prop master deals with any object an actor uses (like a cane or an umbrella), while the set decorator works with intransigent items (like a couch or bedframe).

insufficient budgets. The pigment can't be expected to brilliantly mix itself. So while paint is cheap, a painter's touch will add immense value to a production.

For the main sets in *Twin Falls Idaho,* each room was designated a color that represented the character or characters who lived in the space. The twins' hotel room was a pale green. This gave the feeling of rebirth and splendor on the one hand, and decay on the other. Penny's apartment was a deep purple with contrasting lavender stripes. The purple was to emphasize her false sense of royalty, and the stripes were meant to appear as a circus tent pattern when the twins performed their acoustic guitar number. The other main set was the twins' mother's house, which we painted pumpkin orange, an allusion to the twins' birthday, eventually revealed to be Halloween. We were shooting on such a tight schedule that several of the newly painted walls weren't completely dry when we rolled camera.

Northfork's color palette was built on a gray scale. Death and change are, to our minds, a gray zone, and that's where we wanted *Northfork* to reside. To achieve a desaturated effect throughout the entire film, we decided to shoot using color film but to have everything that appeared on-screen fit within ten shades of a gray scale. Color film as opposed to black-and-white would give us the richness we were looking for. We imagined cool grays next to warm grays; this couldn't happen in black-and-white. Plus the fact that selling a black-and-white film in today's market is very difficult—silly but true. Buildings, clothing, accessories—anything and everything that was brought onto the set—had to fit somewhere in the gray spectrum. We gave each designer and builder a gray-scale card and told them never to stray from it. This turned out to be a much taller order than we originally figured. We hadn't noticed how much color there is in the natural world until we tried to mute it. Whether it was the red-and-blue flaring off the American flag or the hunter-safety orange from the diner booths, we were constantly painting or covering our surroundings. To make the diner scene work, we even had to design gray ketchup bottles and Campbell's soup cans.

Campbell's Soup labels were reworked and printed in gray scale to fit the color scheme/*Northfork*

Beyond infusing our films with a specific color palette, we have used a painterly vocabulary to open up our films' cinemagraphic possibilities. As film and painting are both created inside a confined visual space (even the widest IMAX screen has edges), filmmakers can learn invaluable techniques from the master painters of the past. Envisioning the set design for *Twin Falls,* we referenced the works of Vermeer. We have long admired the way he holds light accountable when it enters a room or when it touches his subjects. While some painters sneak up on you, Vermeer's talent is so overt that one need only glance at his paintings to take in his uncanny representation of light. We laser-copied a few choice Vermeer paintings and handed them out to the production designer, art director, costume designer,

Sunny sings Billy Idol's "Eyes Without a Face"/*Jackpot*

and makeup artist, to assure that the creative team was synchronized. We thought the twins' hotel room should have a particularly Vermeer-like illumination.

On *Northfork* the painterly aesthetic was supplemented by a black-and-white photograph: a shot of the dam at Fort Peck that was featured on the cover of the very first issue of *Life* magazine. We were drawn to the irony that in our film about death we used the dam that was first in *Life.* Moreover, it has a really amazing, colossal cement spillway that very few people have ever seen because it is so remotely located. In fact, Fort Peck Dam is still the largest hydraulic earth-filled dam in the world, constructed in the 1930s and finished in 1940 under FDR's New Deal programs. Migrant workers for the huge project lived in shantytowns, some of which were drowned when the dam was completed.

We conceived *Jackpot* looking to Andy Warhol for guidance—illustrating his famous prophesy about fifteen minutes of fame by showing the other forty-five minutes of failure as experienced by karaoke singer Sunny Holiday. We designed the title sequence with Warholian flair, horizontally panning the credits written in a hot pink Cooper font. The color pink became the driving force, from Sunny's Mary Kay cosmetics car to the blown-out pink room of Tangy, a Lolita-esque girl. When you use as powerful a color as pink, you add another layer to the subtext. All colors have their own definition. In this case, pink represented Tangy's purity, innocence, virginity, and lack of sexual experience. *Jackpot* was essentially a road movie with a shooting schedule of fifteen days, so we knew we wouldn't have much time for any exacting production design. But we did want to create simple pop art motifs that would add some context to the run-and-gun filmmaking style. Our main request was for Christmas lights to decorate the karaoke circuit—we thought small twinkling lights would serve as stars for Sunny Holiday's wishes and dreams. In keeping with Warhol's thematics, we edited *Jackpot* with repetition in mind, similar to what Warhol did with his celebrity silk screens—reprinting an image over and over until the ink runs dry and the image becomes weak, losing its power. With the use of the tape deck, George Jones's song "Grand Tour" keeps recurring, as do the karaoke bars, the bathrooms, the highway signs—all of Sunny Holiday's world is a retread, including the songs he sings.

A Visual Screenplay

We believe a film's look is every bit as essential as its dialogue. In the early stages of writing a screenplay, we'll discuss what it is about the story that is visually stimulating and what we can add to the story that later, in pre-production, can be designed for little money. We ask ourselves a series of questions: Does the concept elicit a specific time in history? Wherever the story takes place, what are some of the defining details of its surroundings? What is the weather like and what time of year is it? We strive to make our screenplays the blueprints for our productions. We intentionally write long scene descriptions because we want the cast and crew to share in the visual design.

When we were thinking visually about *Twin Falls,* we conceived of a film made up of tableaux, unfolding in a few locations in a somewhat modern setting during the early part of fall. The prostitute, Penny, we envisioned with raccoon eyes and berry-stained lips. We wanted her to appear withdrawn, as if hiding from the sunlight. As her relationship with the twins becomes more vulnerable, we wanted her makeup to lighten. We included these specific instructions in the scene description of the screenplay along with objects that heighten details of the twins' story. For instance, Blake and Francis's suitcase is described as "a brown weathered guitar case," foretelling their knack for acoustic guitar. We wrote of the twins' hotel bed as "two iron-framed single beds conjoined with a belt," buttressing the sense of conjoinment. Also in the screenplay, to save money and cut back on exposition, we showed a close-up of the twins' birth certificate, explaining who they are and where they are from. Interestingly, many in the audience would miss the close-up shot of the birth certificate, wondering about those details in discussions after seeing the film. Lesson learned: it's difficult for an audience to read such documents. Unless it's on a billboard, try and put such vital information in your characters' dialogue.

Show or Tell

Essentially you have two choices when making your film. Either you're going to show it to your audience or you're going to tell it to your audience. It's a delicate balance between the two. Since movies are a powerful visual medium, we always choose to show it rather than tell it. In *Northfork* there was an opportunity to visualize an entire joke told by Walter (James Woods). The joke deals with a couple stuck on the roof of their house after a flash flood. They wait two days, hoping for a sign from God. We felt the joke would have a greater dramatic impact if it was imagined. To see the couple waiting in vain on their roof in the middle of a lake injected more humor into the movie. If we hadn't decided to visualize the joke, it might have been lost in the cutting room. Always remember to look at everything in your screenplay and decide whether it is best told visually or through dialogue.

Construction

With indies' small crews and little money, building anything for interiors or exteriors is a bit of an undertaking. Preferring to spend what money they have renting a space and decorating it, the vast majority of independently financed filmmakers avoid construction altogether. It need not be so. In fact, more often than not, the reason builds are dismissed outright is mainly financial but also because no one is capable of drafting proper architectural plans and then organizing their execution. Actually, building a set will sometimes be more cost-effective than renting, particularly when the set is to be damaged or drastically modified in the course of filming. But someone or preferably a few someones will need to know the basics of architecture to handle anything beyond a rudimentary structural build.

In northern Montana the winter months aren't very forgiving, and we knew building any kind of set would put *Northfork* up against the elements. But we also knew that for certain key scenes in our screenplay, builds were the only way to get the shots we envisioned. We realized we needed a production designer who not only understood construction but also the terrain and severe weather conditions. Our father is a Montana native with lots of building experience. As we began contemplating who could pull off the construction, hiring our dad to help design *Northfork* made sense. We knew the specifics of the structures we wanted built; we had previously sketched them out. We were relying less on our dad's design ability and more on his knowledge of construction: he had to take our sketches and translate them into the permutations of building. As preproduction got under way, our dad's experience proved invaluable. He was able to bid for materials at a

The skeleton of the ark was ninety feet long and took four weeks to build/*Northfork*

local's price. He knew an Amish lumber mill that supplied the siding for the homesteads at a discount. He had a relationship with local supply yards that bid the ark at a very reasonable price, much lower than the bid from the yard in Los Angeles.

As construction rose around the plains of Montana, our dad and company literally dug their own graves, shoveling out forty-odd holes to form the cemetery. They also erected from scratch a ninety-three-foot ark containing the Stallings' house. They also built a church without a back wall that looked onto a pasture of cows and an outhouse that served as an unexpected confessional. Later the roof of the Stallings' house was removed and surreally set afloat in the Willow Creek Reservoir while James Woods tells the inhabitants that this is their "sign from God." All in all, the point is: Don't be afraid of exploring the possibility of building your own sets. Ingenuity is an independent filmmaker's best tool.

Makeup and Hair

It's important to hire the most experienced makeup artist and hairstylist you can find. This will make all the difference in the comfort and confidence of your actors, particularly for the veteran actors who have an expectation of professionalism in the dressing room. Sometimes, veteran actors will insist on bringing their favorite makeup and hair person to assuage their anxieties. Since well-established actors work on indies for practically no money, they at least expect to look their best. It is one thing if a character is a bit south in the beauty department, but it's another matter when an actor looks orange because an inexperienced makeup artist applied the wrong shade of foundation.

We have been fortunate to work with a very talented and experienced makeup artist named Jo Strettell. She had a background doing the makeup for high-end fashion shoots and was able to use her knowledge to create numerous looks for our character Penny in *Twin Falls*. From a coal-eyed hooker to a natural sun-kissed girl, Penny was transformed by Jo to match the mood of each scene. With so many makeup changes and a nonsequential shooting schedule (which is the norm for most films), Jo had to work very closely with the other departments

Makeup artist: Whether applying foundation or gluing fake eyelashes, the makeup artist has a goal to enhance the actor's immersion into his or her character.

Hairstylist: Cutting and blowing, shearing and coiffing, you get the idea. It sounds simple, but an untalented hairstylist can ruin an actor's believability. Particularly for period pieces, the hairstylist is vital.

to make sure Penny's makeup was cohesive throughout the shoot. For the makeup of the Siamese twins, Jo's attention to detail made a huge impact on the film. Although we are technically identical twins, we do have some notable facial differences. Jo was able to apply makeup to even out our faces, making us appear incredibly symmetrical. It required her to understand our skin type and tone.

Sometimes you may be able to find a makeup artist who also does hair or vice versa. A person who can confidently handle both jobs is very beneficial on the days when there are a lot of actors required on set. On our first two films, Jo oversaw both the makeup and hair. On *Northfork,* we had both a makeup artist and a hairstylist. Whoever you hire to handle makeup and hair, be sure to discuss the overall look of the picture. It's important for the makeup and hair person or people to strive for a well-defined visual.

Costume Design

Costume design is basically the production design of fashion. All of the same general design considerations are present in both: color, texture, shape, location, period of time, social rank. But where a production design element may be speaking to an overarching theme of the film, an article of clothing should always, at least in part, be character specific. For example, while the gray fedoras donned by the Evacuation Committee in *Northfork* were in keeping with the gray scale of our film, the hats were also telling the audience of the characters' time and place. Clothing should tell the audience something significant about a character's world, perhaps even something subconscious in the character himself.

Comprehensive costume design in the independent realm is hard to find. Most first-time filmmakers do not know the difference between a stylist—

someone who picks out clothes—and a **cos-tume designer,** who not only picks out clothes but can design and construct them as well. We have been fortunate to work with people who understand the construction of costumes. They understand how things are made. They know fabric. They know stitching. They know what fashion is by creating it.

In all our films, the characters have had some piece of clothing specifically described in the screenplay. It is the costume designer's job to seek out the clothing described and add all necessary accessories. Beyond following what's prescribed in the script, a skillful costume designer will find a style in the story's architecture and transfigure it to help fashion each character. On an independent film, thrift shops and home closets are often the only affordable place to go

Costume designer: The costume designer creates an overall look for a film's costumes, including palette, texture, and cultural, historical, or social references. He or she is then responsible for selecting clothing and accessories, and also for designing and making original pieces. The costume designer may also work on set, during filming, to make sure the clothing works with the landscape or set design and lighting, and to handle the actors' and director's costume requests.

for costuming the cast. Still, we have tried to do some design in each of our three films to give the characters a unique look. A talented costumer will help you maximize a meager budget.

The first thing a costume designer does is read and interpret the script to chart the continuity of the wardrobe and evaluate the number of wardrobe changes each character will need. Next, he or she comes up with an overall look for the costumes, including palette, texture, and cultural, historical, or social references. The costume designer then presents the wardrobe concepts to the director, producer, and actors using research materials, fabrics, color samples, and sketches. Once the look is approved, the costume designer

Script supervisor:
The script supervisor is in charge of making sure the continuity of the film is being tended to. Typically, a script supervisor will do a continuity breakdown, noting all elements of the story from costumes to props to hair color that must remain the same throughout the shoot. The continuity breakdown is given to each crew department. On set, the script supervisor is there to ensure that all those little details of continuity are executed.

Wardrobe supervisor: The wardrobe supervisor is responsible for the continuity, maintenance, and cleaning of clothing.

estimates a realistic budget for purchases, rentals, construction, and cleaning. No matter how low the film budget, chances are the actors will not own all the necessary wardrobe. There are continuity requirements that require doubles or triples of an outfit, such as in a fight scene. And while rental houses are often generous with low-budget films, the cost of cleaning is unavoidable.

During all of preproduction, the costume designer should keep in close communication with the director and with the production designer and cinematographer to make sure that all the wardrobe choices mesh with the colors and textures of the rest of the production. The costume designer will present fitting photos to the director, and make any further adjustments to more accurately communicate character and tone. When filming commences, the costume designer will be on set the first time each costume is seen in front of the camera to make sure that the clothing works with any last minute surprises in landscape or set design, lighting, actor requests, or director's observations.

The costume designer is also in charge of staffing the wardrobe department. On an indie, there may be just one or two other people in wardrobe, the most important of whom is the **wardrobe supervisor,** responsible for the continuity, maintenance, and cleaning of clothing. Even on an exceptionally small film, there will be at least one other person in the costume department, usually a **wardrobe assistant** who helps the actors get dressed, maintains the wardrobe, and keeps track of the money spent. This person can also act as a **set costumer,** charged with keeping the clothes in perfect order during filming to ensure continuity throughout the shoot.

For *Twin Falls,* we knew Blake and Francis would have the "freak" label no matter how we dressed them. To counter this as much as we could, we dressed them as gentlemanly as possible, presenting them in the most socially conservative attire. On the other hand, Penny, the

> **Wardrobe assistant:** The wardrobe assistant helps the actors get dressed, maintains the wardrobe, and keeps track of the money spent.
>
> **Set costumer:** The set costumer keeps the actors' clothing in perfect order during filming to ensure continuity throughout the shoot. On an independent, this may be done by the wardrobe assistant.

prostitute, we wanted to dress as a prototypical fashion whore, a designer label–monger with secondhand clothes adapted to fit her nightlife. The costume designer on *Twin Falls* (and later on *Jackpot*) was Bic Owen. She had a clothing designer's background, having designed in England. Although she had never designed for a movie before, Bic had created her own line of clothing and understood the basics of filmmaking and what was expected of her. She brought a great enthusiasm to the set that wasn't dampened by her paltry budget. If items of clothing were too costly, she would make them herself. If the fabric didn't come in a desired color, she would dye it. One afternoon we all went down to the Garment District in downtown Los Angeles to buy the cheapest suits we could find, knowing that we needed to rip them apart and reconstruct them to fit the twins' frame. Calling upon her experience as a seamstress, Bic was able to make a most debonair conjoined suit. That's what a real costume designer should be able to do.

Irwin's bedside table and the stuff of his dreams/*Northfork*

Northfork called for the most elaborate costume design we had ever encountered. The sheer size of the main cast, some fourteen principals, meant a large wardrobe closet and an overworked costume designer. Fortunately we had hired a young buck, Daniel Glicker, who rose to each and every challenge. One of the major considerations was how to fashion the vagrant angels. The angels were all manifestations of various items near Irwin's bedside, but we weren't sure how to best dress a Cup of Tea. We wrote the character as an Englishman with a snippy tongue. Our visual idea was to dress him like a version of the Cheshire cat from *Alice in Wonderland,* forever in leisure wear. Danny came along to add his vision and talent, making actor Robin Sachs the man of the house.

For many weeks we had debated how Flower Hercules should be dressed. We had written the part specifically for Daryl Hannah, and now the challenge was to get the beautiful, long, and lanky girl to look like a hermaphrodite, as a flower would be in nature's garden. We didn't want to portray Daryl as overly masculine, squeezing her frame into an awkward costume. So the idea we had was to make her appear as a cross between Prince Charming and Joan of Arc. A perfect marriage, if you will. Daryl was game for anything and allowed us the freedom to truly transform her. Her makeup was rendered neutral and her hair nicely tucked away; our hairstylist chopped into a wig, creating a boyish cut. We played up the wig, having Daryl fuss with it during her scenes with Irwin, giving the appearance that she was bald underneath it.

Our character Happy was based on the *Antiques Roadshow*. He is the appraiser and has a "don't touch" attitude. He is actually a double amputee and may have touched too much. Being our heavy-handed character, he is the angels' moral compass, and the spectacles he wears are representative of those lying next to Irwin's bed. Cod the mute played by Ben Foster is the music, so Danny had stitched musical notes onto his jacket. A simple detail that gave you Cod's musical past.

One of the most unusual costumes we dealt with on *Northfork* was the teetering dream-dog named Flaco. When Irwin is searching for his band of angels, he spies Flaco, who shows the boy the way to the angels' domicile. Flaco's inspiration came from a street performer parading in a carnival on the streets of Brazil while we were publicizing *Twin Falls*. This was another CGI dilemma. Like Blake and Francis, we felt a more organic creation would serve the story set in the '50s. It was an extraordinary-looking thing, made out of leather and resting on four tall stilts. We admired the ingenuity of the costume. It was at once haunting and irresistible, formidable yet rickety. Using our memory as a guide, we had designer Gary Tunnicliffe, who also worked with us on *Twin Falls,* create a costume meant to look like a Buddhist temple dog carved out of wood. Gary built Flaco entirely by hand without the use of any special effects,

The hairdresser chopped a wig up to make Daryl Hannah's character more androgynous/ *Northfork*

Many thought Flaco was CGI; in actuality he was an actor walking on stilts/*Northfork*

using dyed Styrofoam to resemble antique wood, leather, and much embroidery. The costume was worn by an actor, and it completely covered his body as he teetered on stilts. The effect is of a fragile, tender creature that would catch the eye of a little boy, a kind of lost puppy that our little boy, Irwin, could relate to and follow.

David Mullen and the first AC/*Northfork*

9 | Camera

We have just driven down to the Cantina off Las Palmas in Hollywood. It has a circular counter where customers sit and eat, a throwback to a 1940s diner. As we walk in with our camera bags, Annie Leibovitz is directing traffic as several men place pulse lights around a corner canvas booth enclosing a Formica table. A giant black screen on wheels is maneuvering behind the table, creating a black backdrop. We approach Annie and she addresses us with respect, asking if the lighting will suffice for our needs. It does and we begin setting up.

About an hour before, we had received a call from Annie Leibovitz's assistant. She was frantically looking for someone to roll film to supplement Annie's shoot. It was a last-minute idea. The makeup artist on the session,

Incident light meter: A rectangular device about the size of a television remote control that measures the light gathered on a three-dimensional object—most often an actor's head. By holding the incident meter by an actor's face while pointing it toward the camera, its reading will tell the average light coming from all directions hitting the face. The light meter is used in film and photography. However, lighting a shot for film is a bit trickier than for photography. Assuming you want to see your actors, lighting for film must take into account that the film is being exposed at the average rate of twenty-four frames per second.

who was Michael's girlfriend, recommended us for the job. Truth be told, before this moment we had never been hired professionally to shoot anything. Our résumé includes various odd jobs bagging groceries and one short film unknown to Annie Leibovitz. We begin to unpack our cameras—one is the Arriflex 16S (a 16 mm camera); the other is a Bauer super 8.

The German-made Arriflex 16S was our first experience with a real movie camera. It was one of the cameras of choice during the Vietnam War and (of the same era) for NFL films. While considerably noisy, the Arriflex became popular for its durability and clarity of picture; it was ideal for capturing bombs exploding or quarterbacks throwing them. When we got our hands on this camera, we were excited because it brought us closer to the type of cinematography we imagined. Up until then we had been mostly shooting super 8 with our Bauer camera, a nice picture, too, but a long way from feature filmmaking.

We take off our lens caps and mount the Arriflex on a tripod while leaving the Bauer super 8 handheld. We are a little nervous racking focus for a legend of still photography. Annie is checking an **incident light meter** she's holding above the Formica table, leaning into the canvas booth around which the shot is centered. The meter is telling her some valuable information.

We signal to Annie that we are ready to roll film. She is pacing about, planning where she wants to position herself. She pulls one of the lights back

Cinematographer David Mullen meters the light/*Northfork*

a little, pushes forward the black screen, and steps backward, looking satisfied for a moment. She then turns to us with an intense gaze. "Whatever you do," she says, "don't stop rolling." We nod our heads, but it is harder than it sounds. The Arriflex takes a load of a hundred feet of film, which lasts for all of three minutes if you're running a standard twenty-four frames per second. The Bauer super 8 takes a load of fifty feet, and at twenty-four frames per second lasts half as long. Switching a load takes a little practice but can be done quickly if you're experienced. We are sort of experienced, but one mistake could lead to some serious downtime. The key is to keep some tension on the film as it goes through the guides. Once the **torque motor** has it in its grip, you're ready to go.

Taking a seat at the now fully lit booth are Steven Spielberg, David Geffen, and Jeffrey Katzenberg, and this is their first publicity shoot since they announced the creation of DreamWorks twenty-four hours ago. They ask us how we would like them to sit; Annie waits for our reply. We put Steven on the left, David in the middle, and Jeffrey on the right. We load our cameras with raw film as Steven looks on and tells us how much he wished he had an Arriflex 16 mm camera when he started.

We begin to roll film as Annie flashes picture after picture. Our film load doesn't last long, so we are constantly reloading, but we have our cameras staggered so one is always up. Steven, David, and Jeffrey ease into their seats and, realizing they'll be here for a while, begin to discuss company plans. It becomes apparent to us that DreamWorks is still just an idea like any idea, but that this idea will soon become a monumental reality. Yet there is still something homespun about the whole thing. They discuss placing their studio in Santa Monica and how long it will take to construct it. It's an intimate conversation, filled with enthusiasm for their new venture. We keep rolling film as Annie prowls around angling for the next shot. Somehow everything seems equalized as we stand behind our cameras. We have a job to complete, and it dawns on us that everyone here started somewhere.

Learning to Shoot

Because we are not cinematographers, we had to do some studying to be actively involved with the cinematography of our films. Before we ever made a movie or even a real short, we were living in a cheap New York hotel room dreaming of making movies. We were on a diet of pizza and orange juice, with any leftover money spent on buying and developing 16 mm film. We disliked the look of video, which back in the early 1990s was nowhere near the high-definition quality of today. And even as cinematic as super 8 could be, it still felt miles away from 35 mm filmmaking. But 16 mm, we found, was actually a reasonable alternative to 35 mm—it diffuses a little bit in blowup, but it still retains a great deal of clarity when projected on the big screen. Moreover, 16 mm offered some advantages over 35 mm, such as a smaller, less-expensive camera and cheaper film stock and development costs. We started making handmade shorts inside our hotel using our Arriflex 16S. The camera had three built-in lenses to choose from: 5.7 mm, 12 mm, and 24 mm. A lens is identified by its **focal length,** which is measured in millimeters—the lower the millimeter, the wider the angle. All three lenses on the Arriflex were relatively wide angles, providing not much flexibility but enough to learn the basics of camera work. While one of us composed the shot behind the camera, the other would perform a solitary activity like sleeping or shaving. We used the hotel room's natural decor— drab curtains, an old radiator, a freestanding bathtub—as the backdrop. These shorts were in many ways the precursor to *Twin Falls Idaho.*

After we made a handful of our two-man hotel room movies, we felt it was time to make a full-fledged short film—to do so, we needed to find a cinematographer. We met David Mullen through a fellow filmmaker and later found out he was getting his master's at CalArts, while Michael was just finishing a bachelor of fine arts. We gave David our first short screenplay, which was fifteen pages long. He called later to say he was interested in working with us. We told him we didn't have much in the way of money. All he asked for were expenses for the location shoot in northern California, "so my wife doesn't think I'm taking a vacation." As we began to go through our storyboards with David, we realized we had found a visual collaborator. He was just as eager as we were to explore an architect's design or a painter's use of light and to apply the knowledge to cinematography. Whether it was aeronautics, photography, or fine art—really, you name it—the three of us were exploring unique ways to enhance the visuals in the screenplay, and David equally had a lot of great ideas. David had more experience and knowledge of the camera, but he didn't use that against us.

He said one thing that has stuck with us: "Don't be afraid to ask the dumb question."

Storyboards

The time constraints intrinsic on an independent film shoot can be allayed somewhat by prior **storyboarding** of the screenplay. The sketched rendering of each scene from the camera's point of view gives the filmmaker and cinematographer a starting point for each setup. Considering how much work it is just for the basics—any setup involving a dolly or a large configuration of lights will take a couple of hours or more to get right—there really isn't much time for experimentation. The last thing a filmmaker can afford to do on an indie is expend a large amount of time searching for anything nonessential. This is why a visual map to the production shoot is so useful. Storyboarding is the primary way a filmmaker can preplan the composition of a scene.

The use of storyboards has made our ambitious shooting schedules manageable. We have been able to avoid unnecessary **setups** by combining shots in the storyboarding process. The boards helped all involved visualize our movies before being on set. And even when some of the boards have felt a bit off, at least, even then, we knew we had a visual aid on what not to do. Having storyboards for *Northfork* was critical to shooting the film in twenty-four days in Montana. With locations, weather elements, and the shooting schedule so tight, we had to have a very specific plan of attack.

On our first short film, we drew the storyboards ourselves. Since then, our DP, David Mullen, has drafted them with us. He is a talented sketch artist who makes the boards close representations of each shot's possible composition. But getting started with storyboarding doesn't require any kind of fine art training or even drawing ability. The goal is to solve the visual questions in your screenplay. Even if you draw stick figures standing in a rectangular room, it's a positive step toward an understanding of what's to come.

The Twin Tableau

The major obstacle in *Twin Falls Idaho* was the immobility of the twins. The twins didn't have the ability to get up and walk across the room without exposing their additional arms and leg. So we needed the look of *Twin Falls Idaho* to be painterly, emphasizing the use of natural light. If the shot was to be static, at least it could be beautiful. We specifically had in mind the works of Vermeer, the great Dutch master painter's use of natural illumination, adding to the mix Edward Hopper's use of artificial light sources in night scenes as well as his expressions of loneliness inside a cityscape, and finally the early German expressionist Edvard Munch's psychology of colors. There was this sort of sickly green that Munch sometimes employed for the color of background walls. Green has many representations from decay to disease, from repose to rejuvenation. We wanted to paint the hotel room in monochromatic greens, which would allow us to change the mood of the room by altering the color bias of the lighting as the story dictated.

We briefly discussed whether the film should actually be shot in black-and-white, which would have certainly been visually dramatic. There was a discussion of a low-rent look, very grainy. But David Mullen, our cinematographer, advised us not to put the grain on the film itself, but rather to put it in the set. He suggested we design the dirty and dingy look we had in mind. Making the celluloid grimy would only create a distance from the audience and potentially block the viewer from seeing the picture. There were also financial reasons for not shooting in black-and-white: exhibitors want to screen color films—it's a mentality that goes back to the transition to color cinematography in the 1950s—thus distributors are less likely to pick up a

Skip-bleach process:
The skip-bleach process is a method of film development that bypasses the bleach bath. Typically, 35 mm film is put into a bleach bath to remove the silver granulars inherent in color film. By skipping the bleach process, a film retains more of its silver, which will make the images retain intensely rich blacks.

Flashing: Flashing the negative is when the film stock is exposed to light either before or after the image is captured in the camera. The effect of flashing knocks down the overall contrast of the film, making the imagery more muted than it would naturally be.

black-and-white film. And, obviously, the use of color symbolism would have been rather impossible on colorless film. The solution was to shoot in color but to desaturate the image enough so that it had some of the mood and tonality of black-and-white photography. The question then became how do we best **desaturate** the image?

We did a test using the **skip-bleach process.** This was a step in the right direction. We next tried **flashing the negative.** There is a way to flash film in the development lab that allows for manipulation and is essentially a safeguard. But it is costly and all too reversible if an investor were to disagree with our preference. So we decided to use a device called a Panaflasher, which connects to the camera and will flash the film irreversibly. But this was risky. If the flashing went too far, the footage would be ruined. This was a relatively new process. The one film we looked to was David Fincher's *Seven.* But that was a multimillion-dollar production—no independents were doing this process; and with a half a million–dollar budget, we decided this process would best be kept a secret from the producers and financer.

Once we had settled on the desaturation process, we discussed the color schematics. The film should begin in very cold blue-green tones—almost as if the scenes were underwater—and move into warmer colors as Penny be-

An HMI light is positioned to illuminate the interior of a 1947 Ford sedan/*Northfork*

came friends with the twins. We wrote it into the shooting script that the first interior scene when Penny meets Blake and Francis would take place at twilight. To get this effect on set, David bathed the room in very soft, dim blue lighting—and when the twins stepped into the small bathroom to get Penny a glass of water, he had the bathroom window covered with a green plastic curtain so that the light shining through was a very dim emerald. Between the blue dusk falling in the main room and the soft green light in the bathroom, the effect on film was a watery, dreamlike feeling.

Ten days after we **wrapped,** a small group of us went out to an abandoned cliff-side road overlooking the Pacific Ocean to shoot a dream sequence. In the dream we see Blake and Francis, no longer conjoined, riding on bicycles next to each other until at one point they take different paths and separate forever. The dream comes between the desaturated scenes of the film and the epilogue with its normal color saturation. We shot the sequence in the super 8 format, using Kodachrome 64; the weather was rather foggy with a hot, hazy background—beautiful for filming. Later we transferred this footage to 35 mm by rephotographing the image as it was being projected onto a white screen. The burned-out background from the weather and the contrast of Kodachrome really enhanced the images' surreal quality.

The Grand Tour

In the summer of 2000, we approached our *Twin Falls* cinematographer, David Mullen, about another low-budget feature-length project that we wanted to shoot quickly in some form of digital video. The main character, being a down-on-his-luck country singer seduced by his dream of fame, didn't deserve 35 mm, or even 16 mm, or even the coolness of 8 mm. Or, rather, film didn't deserve him. We wanted to use a format that commented on our character. High-definition video seemed well suited for this subject matter. The word that came up the most during our discussions of a look was "hyperreal"—we didn't want the reflective, poetic qualities that film gave us for *Twin Falls Idaho,* but something more immediate, something both glamorous and somewhat tacky, something a little too shiny and new. The lead was a country singer who found he could perform on the karaoke circuit, able only to imitate people he wanted to be. And the closer he could imitate a famous country singer, the more he would be rewarded. Thus, the camera we thought to use was the 24P HD camcorder—essentially, imitation film. It was the camera that tried the hardest to imitate film: a perfect complement to our character. The viewer would look at the film trying to see if it would expose itself as video, just as the karaoke crowd would examine our singer to see his flaws and limitations.

While we were all excited about shooting in mini DV, we had some technical concerns about using any consumer-style camcorder. David was worried that since many scenes were low lit and since one of the two leads was a very dark-skinned African American and the other was a very light-skinned Caucasian, we would have problems keeping the contrast down. (David's skin tone is somewhere in between so we can't really accuse him of overreacting.) We wanted to be sure that the camera had all the professional features we might need to control contrast and exposure. The other concern was that the DV camera wouldn't have enough mass for doing smooth and slow pans or tilts on a tripod. It wasn't a huge concern, though, because most of the shots were going to be static compositions or, at most, have minimal camera movement.

Things were moving at a fast clip as we researched the DV camera further. At a stage at Paramount Studios, we saw a lighting test with the 24P HD camcorder. The demonstration suggested that low-key film-style lighting techniques could be employed when using the 24P HD camcorder, and that it handled dark areas of the frame very well, which was our biggest concern. We also went to EFILM, a company that does laser-recorder work transferring digital to 35 mm. We saw a projected demo of different video formats recorded to 35 mm—material that originated in a variety of video formats, such as NTSC, PAL, mini DV, digital Betacam, and HDCAM. By far, the best-looking footage was shot in 24P HD. **Standard-definition interlaced-scan video** formats produced noticeable artifacts in the image, creating warbled diagonal lines. Fortunately, we got the camera we were hoping for when we made a deal with Sim Video, a Toronto-based video rental house, to allow us to shoot on their new 24P Sony HDW-F900 camcorder. We also made a deal with EFILM to do the transfer to 35 mm when the shoot was complete.

Production began on August 14, 2000, and we shot the movie in fifteen days in various locations in Los Angeles, mainly in the San Fernando Valley. When you mix a small crew, a video camera, and San Fernando Valley, you are instantly labeled a porn shoot. While we were shooting, a porn news van pulled up and asked us what porn actors or actresses were in our movie.

With no time for any elaborate set designs, our main visual concept was that the night scenes in the karaoke bars would be richly colored to contrast with the more mundane settings encountered in daytime—to create a sort of low-rent glamour for the karaoke contests. We even went so far as to use the Sony camera's internal star **filter** for some musical numbers, something David switched into as a joke. But when he showed it to us, we saw it as a great way to enhance the sort of retro-1970s, television-variety-act quality of the scenes. In fact, the first shot of the movie was the result of another joke David had made. When trying to think of a new angle to shoot our lead, Sunny Holiday, sitting in his pink Cadillac listening to music, David suggested that the only angle we hadn't shot yet was from inside the tape-deck slot looking out at Sunny. So later that night in our hotel room, David carved a slit into a shoe box and mounted the hi-def camera behind it. We had Jon Gries (Sunny Holiday) staring down while popping a cassette into the cardboard hole. Because it was such a restrained field of vision, the shoe box worked perfectly as the cassette player.

Because the production was moving around almost on a daily basis, we needed a compact assortment of lights. Our lighting package consisted mostly of Kino Flos, Dedolights, a few 1200-watt HMI PARs (our brightest lamp, like a big spotlight), and a few small tungsten units (halogen bulbs, very bright and portable). Most of the bar locations were lit with a couple of Kino Flo tubes that were covered in party gels and dressed into the set, plus strategically placed Dedolights, often in the shot as well. What really helped

One of many bathrooms we filmed during our bathroom, bar, and bedroom tour/*Jackpot*

the lighting, though, was the use of smoke, which raised the ambient detail in the room. Every karaoke bar sequence had a scene in the bar's bathroom before the performance, since this was Sunny's dressing room. To keep these little rooms interesting visually, they were also dressed with colorful Kino Flo tubes taped in odd places, as if built into the location. We ran regular household power at most locations, except two: an empty field at night and one bar that had almost no available power. For those two days, we used a generator. In one scene involving a police arrest, we used revolving police car lights and two flashlights. One flashlight was covered in an **ND gel** so that when it was pointed at Sunny's face, it would be normally exposed, while the

ND gel: A gel is a sheet of dyed plastic, and ND stands for neutral density filter, which is gray in color and affects all colors equally by reducing the amount of light.

other, ungelled, flashlight was allowed to really overexpose Sunny or flare the lens as it moved with almost every light in the shot, whirling or moving or rising and falling in intensity.

We had to work quickly, shooting at multiple locations per day with a small lighting package, so one technique David used was to set up the camera and HD monitor and look at the location in natural light, to determine the minimal amount of lighting we needed for the scene. Sometimes we were happy with the natural light in the room and we didn't add any lighting at all. But for the bar locations, plus their bathrooms, the room was more or less "created" by the colored lights that we added, shining through smoke.

Even though *Jackpot* was shot on video, it was true run-and-gun filmmaking. We treated it like film, lit it like film, and probably had the same amount of stresses due to the newness of the hi-def technology. The major benefit of HD is its cost-effectiveness (though later transferring to 35 mm for exhibition will be costly) and the speed of setup. There was a wonderful yet exhaustive energy using a format that allowed us to shoot a feature this quickly. We had to live with the sacrifices one makes when only shooting a few takes per scene, but we were hopeful the magic would be captured when the whole piece was assembled.

The risk and benefit of shooting on video should be weighed carefully, because being able to shoot endless footage on the fly can make a good script go bad. Telling a great story is what counts, so whatever format you shoot on should support that intention. This HD format seems to be catching on, though, and we should be seeing a lot more HD features. Already network and cable television are in the midst of an HD explosion with more and more content being shot on this format.

The Gray Garden

With its period story and its poetic textures, *Northfork* called for 35 mm film. It deals with the limbo between life and death, so we wanted to shoot 35 mm in a very extreme way, by muting almost all of its naturally vibrant color. We briefly looked into the possibility of making a digital intermediate, which is technology allowing extremely precise manipulation of color and contrast in digital transfer after a film is edited. But after looking at some tests and the high cost of an intermediate, we decided that a more organic, photochemical approach was better for our 1950s story, which needed a noncontemporary feeling. We wanted to achieve a faded, monochromatic look for *Northfork,* even more radical than that of *Twin Falls.*

Our visual references were varied, and we began to create a schema with David. We were drawn to the wide-screen country landscape paintings of Andrew Wyeth, early color processes like **autochromes,** the black-and-white portraitures of Robert Frank—we had a photo book we have long admired called *The Americans*—and, more broadly, David introduced the black-and-white documentary photography of the Depression era. Since the story takes place on the windy plains of Montana, at the base of the eastern Rocky Mountains, we felt that the 2.35:1 **aspect ratio** (**CinemaScope**) would best capture its grandeur. David was worried that shooting in super 35, which uses more of the film area than standard 35 mm, would cause a problem when it was transferred by an **optical printer** and then blown up to **scope** through **dupe elements.** We feared this would

Dupe elements:
A second-generation negative used for making copies of the film and transfers to other formats. "Dupe" is an abbreviation for "duplicate," a copy of another piece of film. Since the original negative of a movie is highly valuable and delicate, copies are made onto intermediate duplicating stocks, for archival protections and for making large numbers of release prints without risk to the original.

Anamorphic lens:
A camera lens that compresses a widescreen image to fit in a standard film frame. An anamorphic lens on a projector then decompresses the image to its normal width when shown on the screen.

degrade the image too much, especially when combined with the heavy image manipulations we had planned. So we opted for standard 35 mm shooting with Primo **anamorphic lenses** from Panavision.

To desaturate the image, we used a number of techniques. The most effective one was to simply art-direct each scene in as colorless a way as possible, although this doesn't work well for wide scenic shots. Fortunately, the great plains of Montana were stark and monochromatic during our winter-land shoot, frosted by Mother Nature's hand. Wherever needed, we painted our locations gray, usually interiors. We went as far as to sew together a black-and-white American flag and, in a diner scene, make gray Campbell's soup can labels. The costume design was also entirely in shades of gray.

Expanding much further on an approach used in *Twin Falls Idaho,* we decided to flash the negative (using the Panaflasher) to soften the colors and contrast, going as high as a 20 percent flash on most day exteriors. We combined this with ProMist **diffusion filtration** (which softens the image with a mistlike effect), and most of the sets were smoked as well. We pulled back on the diffusion for the extreme wide shots, so as not to lose the subtle details in the rolling hills, distant mountains, and stormy skies above. In fact, much of the weather we encountered on our twenty-four-day shooting schedule was quite bad.

What helped us cope with *Northfork*'s unpredictable weather conditions and grueling shooting schedule was an additional cinematographer and director referred to collectively as the **second unit.** A second unit is typically a stand-alone mini film crew with its own cinematographer and director with all the necessary film equipment to shoot. Technically, we had what is termed a **splinter unit** because the DP and second unit director relied on the first unit's equipment for such things as camera lenses and extra crew. We referred to them during the shoot as the second unit, because they did have a second unit director, which usually isn't the case for a splinter unit. After the first unit would complete a set of shots, we would make a list of **insert shots,** additional coverage we felt we may have missed after we left a location. Mostly, the second unit spent its time shooting exterior shots of the Montana plains. This allowed the first unit to move quicker and focus on actor performances.

A second unit can be a great addition to a film shoot if it is well thought through. But be cautious, if equipment is in short supply (which is almost always the case on an indie), the second unit can drain valuable resources from the main production. The fastest way to get a splinter into the side of the production is to have your splinter unit taking much-needed equipment miles away from the movie set.

Coach Woods with the Evacuation Committee/*Northfork*

10 | Producing

"Well, if it ain't the bottom feeders."
—Ursula, the octogenarian waitress in *Northfork*

We had just ordered monster tacos from Del Taco off the main strip in Great Falls, Montana. We forget what number the combo meal was, but it included two tacos, large fries, and a large Coke. When we were writing *Northfork*, we'd split the number 2 at McDonald's: two cheeseburgers, fries, and a Coke. In both instances the underlying fact was the same: we were dead broke. But unlike our McDonald's of the past, this time we had seventy mouths to feed, not just our two. And the hungry mouths belonged to seventy members of the hardworking crew from *Northfork*. We ate our tacos on the side of the street. They weren't much more than pouches of grease.

Emotionally, we were sunk; we felt we were as low as we could get. The only thing lower than us was whale shit. How were we going to deal with

Personal guaranteed loan:
In independent film financing, a personal guaranteed loan is when a bank or an investor makes a loan to X Production, and a person (usually the filmmaker) personally guarantees the repayment. This is a very risky loan for the guarantor because all personal assets are on the line if payment is defaulted.

tomorrow morning and a production with no money? We had just given the crew their per diem out of our own personal bank account. Our families were back in Los Angeles, and whether they knew it or not, they were now part of the struggle. We had already signed a **personal guaranteed loan,** which means if we couldn't repay, anything we owned in our names was up for grabs. To put it in Las Vegas gamblers' terminology, on the roulette table we had just shoved everything we owned on the color red and the ball was about to drop. In Great Falls, Montana, there isn't even a millionaire you could sleep with to pick up the bill. We are filmmakers who can't turn to the producers and ask what the hell are we going to do: we are the producers.

What a producer does on one project may vary on another, but generally producer responsibilities include the following: obtaining financing and the cast, overseeing how the financing is spent, planning the production, hiring the crew, negotiating equipment deals, overseeing location scouting, making sure the film is on schedule, keeping a general overview of the film's progress, supervising the film's postproduction, and overseeing the sale of the film once it is completed.

Giving proper credit to who did what is very important to us. On a successful independent film, a producer credit will elevate the career of that person. The slate of producer credits is always the hardest to nail down. In a few situations, we've been contractually bound to give credit where we wouldn't have otherwise. Through the trial and error of three films, we have come up with a slate of producer titles that we feel represent the different capacities of the chameleon-like producer. Other filmmakers may use these titles to represent different capacities, but for our needs the following delineation has worked quite well.

PRODUCER | The person on and off set making the big decisions of finance and logistics. The plain "**producer**," without a prefix, is the one most in charge of the business of making a film; his or her word is usually final, and crew decisions are all subordinate to the producer's. In our films, one of us acts as the producer while the other directs.

EXECUTIVE PRODUCER | Often an **executive producer,** referred to as the EP, is someone who helped procure money for the film but, creatively, sometimes has nothing to do with its making. An EP may be involved with some of the creative decisions and cast, but the involvement is usually limited to financial matters.

Credit check:
Producer is the loosest of all job titles on a film set. The role of producer can span from creative to purely financial depending on who is controlling the project. If the producer has optioned a book and hired a writer/director team, he or she is probably going to have the final say on all matters creative and otherwise. On the other hand, if the project is the brainchild of, say, the director (which is the case on most independents), then the producer's role, in theory anyway, is accompanying the filmmaker's vision.

CO-PRODUCER | We reserve this title for either someone who has contributed financially when we were in a pinch or someone who has performed beyond expectation in a lesser position. For instance, we gave a **co-producer** credit to the line producer on *Northfork* because he had stuck with the production through thick and thin and performed well under pressure. On the other hand, we bestowed this credit in another instance for a much-needed six-week loan that allowed us to continue work on the film. It varies from situation to situation. The general idea is that a co-producer has supplied a meaningful lift to the film, be it sweat equity or, well, equity.

LINE PRODUCER | After the producer, the **line producer** is the most important business and logistical person on the set. He or she is basically in charge of running the shoot, which includes making sure all guild contracts are filed and overseeing the production manager and accountant to ensure the film isn't exceeding its budget.

ASSOCIATE PRODUCER | Like a co-producer, an **associate producer** is a discretionary credit. If someone comes in with a small amount of money or if there is someone we feel deserves some further recognition, an associate producer credit may be given.

Giving Credit

On a film the producer credit, as we have discussed previously, is the most abused credit in Hollywood. Just like the term *independent,* it has many definitions and meanings. This credit has probably caused more legal wars than any other vanity credit in the history of filmmaking. Our pictures have been littered with more producer credits than we care to name. A few people received the credit for financial support, some by just being in the room. Only a handful of people we've worked with have actually earned the credit.

How does a real indie producer earn the credit? Producing feature films is a tough and difficult job, but producing independent feature films is in a whole other category of producing. The independent film producer is a gambler, a magician, a manipulator (in all the best ways), a shrink, a faith-based healer, and so on. In short, the producer takes on a lot of unnamed, thankless duties during the production of an independent film. If you're the producer, then it's your job to make everyone happy.

The independent producer is in an odd position, stuck somewhere in the middle of creative and financial matters. The best indie producers balance the two and keep the artistic vision intact. The worst of them are solely concerned with the business end of filmmaking, forcing the filmmaker into bad creative choices. An independent producer has to be creative in his or her own right. The producers should have the director's interest at hand and should assist him or her in making a great film—not second-guessing the creative choices. Talented directors are highly collaborative people and surround themselves with people who will facilitate their vision. Suggestions and alternative ways of doing things are great to present to the director but should never be an unalterable demand.

On our films—the ones we've directed as well as acted in—we have run the gamut with all types of producers.

Fist Full of No Dollars

We sat in the rental car in Great Falls, Montana, eating our deal-a-meal, contemplating what to do. We had run out of money and there was none coming. Five weeks prior, we had been in a very similar position. While settling down in our hotel room after our location scout outside Augusta, Montana, we got a phone call from our representatives in Los Angeles saying that the financing had fallen through. *Northfork* wasn't going to be financed, and certainly not anytime soon. Their advice was to close up shop and return home to Los Angeles. To us, that was *not* an option. We had worked too hard, too long, to turn back now. Not only that, but James Woods was driving up and had already reached Salt Lake City, Utah. Our representatives didn't understand that this was a train that couldn't be stopped. Most of the cast and crew were already in Montana. And even if we could stop the train, it most likely couldn't be started again. Not with the cast and crew we now had on board. We had already sunk a hundred grand of our own money in preproduction. That was money we would never get back. We needed a completed film, and that was the only option as we saw it.

We started doing everything we could to raise the financing ourselves. It felt like we were working the lines of a telethon. One of us was constantly on the phone on and off set. We were filling out late-night online credit card applications, trying to extend any credit line that we had already extended. Actor and friend Jon Gries was back in Los Angeles trying to garner interest from a few studios, searching for private equity, calling his long-lost uncle for a loan. We were e-mailing everyone still photos of the scenes we had shot to show the production value of *Northfork*. (But a picture is only worth a thousand words.) We were thinking of every angle possible. We even asked our dad for some help, and he generously gave us several of his personal credit cards. Not only was he personally financing our ninety-foot ark, but now he was an equity investor in the picture. We were attempting to raise money in any way conceivable, short of setting up a lemonade stand. And we were starting to feel that we might have been holding the biggest lemon.

We didn't even think about quitting. Instead, we continued on. The go-for-broke filmmakers in us overrode the producers in us who had just heard the bad news. We had no money to make *Northfork*. When we say we had no money, we mean "no money," meaning zero. Most low-budget productions that say they have no money are referring to the fact that they have very little money or that they can't afford expensive toys like a crane for the camera and so on. Having absolutely no money was what set this experience above and beyond any experience we'd had on our two previous pictures. We had heard of other productions losing financing and having to either quit in preproduction or shut down while shooting. We had never thought that was going to happen to us.

Insufficient Funds

After we finished our Del Taco combo, we both retired to our rooms. The next morning we would have to face the crew. We had to be honest and communicate the financial problems to them. Up until this point, we were purely running on faith that we would find an investor to finance *Northfork*. But we hadn't and the production couldn't go a day longer. Earlier in the week, we had been approached by our first assistant director, Andy Coffing, after he heard that there may be money problems. We knew the news was leaking out to the crew. Andy would go down with us; he was there just to see if he could help.

Ben Foster, who was cast as Cod, the mute gypsy, eventually took us aside, saying he had heard we were having financial difficulties. He offered to give the production some of his savings. It was an incredibly kind gesture, but we couldn't accept as we were already taking his talent for little money. Not to mention we had to downplay our financial troubles. We didn't want it spreading more among the cast. But it was starting to—the news was leaking fast, among a select few. Fortunately, the news had gotten to people who wanted to help us. We were most concerned our financial woes were known by the crew. They had been working hard and were loyal to making *Northfork* the best movie that they had yet worked on. They were a generally happy crew, having such a good experience in Montana that they hadn't cashed their checks. One reason was the remote locations—there weren't many banks around. By not cashing their checks, they didn't catch on to the financial problems. Because if they had, they would have seen them bounce. The little per diem we were giving them was good enough for the time being. As long as money wasn't coming out of their own pockets, they seemed pacified. But then the check to the head of transportation was returned with the words INSUFFICIENT FUNDS stamped on it. Oh dear.

The Filmmaker Produces

A filmmaker is inherently a producer. It comes with the territory, especially when you have written the screenplay, too. We had budgeted *Northfork* at just south of $2 million. We knew going in, if we made it for anything more, we probably wouldn't be able to sell it. The commercial appeal of *Northfork* was limited, of that we were confident. So, just as we had for *Twin Falls* and *Jackpot,* we went through the screenplay and made necessary cuts and consolidations

Michael Polish does a camera test/*Twin Falls Idaho*

to match the budget. A period piece set in the early 1950s is costly by its nature. Having the story center around the evacuation of most of the residents of Northfork was a conscious choice. It allowed us to conceive of a period piece without the expense of hundreds of extras and tens of sets. Also, the $2 million mark is the cutoff for SAG's low-budget actors' agreements. If our budget were to exceed $2 million, we would no longer be qualified for the SAG breaks, meaning the actors would have to be paid substantially more.

Our desire to shoot *Northfork* in Montana was resolute. To begin, it is the place we have visited most since we were born and old enough to run free. In a way, Montana represented our imaginations. There were no boundaries, while our life near Sacramento was full of constraint: in high school, time allotted to art was an hour (really fifty-five minutes) a day and that was an elective.

In the financing stage of *Northfork,* we had many offers to go across the border to Canada, offers that would have increased our limited budget. But we felt this movie was about Montana and taking it to another place would be a compromise. Although most of the viewers wouldn't have known whether it was Canada or California—for instance, *Legends of the Fall* was shot in Canada, but most believe it is Montana. Parts of Montana and Canada are mirror images

Location rebate: Many places outside of Hollywood give substantial incentives to lure American film productions. It is estimated that one quarter of all Hollywood films are now shot in Canada, and a large reason for this are the Canadian film-friendly incentives, such as: waiving permit fees; assisting in location scouting; assisting in liaising with municipal and other government departments; providing free or discounted facilities—parking, police, and other civic facilities; providing tax credits; and assisting with accommodation. Even a small-budgeted indie can save thousands of dollars with location rebates if the producers are savvy and interface with the local film commission.

of one another. But, true, the feeling of Montana can't be duplicated. And most important, if we felt our location was disingenuous, we were certain our film would feel that way, too. As it turned out, it was our family and the people of Montana—as the weather and financial forecast varied day to day—who immeasurably helped us get our movie made.

After scouting locations for *Northfork* two years previously, we decided the best time of year to shoot would be the Montana that was just coming out of winter. The landscape would still appear dead, but the harshest of the elements would have passed. We were going up there to shoot some of Mother Nature's best work as our backdrop, and she had to be on her best behavior. But what we were unaware of was her schizophrenia; in a single day we could have a morning blizzard and a seventy-degree afternoon without a single cloud in the sky. Fortunately, her mental illness seemed to come and go as we needed it.

With a shooting schedule of twenty-four days and a budget of roughly $1.8 million, we were more preproduced than with our previous two pictures. Our confidence had grown from the other two experiences. Although there were enormous expenses incurred getting to Montana, once we got there, the state really worked with us. This was the off-season for tourists, so any money we injected into the local economy was welcomed. We rented a block of hotels for a discounted rate, we got open-ended plane tickets at a bargain, and generally everything in Montana is less expensive than in Los Angeles. Additionally, there is no sales tax. We met with the Montana Film Office, who were very helpful in securing us permits and getting us great deals on workers and supplies. Being that it was the winter season, the locals in northern Montana rarely see any business from tourism. They welcomed our crew at every tavern and restaurant we passed. There was one in particular, the Sip-N-Dip in Great Falls, featuring tap beer and a glass-enclosed swimming pool for the voyeuristic inebriate, that we frequented quite a bit.

Resources

We shot in Montana because we had access to resources. We knew the people, we knew the land, and we were able to use that knowledge to our advantage. As an independent producer, you not only have to stretch the dollar, but you also have to be resourceful. When shooting *Twin Falls Idaho,* the hardest set to obtain was the one for the hospital. On a limited budget, shutting down a wing of a hospital would be way too costly. Plus finding one that would let us shoot would be nearly impossible.

We discussed the location problem with everyone we knew. It was our last location to secure and a major point in the movie. This was a scene you couldn't rewrite to take place anywhere but in a hospital. We finally posed the problem to Jon Gries, who had in the past filled in the holes when we needed to find actors or work out production issues. He remembered that the show he was working on called *The Pretender* had a hospital set on a soundstage in the valley. The show was on hiatus, but the set remained and was a fixture on the show. This was the best-case scenario: a soundstage with a hospital set. Jon called the executive producers and asked if it was possible for us to use the existing set. The problem was that this set was wrapped in corporate red tape from NBC, who aired the show, to FOX, who owned the show. Jon had the confidence to ask

Free ninety free: Start with free and go from there when conceiving of how you're going to shoot your movie. Your house and your car can be two locations that will cost you nothing. It's about using your own personal resources first. You don't have money, so you're going to have to spend yourself. Take advantage of the stuff you've already spent your money on.

for anything, but his voice was a bit weary when he found out whom we needed approval from. Knowing what we had, we waited for an answer, all the while composing a letter to NBC and FOX, telling them how important this would be and how much it would mean. We thought we didn't stand a chance to get approval from a corporation like FOX. But within hours they said yes. All we needed was to hire a security guard.

Facing the Tribe

We were shooting in Great Falls, Montana, at an abandoned elementary school. The **call time** was very early. We were at the end of our shooting schedule for *Northfork,* and our financial problems had reached critical mass. We drove together, the first time in the entire shoot. We needed each other's support. We knew this could be the final day. We had made it pretty far on no money—but now everyone knew the reality of our situation. The cast and crew had every right not to continue working. It would be their decision to make.

We stopped at a local gas station on the way. They had a makeshift coffee shop that served gourmet coffee. We arrived on the set and sat in the car for a moment. We didn't even sip our coffee. We could see some of the crew waiting for our arrival. We only had two choices to offer the crew: to quit and go home without a paycheck and an unfinished film or to work for free for the time being, finish the film, trusting us that they would later get paid.

An unfinished film brings you nothing; your chances of getting something from it are nil. We got out of the car. This would be the hardest walk to a set. We remembered that one of the crew, one night out at the local bar, had said, "We would do anything for you guys and don't forget that. We wouldn't be doing half the shit you put us through if we didn't believe in you."

We reached the set and took each key crew member aside, cutting a personal deal with each of them. Each one agreed to forgo a paycheck in the short term. We had treated them as our family, with respect and equality. And like a family, when the shit hits the fan, they were there for us. They all worked hard on the film and knew they wanted the film to be seen, not canned. This isn't to say that we didn't have some detractors. Actually, there was only one, but we don't know where he is. Probably wearing a grizzly coat (that's Montanan for he was eaten by a grizzly).

The Polish Brothers give Duel Farnes direction/*Northfork*

11 | Directing

One thing that is clear about directing independent movies is that it requires you to be multifaceted. You're not the typical **director,** in the sense of what the highly coveted credit in the Hollywood system means. You are a filmmaker; your job requires you to do a lot more than what is usually thought of as directing. Very little of what we do is "directing"—from writing, casting, and producing, what we do is make movies. Your job is better defined as filmmaker than director, because of all the tasks that it takes to produce and direct.

There is probably nothing better than to arrive on the movie set as directors and get our bagel and coffee served as we discuss our first shot of the day. But as an independent filmmaker, you're responsible for that bagel and coffee, and if you want it, you have to go get it. Funny enough, you probably even went to the store and bought it on your credit card.

The Vision

A director needs a vision. A vision is the way you see your picture: the acting, the set design, the music, the editing. Anything and everything creative. It's your choice; it's your world, and how do you see it expressed? This is a vision that all involved have to see and be inspired by. If this takes referencing photography books or other movies, then show those to all key crew members. It's your vision and you want everyone to see what you are seeing. Whatever it takes, show the pictures you have in your head. Inspired people—whether they are blind to your vision or not—go a long way toward helping you achieve the picture you want. We are pretty sure not everyone involved in *Northfork* understood why we wanted the red Campbell soup can labels in black and white. When you saw a line of them, it did look strange and out of place, but what was explained to all in great detail was that this was going to be a movie about the limbo between life and death: a gray area. So all the elements were to be gray, and no color was allowed. Gray was a hard vision to convey. There are warm grays, there are cold grays. We explained our gray concept to key members of the crew. We had ten shades of it on a color chart. This was our vision. A black-

Dream shot: It may be tempting to try to shoot an impossibly elaborate shot, one that requires hours of setup and rehearsal of the complex camera move. Many first-time directors want to shoot a shot that has never been accomplished. But chances are it has been done before. And, besides, the elaborate shot is all too time-consuming on the budget of an indie. The end result is usually something less than was intended, which will only draw the audience's attention away from your story.

and-white movie shot on color film. *Northfork* was going to be our most visual film, and it was going to have the most dramatic look of any of our previous movies. The color scheme was simple. So when color mistakenly popped up, like on the bumper of one of the Ford coupes, there was the AD telling us that. While shooting *Northfork,* we explained to the six actors who made up the Evacuation Committee that they were to be dressed in identical black suits with fedoras and would be driving identical black Fords. Why? To evoke power. Their uniformity created by repetition was a visual motif we employed throughout the film. When the crew knows your vision, they protect it, and you end up with forty or so people doing quality control.

The vision of how to best direct your movie will come foremost from your interpretation of the screenplay. If you have written your own screenplay, then you probably have already envisioned the movie playing out in your head. Your vision for directing your film may not be directly written on the script pages, but you have likely imagined how the characters interact, how they speak, the locations they reside in. If you didn't have a hand in writing the screenplay, you should definitely discuss your concepts with the writer to learn his or her intentions in telling the story, what tone or what mood the writer is trying to convey. As director, you are in charge of bringing the screenplay to life visually and aurally, and whatever that ends up becoming is, in essence, your vision.

Once you are in preproduction and moving toward production, there will be thousands of questions you will have to answer as a film's director, all related to your overall vision. You need to be very clear about what you want to achieve and how you want it executed—this isn't the time to be indecisive. It's better to make a wrong decision and correct it later than to never make a decision at all. During production, we have faced many daunting choices, which were usually caused by the time constraints inherent in a low-budget film schedule. We've had to condense lines of dialogue and shorten complete scenes while we were shooting. On the *Twins Falls Idaho* shoot, there was a scene where Penny questions the size of her butt. We were so exhausted from directing while simultaneously acting in our conjoined suit that we almost said "Forget it" to the scene, because we had fallen behind schedule. But the writer in us said, "Let's shoot the scene in one take, and if it doesn't work out, we'll cut it in the editing room." Another pressure moment was the "nick in the paint" scene in *Northfork,* where Willis gets upset when he discovers a blemish in the door of his brand-new polished Ford. We were so pressed for time that it almost seemed impossible to get the scene shot. But we persevered and got the shot in one take. In both the *Twin Falls* and *Northfork* pressure instances, deciding to shoot the film paid off. Both scenes made the final cut. We were able to shoot those scenes so quickly because we knew which camera angle (or coverage) we wanted for the scene. Those are the type of on-the-fly decisions a director must make on an indie. Deciding what compositions are essential is your job as director; your cinematographer will always give you suggestions, but at the end of the day you have to decide what is most important to the scene. Several times we have found ourselves in the position where we have only had time to find the best angle for a scene and to give it one take—a oner. We take no pride in this method; it's a last resort and gives you no other choice in the editing room. But that is a decision you'll make as a director, and you'll make many decisions as a director that you'll have to live with.

Don't be afraid of communicating your vision and enforcing its execution. It's a privilege to be a director, a privilege that can be taken away. This is your film, your chance, so prepare yourself by knowing the material as best you can. Know what the screenplay is trying to communicate and guide it to the big screen. Take care, and respect the written word; it will always take care of you and tell you what you can and cannot do.

Losing Your Vision

It doesn't take much time to start seeing your vision being compromised, because of the real lack of time and money. We were as prepared as one could be on *Twin Falls Idaho,* but once you walk on the set, it's a whole new beast you must tame. We aren't talking about the conjoined twins. We are referring to the picture; it's coming to life and if you don't tame it, it will beat you up pretty good. Because of the actors' interpretations and so on, your vision will change. It won't come to life exactly the way you have envisioned it. Sometimes it changes for the better, sometimes for the worse. Not to dwell on the negative, but each day you will lose a bit of your original vision. It just happens (it's the nature of the beast). When we walked into Penny's room on the set of *Twin Falls Idaho,* what we saw and what we wanted were quite different. Instead of a room lined with hundreds of strands of fairy lights, there were just a few strands hanging around the room. It didn't quite support Penny's line of dialogue: "It's Christmas every day." We couldn't stop the production, run down to the store and buy a hundred boxes of Christmas lights (also, it was mid-June). To get Penny's room the way we had envisioned it would have taken hours and put us behind schedule.

We had to learn to forget the picture that we envisioned and start creating a new picture with what we did have. It's difficult because you have lived with your ideas for a long time, and to start replacing pictures, ones you're not that happy with, can really contort your vision. You start to think that your picture is coming apart at the

Framing: Framing the shot is what a director should keep at the forefront. The only things that exist are what are in your frame. If it's not in the frame, it's not in the shot.

seams. Fortunately, we had each other to consult with over our losses. What we had to remember was that though we may have been losing some of our texture and layers in the story, we weren't losing actual scenes in the script. That is something we never lost, except as a choice in the editing room. If we had to put a percentage on how much of our vision was stuck to the celluloid, we would say around 85 percent. You should be prepared to know that you will lose some of your overall vision, but if you're not losing your story, you will be okay.

First-Time Director

Nothing fully prepares you for directing your first film. This is your first time at the controls. You pretty much have everything stacked up against you. We believe the key to success in being a first-time director is TIME. There is no greater enemy to the first-time director, nothing you're fighting with more. You just will never have enough of it. And when you're making key creative decisions, like an actor's performance, you can do only so many takes before you have to move on to the next setup. You can't afford to have fifteen takes of an actor. Well, you can, but it isn't time efficient.

How you plan your overall **coverage** of a scene can save a lot of time. A three-page scene will not be played in a wide shot; you know you have to jump into a tighter shot a few beats into the scene. And from there you will probably jump closer, possibly a two-shot or a close-up. Pre-editing the scene is dangerous, but with

Coverage: "Coverage of a scene" may be defined as filming the action of a scene from different angles and shot sizes in order to edit it in the most effective manner to tell the story. Often the action filmed overlaps that covered by a different angle to allow flexibility in cutting. Also, a scene may not need to be covered, or it may be covered unconventionally.

Michael Polish and Andrew Coffing (first AD) check the playback from the set/*Northfork*

such limited time, some scenes allow themselves to a pre-edit of sorts. If you know that certain dialogue is only going to play well in a close up, then don't waste time getting the perfect line reading in a wide shot. Move on and make the note that in the close-up is where you are going to get the reading you want. We are not saying skimp on coverage—you and your editor will want every option when in the editing room—but when squeezed for time, have your priorities in order. An intimate scene doesn't play in a wide shot and a fight scene doesn't work in an extreme close-up.

Twin Falls Idaho was our first time directing. We were acting for our first time, too. Being actors in our movie gave us perspective from in front of the camera. But usually the director is behind the set, either watching the monitor or viewing the action beside the cinematographer. It was difficult at times not being able to view a scene instantaneously. Our only recourse was to tape it on video and watch it on playback. This proved to be adequate; but there is something strange about directing yourself in a movie. Michael would have loved nothing more than to stay behind the camera; that's where he is most comfortable. So the challenge was for Mark to keep us on course. We started to direct each other. After each take, we would discuss our believability as Siamese twins. This was our overall concern during production, and the major directing choices were made to reinforce believability.

Directing the Actor

We have been blessed to work with some of the finest actors there are. Every actor has one thing in common when they work in our movies: there is no big paycheck and, therefore, they are doing it for reasons more substantial than money. In *Twin Falls Idaho* we got to witness the subtle acting brilliance of Patrick Bauchau. Patrick was our first contact with actors that have weight. His technique, or method, of acting was developed through the French New Wave. Fresh off his plane from Paris, Patrick walked on the set not knowing a lick of his lines. With an allotted time of an hour to get his first scene done, we remember thinking he had a good amount of dialogue and we may be here a lot longer. We didn't know how long. We were already a bit behind in the schedule. But Patrick quickly found his mark, scanned the sides a few times and was ready to roll. This was Patrick's process: to learn

Sharing storyboards: Discuss the shots with the actors and show them the storyboards. It helps them visualize what each scene will look like. When an actor knows beforehand that we are shooting a wide angle, then that actor understands the space he or she will occupy. It's important to involve the actor in the visual language, to show how he or she will appear throughout the film.

the lines mere seconds before he was to shoot. It made us a bit nervous, but it made Patrick's performance real and believable.

We've also worked with Leslie Ann Warren, who played our mother in *Twin Falls Idaho.* She is a veteran actor who has given her talents to independent filmmakers. She was the opposite of Patrick; she came fully prepared, going over her lines and character choices while her makeup was being applied. When she came to the hospital set to do her critical scene, where she sees the twins she had given away at birth, we had prelit and set up the shot without any rehearsal. At that point we had zero time. Leslie walked on the set and you could see she was a bit uncomfortable. What we failed to realize was where the camera was; we were shooting Leslie's bad side. Rather than call attention to it, she did the scene perfectly and we moved on. It's difficult on such limited time to have full rehearsals and allow the actor to choose their best side, or choose their own mark to hit. If you leave them up to their own devices, they will walk all around the set, sit down, get up, go across the room while saying their dialogue. This would take a hell of a lot of time to cover. You have to limit their choices, just like you have to limit your own as a director. It's not putting them in a straitjacket; it's educating them on the shot. Telling them that less is more and the more coverage you have to do will only lessen their performance.

We had written *Jackpot* with two actors in mind: Jon Gries and Garrett Morris. We knew these two actors were team players and that is what was needed for a movie that spent a majority of the time in bars and bathrooms. We also worked with both in *Twin Falls Idaho,* and their dedication to the craft was never in question. These guys were believable partners as karaoke singer and manager partially because their friendship existed before we wrote the screenplay. Their natural chemistry was what we needed to capture in the fifteen days we had to shoot the movie. What worked to our benefit was that

Garrett Morris as Lester "Les" Irving/*Jackpot*

these two actors had television experience; both had been on the sitcom *Martin.* Television schedules are brutal and the actors need to be on their game; episodes are shot very quickly and, therefore, actors have only a few takes to get each scene right. *Jackpot* had a similar shooting schedule. We were shooting an average of five pages a day, with only a few takes allowable per scene. It was a tighter shooting schedule than a movie of the week, which are notorious for their quick turnaround times. One advantage was shooting *Jackpot* on hi-def video; this allowed for quicker setups, making the many pages we had to shoot each day possible. This was also a comfort to the actors, knowing that it wasn't film a bad take would be wasting. The inherent insecurity most actors have of wasting film disappeared from the shoot. We could just keep rolling tape until the actor got it right. However, this freedom didn't allow them to improvise; it was quite the opposite—we stuck tightly to the screenplay. There was no time to interpret the scenes differently than they were written. Garrett Morris and Jon Gries were focused, and once they said their lines, it was on to the next location.

Working with Garrett Morris was a treat; he's a real natural performer. In our first conversations with Garrett, he asked us, "How do you want me?" We kindly suggested his character, Les Irving, should wear Malcolm X–style glasses with a short-brimmed hat, which he later termed "stingy," and a Brooks Brothers–inspired suit from the Blue Note heyday. Garrett never wavered from our idea to create a strong presence for Les Irving. Les had to have the appearance of knowledge on how to guide his protégé to stardom.

Whether he was wrong or right, Les had to have the power of belief—he knew in his heart how to manage Sunny Holiday down the road to fame.

As directors, we had to make sure Garrett was confident playing this role as a reserved manager. We explained to him what we wanted. Changing some of his acting tactics proved to be a valuable lesson. Garrett has spent most of his years acting as a comic actor. His animated style of comedy is how he is known. Like many comedians, Garrett uses body language to help convey his every thought. We would watch in delight as Garrett plunged into a page of dialogue, memorizing chunks of text in minutes. But we directed him to slow down—with every take, we would ask for a slower version: years of him ranting as an animated comedic persona had to be curbed. We started taking things away from him. Most notably was his ability to talk with hand gestures. Instead of waving his hands to enhance his character's speeches, we said, "Sit on your hands; you can't use them." And we kept him to it. Toning down Garrett's body language was the most successful direction we could give; it changed his whole character dramatically. Les became much more reserved and focused, and this changed the way the other actors responded to him. It was a much more serious Garrett than anyone had witnessed before, and it was the respect that he needed to make Les Irving work.

The Heavyweight

"You fucking want to go work on a Jennifer Lopez movie, or do you want to be here with real artists? You need to shape up...want to work for free, or do you want to make some real money? You want to work for free, of course! That's the deal. Free is good."

—*James Woods* (schooling an actor for complaining
about the weather on the set of *Northfork*)

James Woods takes a moment to commend the dam workers/*Northfork*

Many people had said many things about James Woods before we began working with him. Some good things, some bad things. Most memorably was
that he would run the set if you weren't a strong director. You always hear
things about actors and their tantrums, but we felt we are not ones to judge;
everyone has their bad days, and at this point we could only be grateful for
his services. And if he were to attempt to take over, we would deal with it
then. Sure, we were a little nervous, but we knew once in Montana anyone
with an attitude problem would soon be dwarfed by the landscape and realize that they were just part of the food chain. We had watched *Once Upon a
Time in America* way too many times to count. James Woods's mesmerizing
performance as Maximilian, a sadistic Jewish gangster, was breathtakingly

real. That was the role that introduced us to James Woods the actor. Since that day back in the early 80s, we had watched James in quite a few movies. Most of his characters displayed an explosiveness; they were intense, to say the least. So with that in mind, not knowing James that well, we had to think about how much of James is in each character he portrays. Walter O'Brien, the character he was to play in *Northfork*, didn't have any of those trademark explosive qualities. James would have to find restraint and bottle up the emotions that he was known for. We had spoken only briefly about character with James; we felt he understood *Northfork* and his creative character choices for Walter would be fine.

While filming *Northfork*, each morning we would greet each other and walk to the set. From the first day at the Fort Peck Dam, James told us he would not get emotional and cry in the scene in the outhouse. This was a pivotal scene where Walter finally confronts his wife's death. There really wasn't any other way to play it but to get emotional. But if James wasn't going to cry, then we weren't going to make him. We didn't know what we were going to do. We knew what the scene needed, and James wasn't going to deliver. We were worried. Every morning we got the daily reminder from James that he wasn't going to cry. Each time we would just nod our head and agree with him. What we didn't want to do was engage and start a disagreement with him. Not for the fear of pissing him off, but we still had another two weeks before we got to that scene and maybe his mind would change. We hoped.

Throughout the shooting, James provided the security for all the actors, especially the

Icing: Filmmakers often make the mistake of calling out their principal actors to set or location before they are actually needed. There's a level of respect that must be shown to actors. Most actors resent being called to the set only to be sent to their trailer to sit for hours. Don't ice your talent; get them on set when they're needed.

members of the Evacuation Committee. Besides Mark, James was the only actor present the entire length of the shoot. He would come to the set on days he wasn't working to take photographs or hang out to see what ideas we had for the rest of *Northfork,* for scenes that he wasn't even in. James showed not only the other cast members but also the crew that he was dedicated. On and off the set, he is probably one of the most intelligent actors we have ever worked with. When you hire someone with the stature of James Woods, you get their many years of professionalism. He wouldn't have worked as long as he has if he wasn't a pleasure to work with.

As the days went on, James was sinking deeper into the character of Walter O'Brien. He became more comfortable with his character and with us guiding him through the story. It was deathly cold, and it was going to take some time for James to warm up to Walter's calm demeanor. Walter had the weight of death, he carried guilt on his shoulders—with a face drained of color and a posture stricken by years of grief. James understood his understated role as Walter. He started to articulate off camera exactly why Walter was remorseful about his wife's death, and he began to go into details about the conflict of exhuming a dead body. Though Walter's son, Willis O'Brien, was to be the voice of his stubbornness, James held Walter in check and eternalized his sadness. When we finally reached the emotional outhouse scene, he didn't need any direction. We didn't know how he was going to play it, but James was going to do what he felt the scene needed. He had been in Walter's shoes for two weeks now, and all we could do was witness this moment. We sat back, nervous, but sure James would make the right choice. He did. He gave it all up and cried. James played the scene better than we had imagined possible.

When he exited the outhouse wiping his eyes, all James Woods wanted to know was, "Was it a Golden Globe or an Oscar moment?" We gladly delivered with, "It was a People's Choice moment."

First-Time Actor

We have a lot of experience working with first-time actors. We have had first-time actors in all of our pictures. Your chances of working with a first-time actor or even a nonactor are pretty good when you're doing an independent. They just come with the territory.

Most first-time performances are made in the editing room, pieced together. Many times first-time actors just aren't consistent in their line readings. The longer the lines, the more difficult it will be. This is something to remember while filming. The chances of getting a complete perfect take are slim. So look for pieces in each take that you know are good. If the actor has five lines, make sure that in each take at least one of those lines is what you like. Trying to get all five lines right at the same time will drive you crazy and most likely won't happen with a first timer.

Sidelines: When an inexperienced actor is having trouble getting comfortable in front of the camera, it often helps to have someone close to him or her feed the off-camera lines. To get the line readings we wanted from Duel Farnes, the eight-year-old boy in *Northfork*, Mark read most of the off-camera lines to him. Having someone Duel related to off-camera helped him relax on-camera.

Final Take

In a way, we really don't direct actors, we observe them. They are very talented people with many ideas on how their characters should behave. Their first priority is to serve the story. They are part of the big picture; they aren't bigger than the picture, and when they lose their way we step in and whisper, "Breathe." We find there is no common advice to give an actor to perform exactly how you may want; you can only go on a feeling, the same feeling you get when you write or read the screenplay. It transcends the page. We have found that the more experienced actors are faster to get to a place of comfort. They have the ability to transform into a character before your eyes. Your guidance as director should be to assure them they are doing the right thing and that you appreciate their effort in getting to a vulnerable place. It's an extraordinary gift to be an actor. James Woods is very different from Nick Nolte, but both are extremely gifted, and both give you everything they have. There are no rules to directing actors—respect their craft and follow your instincts.

Listen

Listen. That is the best thing you can do as a director. Listen to your actors, your cinematographer, your editor—you can't direct unless you know where everyone is coming from. Yes, of course, you are commander in chief, but why bark orders and turn your team in a direction that is harmful to your vision? Nobody does good work when shouted at, and filmmaking is a team effort; you're facing the workload together. On an independent film, the director doesn't have the kind of money to keep the crew hostage inside his or her dictatorship. Most of the time, people work on indies either as a favor or for the sheer experience. When there is very little money being paid out to your crew, being nice and considerate makes the production bearable. Nobody has to show up for work when they aren't getting paid. Remember this before you unload your frustrations on an undeserving crew member.

Everyone who is involved in the making of your film should be inspired to work for you. Remember: you're a rookie. Everyone is going to

Losing your lines: It's not uncommon for an actor to have difficulty remembering his or her lines when the camera rolls. Due to nervousness, this can happen quite a bit with first-time and nonactors. The best thing to do is turn the camera on the veteran actor first, so that the novice actor can get more comfortable digesting his or her lines.

judge you, and whatever you do is going to reflect what kind of director you are and will become. Your crew will probably be more experienced than you and will be concerned with things that may seem trivial to you—like leaving the set at a reasonable hour. The crew and actors will all have interpreted the screenplay in their own way. As director, it's your job to get everyone focused on your overall vision of the film. This requires you to articulate your thoughts in a manner that each crew member can understand. Not everyone is going to follow every thought process or reasoning behind your creative choices. Because it's your vision, as the filmmaker you need to bring everyone on board to execute exactly what you see. You're the director.

Digging the scene/*Northfork*

12 | **Postproduction**

The biggest misconception about **postproduction** is that it means the brunt of the battle is over. In actuality, postproduction is usually the longest part of a film's production cycle. On an independent film, postproduction typically takes eight to twelve weeks, depending on the budget. Postproduction encompasses everything that must be done to complete a film after it is shot: editing, sound editing, and creating the score, the sound mix, and the print master—all essential elements. As postproduction begins, many of the production departments are closing accounts; crew members are dropping off final receipts, the color in their faces returning after the long shoot; but the filmmaker and the postproduction team have lots of work yet to do. It is in postproduction when a film finally either comes together or falls apart.

A filmmaker must plan accordingly, or conflicts will erupt and the budget may implode from unforeseen errors. And it is here that a filmmaker's promise to "fix it in post" must be fulfilled.

At this crossroads in the project, where a film is moved from myriad production decisions to the realm of the editing room, a postproduction supervisor (PPS) is brought in to organize the remaining activities. The PPS must work effectively with the creative demands of the director and also handle the complexities inherent in the technical demands of postproduction. For studio pictures, a postproduction supervisor is rarely involved with the production of a film. Rather, he or she comes on board with fresh energy and exuberance for all the finishing details. But for budgetary reasons, often one of the producers on an indie will take over these responsibilities. On our first film, *Twin Falls Idaho,* one of the producers stayed with the film through post; on *Jackpot* we, as the producers, took on that role; and on *Northfork* we had veteran postproduction supervisor Todd King taking on the responsibility. *Northfork* was the first time we really saw how the job works when properly managed. And with all the financial difficulties we had with *Northfork,* we witnessed how a good postproduction supervisor keeps a film going forward.

The post supervisor helps to steer the course through the many weeks of editing. Once the film is fully complete, he or she will help deliver the film to the distributor. There will be a slew of decisions made in post, all impacting the creative and financial needs of the film, such as where to mix the film, the length of the final mix, and who the mixer will be. The post supervisor will help to control the costs and keep the creative engine running smoothly during this final stretch. The world of postproduction is marked by many technical decisions, all potentially budget draining. Something as seemingly benign as choosing a development lab for the final print will have a big impact on the look of the film. Deciding on who is going to mix the movie can have a huge impact on the budget. The post supervisor must sift through all of the project's editorial needs and demands and create realistic solutions to satisfy the financial parameters of the project.

In selecting your postproduction supervisor, focus on successful independent films in your budgetary range. Find someone who capably handled these budgetary constraints in the past. The importance of choosing a knowledgeable postproduction supervisor can't be overstated. So many technical decisions will have to be made, and most are beyond a first-time filmmaker's scope. That's not to say you shouldn't gain familiarity and even expertise in this leg of the journey. The more knowledge you can acquire about editorial intricacies, the less is left to simple good faith.

Put your lab hat on. This part of the exercise is going to cost you. Film labs consume a big chunk of your budget. From the first day's **dailies** to the **final print,** you'll be dealing with this crucial facility. The cost of processing at a lab is considerable and must be managed at a reputable, hopefully high-caliber company that is attracted to your project or was referred to you by another trusted filmmaker. Take a little time to tour the facilities. You shouldn't choose a lab solely on the basis of the lowest bid. Shop around and ask other filmmakers about their lab experiences. The lab is going to be your constant companion all the way through distribution. If your film is shot on 35 mm, you are going to have different development needs than a film shot on digital video.

We used Deluxe Laboratories for *Twin Falls* and *Jackpot,* and on *Northfork* we used Technicolor. Both of these labs did a great job and were willing to work for very little money. There was a willingness to start a relationship with us, and these labs do high run numbers. They do studio prints and have a lot of inventory coming in, so they can afford to subsidize an occasional indie. Another lab worth mentioning is FotoKem in Burbank. They are known for doing a lot of indies. It's often the first stop for indies—but it doesn't mean it's the only stop. Go where you most want to go, first. For *Twin Falls,* we used Deluxe Laboratories because they had a skip-bleach bypass process we wanted to use. We were comfortable with them because of their previous work. Whatever lab you end up with, if you're fortunate enough to sell your movie to a distributor, it is best if the studio will run copies of your film from the same lab. This guarantees the look of your film will be what you intended. Once we sold our films to their respective distributors, we made all of their prints with the same labs that made their **answer prints.** Distributors are sometimes partial to particular laboratories and often want to change a finished film to their lab of choice. This battle can be won, however. It is important to discuss your lab choices during the negotiation of the distribution deal. Whenever possible, get your lab of choice in writing.

The Answer Print

This is the answer to how your movie is going to look. Everything you've done up until this point is reflected here.

After the negative is cut into reels, it has to be printed with the correct levels of red, green, and blue printer lights to color-correct the image, shot by shot. The process of determining these sets of printer lights is called color timing. In other countries, it's called color grading. The prints that result are called answer prints.

Usually at some point early on in the process, the answer prints are made with the soundtrack as well (also called a **composite print**) so that the sound and image can be judged. The print is projected at the lab with the client and the lab timer present, and necessary or desired changes are noted by the timer. You basically can adjust the overall image in the direction of the three primaries (red, green, blue) or secondaries (yellow, cyan, magenta) plus in terms of density (brighter or darker).

You can't change contrast within a shot nor the color of only selected areas in the frame—to do that, you'd need to color-correct the image using a **digital intermediate,** where the negative is scanned into a digital form, color-corrected electronically, and then recorded back to film. This is starting to become more of an industry standard, but it is much more expensive than traditional photochemical methods.

> **Digital intermediate:** A process where film is scanned into a digital form, color-corrected electronically, and then recorded back to film.

You can adjust overall contrast and color saturation levels for an entire reel by changing the print stock, applying a special development process, or both. There are five different 35 mm color print stocks made, two by Kodak and Fuji, and one by Agfa, but the variations in look between them are pretty slight. Some are more saturated and contrasty than others.

Often it takes at least three answer prints of the entire movie to get something acceptable to the client; after that, often only individual reels may need reprinting with adjustments.

When the final sets of printer lights are determined, more composite prints can be made off of the original negative (called **show prints** now instead of answer prints).

Usually a color-timed **interpositive** (IP) is made at this time. An interpositive is a positive image like a print but looks more like a negative, i.e., very low in contrast with an orange color-mask. It serves as a protection copy of your original negative, a film element for the final telecine transfers, and as a source for striking an **internegative** (IN), also called a dupe negative (dupe for duplicate).

From a dupe negative, large numbers of release prints can be struck without risk to the original negative. Also, since the IP was color-corrected by using the variety of printer lights determined in answer printing, all subsequent generations can be printed at one set of printer lights (called one light printing, which is cheaper). However, there is some mild quality loss through each generation; therefore, prints made off of the original negative tend to look better than ones made off of the dupe negative.

Keep in mind that these techniques will probably fall the way cutting film did. When we started, we used to actually cut film, and by the time of our first feature, we were editing on an Avid system—never to lay a finger on the prints. As the digital age of moviemaking excels, we will probably see less of the answer printing process.

The art of the answer print may be lost in the independent film world, due to the lack of money and because some creative choices, like the ENR process or digital intermediates, may prove too expensive. There have been plenty of times the filmmaker is trying to just find enough money to print the film to make it to a festival.

Opticals and CGI

An **optical** is a postproduction manipulation of picture that includes the title sequence at the front and end of a film. When you see a scene dissolve into another, or watch credits scroll across the frame, you are witnessing an optical. Independent filmmakers with their too-small budgets need to choose their opticals carefully. An Avid allows you to come up with elaborate fades and swipes. The trouble is, once you go to make the transfer, all of the temporary Avid opticals need to be manually redone at an optical house, which can cost a small fortune. *Northfork* was a film about transition, and thus we used about every conceivable transition optical available: match cut, hard cut, fade to black, fade to white, sweeps, swipes, dissolves—they were all in there. We spent $70,000 on opticals for *Northfork*. That's not chump change.

In all three of our films, we have designed title sequences. We feel the presentation of credits, their typography, and the images that frame them are most interesting when they directly relate to the story. For *Twin Falls,* we chose a typeface called Mrs Eaves, which is well known in the printing world

for being the font with the two occasionally conjoined letters, known as ligatures. As the film
opens, in the background, behind the credit
scroll in Mrs Eaves font, we superimposed hospital X-rays of conjoined twins. In this way, in the
title sequence both our font and picture were
setting up the story.

For *Jackpot,* we used our title sequence to create
the mood for our struggling singer, Sunny Holiday, and his adventures. We chose Cooper, a
bubblegum font in pastel pink (the same color as
Sunny's Cadillac), which pans across the screen
like lyrics on the screen of a karaoke machine.
And for *Northfork,* relating to dam construction,
we used the title sequence to allude to the coming evacuation. There is a scene twenty minutes
in where Father Harlan gives Irwin a View-Master,
which shows the history of Northfork the town

David Mullen, high on the job/
Northfork

in black-and-white photography. We foreshadowed this scene in the title sequence, using black-and-white stills that slide up and out of the frame as it
would through a View-Master. These pictures are all of historical dams built
in Montana during the 1900s, directly relating to the story of *Northfork.*

The sister expense related to opticals is CGI (computer-generated imagery).
Like opticals, CGI is a postproduction expense and it, too, can easily absorb a
film's budget. Most independent films use CGI very rarely. The graveyard scene
in *Northfork,* where the camera pans up to reveal hundreds of plots of newly
exhumed sites, was in part created with CGI. During the shoot, we had a small
crew digging grave sites, but with little time and dwindling resources we had
to get the shot before we were completely satisfied. When we mapped out

Sound advice:
The budgetary issues with indies and post-production often make the sound component suffer the most. Set aside enough of your post budget to have high-quality postproduction sound to complement your picture edit. If it's not the case, you will have to work hard to stretch your meager means. The best way to ensure a great-sounding picture is to work with veterans whose previous work you trust and to have enough money in the budget to allow them time to really craft the sound elements.

postproduction, we decided to meet with an optical house that did some CGI work. With a CGI animator we ended up creating a populated gravesite with hundreds of piles of freshly shoveled dirt. The scene turned out so convincingly that at this point we can't remember which sites are real and which are computer generated.

When we finished shooting *Twin Falls,* we met with the indie-friendly post houses. After several meetings that left us nonplussed, we approached some of the bigger sound houses and found that there were some experienced editors willing to work for cheap if they liked the project. The bigger sound houses differ from the indie houses in size, in available equipment, and often in the experience of the sound people working there. This doesn't mean there aren't great indie sound houses, but do your research. If you have the opportunity to work with someone who has an expansive résumé, it may improve your movie. We ended up working with Sound Storm (a now-defunct large sound house), which had done some very high-profile pictures; their walls were lined with framed posters from studio franchises. Even though we got bumped around a bit schedule-wise, they had experienced veterans working on our picture and state-of-the-art sound equipment. And although they weren't making much of a profit working on our movie, they were building a relationship with us so that when we could do a bigger-budgeted film, we would work with them again. The point is, as you plot your postproduction needs, don't be too intimidated to meet with established companies that mostly work with the big studios.

Choosing which sound effects supervisor and **mixing facility** you are going to use are paramount decisions, and there is no substitute for interviewing, asking around, and visiting the locales best known for this specialized work. Your picture editor will certainly lend advice and offer recommendations. Your post supervisor may have contacts and deals already organized for your approval. But remember, it's your film and you have the right to look elsewhere. Try to navigate your project to the most reputable sound house you can afford and work with them on the bottom line of your budget. If your timing is right, and one of these enterprises is indicating a hole in their schedule, you may be able to accomplish a high-quality sound mix and edit for a discounted rate. The earlier you and your post supervisor can develop a schedule, the sooner you can begin the process of contacting the sound companies and determining if their workload may be able to handle your independent.

Sound mixer: Often an overlooked position in terms of production value, the sound mixer is in charge of recording all of the actors' dialogue. Many independent films have a noisy dialogue track because the sound mixer is either inexperienced or forced to record in a cacophonous environment.

It is best when funds for a quality soundtrack are committed to early in your preproduction budget planning and put safely aside. But most independent films cannot afford this luxury, leaving the creators wondering how they will put it all together. Too many projects are forced to sacrifice their postproduction dollars during the filming leg of their journey and, predictably, make poor decisions that create an unpolished finished project. To make an indie that looks and sounds highly professional, always be tough with your dollars during production and keep your postproduction financing commitments intact.

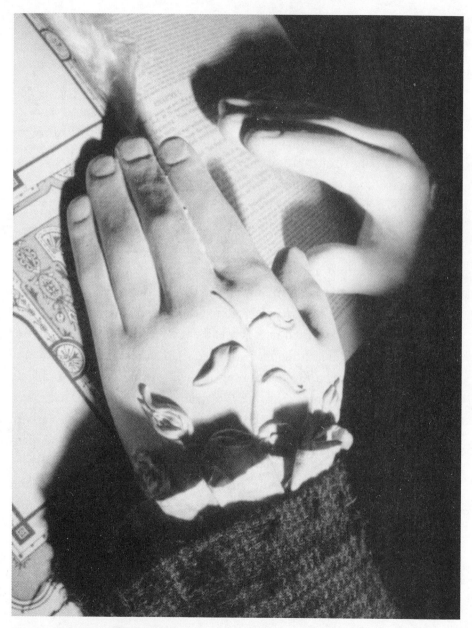

Happy's porcelain hands/*Northfork*

13 | Film Editing

We are sitting in the producers' office interviewing **editors**. All the other creative keys—cinematographer, production designer, costume designer—who will participate in the making of *Twin Falls Idaho* have been hired. We are in our last week of preproduction. The producers have deferred to our crew choices so far, but as we broach the question of editor, the producers insist on having final say. There have been interviews with editors without us present. The first editor the producers had us meet asked us if we really believed in our story. We didn't mind the query, but it was obvious he didn't believe in it. The second editor we met was completely introverted and would nervously look over at the producers when answering one of our questions such as, "What sort of films do you like?" It became obvious to us that the producers wanted to hire another editor—someone who agreed with them. If we

Editor: Behind almost every great film is a superb editor putting it all together. An editor's job, in a broad sense, is to choose the best of the multiple-take performances and assemble all of the choices into one compelling narrative. If the filmmaker is the storyteller, the editor is the objective ear that the storyteller relies on for input and guidance. Any film, Hollywood and independent interchangeably, may be lost in the hands of a weak editor.

delivered an esoteric cut, they would be able to salvage *Twin Falls* commercially with the chosen editor.

As we interview editor Leo Trombetta, one of the producers uncomfortably shakes Leo's hand. It turns out they know each other; Leo was fired from a project they were working on a while back for siding with the filmmaker. As Leo answers a few of our questions (what editors he has a high regard for, what films he likes), it is apparent that his knowledge of the craft matches our enthusiasm. He has an encyclopedic recall of who did what on the classic films we admire. Leo also has a sound editor's background, which we feel is a big plus. After a twenty-minute discussion, we are more than happy to hire him. But we must still convince the producers. As Leo says good-bye to us, we figure it will be a matter of moments before the producers dismiss Leo as an option. But we have one thing going for us, an impending shoot date that requires hiring an editor immediately. We express our willingness to work with Leo, and the producers reluctantly agree, saying they can always hire someone else after production if things go south. With our editor on board, our creative team is complete as we head into the beginning of principal photography.

As production gets under way, the general routine for the editor is the same on every film. When each day of shooting wraps, the film is taken (by your most trusted production assistant or driver) to a lab, taken out of its canisters, and put into a chemical bath for development. Then the selected takes are transferred to videotape (usually Beta SP or ¾″), a VHS copy of which is sent to the set to be viewed by the filmmakers. In a sense, postproduction begins for the editor sooner than it does for everyone else, as soon as the first day's **dailies**

> **Dailies:** The raw, uncut footage developed by the lab and shot, in most cases, the previous day. (Also known as rushes.)

arrive. An editor usually has an assistant who organizes the incoming film. Locked away in a cubicle or a small room, the editor and his assistant begin to digitize the dailies onto a large hard drive connected to a computer. There are various digital editing programs that allow an editor to rapidly scan through hours of footage and make numerous editing choices with the click of a mouse button. The most popular of these is **Avid,** a software/hardware combo, and Final Cut, which is huge in the independent world. Digital editing is an amazing timesaver compared to the manual efforts of the past, where, as recently as a decade ago, an editor used a grease pencil to mark each cut. These were then executed with a razor blade and tape. While the editor watches each take, making preliminary notes as to how the scene might best be assembled, the assistant catalogs the footage into a logbook, noting camera roll number and corresponding **SMPTE time code.**

When the editor receives the day's new footage, he or she, usually after consulting with the director, will compile it into a rough assembly. Each shot needs to be trimmed, removing the slate and whatever else lies before and after. As production progresses, more and more of the film is pieced together. The first cut, which is the combined assembly following the sequence of the screenplay, is the editor's best guess at the overall direction of the film. Although he is making performance choices, the first assembly is really more a preliminary step to editing the movie. The editor is quickly assembling scenes as they land in his editing bay, and his main job at this point is to get the film in sequence. There is hardly any attempt to adjust scene length, because an

editor would much rather remove footage later at the behest of the director than have to go back and reinsert scenes. Therefore, a first assembly may
run as long as four or five hours, depending on how much extra coverage
was shot.

As the *Twin Falls* shoot got under way, we met with Leo regularly at our
lunch time break to discuss the early assembly. Leo became more than just a
by-the-clock editor; he was our quality control. Drawing on his experience,
he told us not just what was cutting well, but also what shots he felt we were
missing. As *Twin Falls* was storyboarded, it made for a quicker assembly, considering the shot sequence was already laid out to some extent. Still, to really
get the scenes feeling right, it takes a good bit of finesse. Each night Leo assembled that day's footage and, by the next day, knew what, if anything, was
missing. Leo then put together a small list of shots we definitely needed and
another list of shots that would be great to shoot if we had time. We were
mainly focused on the shots we needed, but it was incredibly valuable to
have an editor reaching for the high-water mark. The last thing you want to
feel after watching the final assembly is disappointed in not having a larger
shot selection.

The various types of shots a filmmaker and an editor have to choose from
are often referred to as the "grammar" of filmmaking—**close-up, medium
shot, wide shot, dissolve, cut, superimposition, split screen**—and these
differing perspectives will ultimately convey not only what is happening on-
screen, but how that has an impact on the film's characters and, by exten-
sion, the viewer. The editor weighs shot selection and shot duration to find
the best way to assemble a scene, deciding such matters as how long to hold
on a shot; when to cut away, and to what or to whom; who should be in
frame during a conversation; and how to exit a shot (with either a hard cut
or use of a dissolve). Each of these decisions influences what the viewer will

take away from the scene. A device as simple as a close-up can be as riveting as a gunshot when utilized properly.

We have just picked up the developed film from the last shooting day of *Twin Falls,* the dream sequence. The super 8 Kodachrome we transferred to 35 mm looks mesmerizing. In hand-painted celluloid, the twins ride their bicycles in unison and then they separate as a surreal accompaniment to the previous emergency room scene, where the surgical separation is about to take place. It is really the emotional heart of the movie. We drop off the footage to Leo, not saying anything except "Take a crack at it; we'll be back in a few hours." Leo nods affirmatively. When we arrive later that evening, Leo looks emotional. He shows us what he's done with the imagery. He has cut it in a way that makes the scene feel like a silent movie, which is exactly what we wanted. He has enhanced the story and created ambience through his editing. We had written our screenplay with sound in mind, and Leo's sound-editing background has been very useful. He thinks aurally while picture editing, often showcasing in his **temp track** fully rendered scenes complete with audio. Leo has been able to take dialogue tracks from better-sounding takes and fly them into the chosen visual. If an **ambient sound** from the shoot turns out inaudible, he has been able to substitute it with something haunting from another take.

We are nearly done with the assembly on *Twin Falls* as the production has been wrapped for a week. The producers eagerly await the completion of our director's cut. In the Halloween party sequence, we have employed a split screen, used to show the separate points of view of the twins simultaneously.

Temp track:
Temporary music and sound effects added to the soundtrack of a work in progress to create an atmosphere and convey a sense of what the finished product might sound like. Most, if not all, of these effects will be replaced by the sound editor and composer.

It also serves as an efficient way to show twice as much action in half the time while allowing us to make a subtle reference to Andy Warhol's *Chelsea Girls* and to Holly Woodlawn, who appeared as one of the partygoers. One of the producers calls the split-screen effect "too weird." We're not sure if that's a bad thing. Then, after watching **playback** of several scenes **intercut,** another producer suggests that Michele Hicks's speaking voice is "too Jersey" and should be **overdubbed** by another actress. We're not sure how to respond but keep a strong resolve to finish this film our way.

When we are finished editing *Twin Falls,* it comes in at 104 minutes. We are happy with the way it moves, feeling just slow enough, while never dragging. We and Leo believe it is time to **lock picture,** which means the length of the movie is determined and all that is left are sound concerns and **optical effects.** But before we can do this, we have to convince our producers that our filmmakers' cut is the right one for the Sundance Film Festival—where we are hoping to find a distributor. A producer arranges for an evening screening to show *Twin Falls Idaho,* inviting a small crowd of friends and advisers. We have made an independent film, but the producers are beginning to treat it like a Hollywood studio picture. Surprisingly, the audience even gets the absurdity of breaking down an art film into quantifiable categories and openly expresses this to the producers. Generally, everyone liked the film, but the producers are still concerned.

We are still waiting to lock picture. The producers decide to have yet another screening, to make some "final adjustments." We tell our friend Paul Schwartzman about the hoops that the producers are putting us through, so he calls up Jeffrey Katzenberg, who offers to watch *Twin Falls* and give his assessment. We drive over to his hacienda and drop off a VHS copy of our final cut. The next day the phone rings and it is Jeffrey Katzenberg. He tells us how much he enjoyed our *Twin Falls* and how we should work on a project together in the future. At the final screening, when the film is over, we suggest to the producers that they should call Jeffrey Katzenberg if there are any doubts. We offer them his home number. If they want studio approval, now we have it. Finally, the producers collectively agree that they will not attempt to reedit the film.

Reel Breaks

In the twenty-first century, most theaters do not use the well-known reel-to-reel projectors of the past for 35 mm films. Nevertheless, films are still broken down into a number of reels—generally five or six for a ninety-minute film—both to accommodate the older theaters still using the classic projection methods and to simply make the movies easier to transport from location to location. Traditionally, 35 mm movies were edited into thousand-foot reels for ease of handling the rolls on flatbed and upright editing machines. Then, after the film was complete, the thousand-foot reels were spliced into two-thousand-foot reels for shipping and projecting. The classic model used two projectors and would switch from one projector to the other at the end of a reel. Nowadays, most movies are edited on computers, and most labs and film recorders are able to handle two-thousand foot printing rolls, making it commonplace to edit a movie directly onto two-thousand-foot reels. Likewise, many modern theater chains no longer switch from one projector to the other; instead, they splice the reels together, and one full-length reel is laid flat on a platter for continuous projection with no changeovers.

Even with all the advances in projection, for an independent film hoping to make it on the festival circuit, the film will be shipped and shown from reel to reel in the classic way films were shown in the past. Some cautionary rules apply in postproduction when making the critical reel breaks in your project. It is advisable if not mandatory to complete a scene before making your break in the movie. It is difficult for backgrounds and other audio information to make a seamless changeover from one reel to the next. And it is considerably more dangerous to extend a music cue over a change in reels. It is rarely done and usually will result in a bump or notice-able glitch that can take an audience out of a scene. The same rule applies with dialogue. It is pretty much industry standard that when completing your scenes for reel-break considerations, you should allow a second of dead air on either side of the changeover so that no clipping of the language oc-curs during the crossing of reels.

When our composer, Stuart Matthewman, began working on his (and our) first film, *Twin Falls Idaho,* he didn't know the golden rule of avoiding music cues over reel breaks. So, when he was halfway through his finished score, it came as quite a shock to all of us that music couldn't continuously flow at the breaks in the reels. The odd thing was, Stuart had read a hand-ful of film-scoring books, but none of them made mention of reel breaks. We surmised it was a conspiracy among experienced composers to keep the young and hungry composers in the dark. So, now you know the great un-told tale of reel breaks. Keep it to yourself.

The Independent Film Editor

Of all the elements that go into the making of an independent film, the role of the editor is one of the most misunderstood and underappreciated. No better example can be cited than the fact that neither the Independent Spirit Awards nor the Sundance Film Festival has an award for best editing, al-though they both annually give an award for best cinematography. The Sun-dance Festival has even given an award for best production design, certainly a very important element to the artistry of film, but no more important than editing.

Leon's Steak House proved to be a valuable location, used for five sets/*Jackpot*

Editing an independent film differs from editing a Hollywood film in two key ways. First, an indie is usually going to have a tighter schedule, typically eight to twelve weeks, whereas a Hollywood film may take four months or more to edit. Second, an independent film is being put together with the filmmaker's vision at the fore, while a studio film is likely to go through a committee process—test-screened and then reedited to appeal to the largest target group. What makes independent film so rewarding for many editors is working toward an aesthetic goal rather than a commercial one.

While editing techniques aren't uniformly independent or Hollywood, American independent film, borrowing heavily from the French New Wave of the late 1950s, has used its techniques to go further than the simple as-sembly of story. While editing *Jackpot,* we played with the chronology of the story using a variety of **jump cuts.** A jump cut is the joining of two shots

Daryl Hannah as Flower Hercules/ *Northfork*

that are not sequential within the story. The jump cut asks the viewer to take a leap of faith, to believe that this sudden incongruity will lead to greater understanding. Our movie was hitched around the George Jones song "Grand Tour," and we wanted the editing of the film to follow the verse chorus chronology of the song rather than a typical filmic narrative structure. We wanted the plot to move about with the fast-forwarding and rewinding of the song on a cassette, as if the story was almost a thought, a recollection of a favorite song. We employed the jump cut to pace with the driving forward of our main character, Sunny Holiday, as he was doing karaoke contests farther away from home. We were able to go back in his life, abruptly transitioning like an unshakable memory. The jump cuts were, in essence, his memories catching up with him. We spent many days perfecting these time shifts, using jump cuts to bounce in and out of the past, present, and future.

In *Northfork* it was determined early on that the use of dissolves and superimpositions (sometimes as many as four images were superimposed) would convey the hallucinogenic nature of the boy Irwin's fever dreams as well as create a landscape of impressions rather than of concrete reality. Our intention behind the editing was not to differentiate between the dreamworld and the real world once we transitioned in, giving the impression of entering a daydream. The slow dissolve was good for this, making the film appear to melt into the next shot. As it did, we'd reveal the world of Irwin's imagination. The slow dissolve creates a metaphor of landscape, and often a film's essence is wrapped inside it. In one shot of Irwin's bedside table, there are several items, including a cup of tea, a flower, and a Hercules comic, that we carried into the following scene—but personified. In Irwin's fantasy world, he is visited by several gypsies, one named Cup of Tea and another Flower Hercules.

Whatever editing devices you and your editor use to compile your movie, they should keep with the independent spirit that made you write your screenplay. That's not to say that audience satisfaction shouldn't be a criterion when compiling a film, but too often indies are gutted in the edit room, made to pander to the lowest common denominator. The editor and filmmaker should be working creatively to better the piece. Successful independent films usually find their audience through invention, and during the edit is an amazing time to explore your film's possibilities.

Sunny sings "Escape"/*Jackpot*

14 | Music

"The silent threat of violence hangs in the air, along with the smell of the chocolate factory. Chocolate factories, by the way, don't smell of chocolate, they smell of death."

—*Crap Towns: The 50 Worst Places to Live in the UK,*
on the #1 rated crap town, Hull, England

Everyone has to come from someplace, but we like to think the lucky ones come from a place that smells. The composer on our three films is Stuart Matthewman, and he is from a place called Hull, a northern port in the UK, a place to leave. We went there once, briefly catching a boat to Rotterdam, and it was an impressive smell. That whole area of northern England has an industrial aroma that seems to breed music. Whether it be Manchester, Liverpool, or Birmingham, these places produce great sounds. Of course, it's a stretch to put Hull in with the bigger three, but, for us, the little city gave us our composer. Just as the aroma of chocolate raised our composer Stuart, we were weaned on the effervescences of the ammonia factory in our birthplace of El Centro, California. When the morning sunrise is accompanied by stench, it's imperative you turn to your imagination.

So how does one track down and secure a competent film composer for an independent film? By the time we crossed paths with Stuart, he was a long way from Hull. He had already released several huge albums as cowriter and multi-instrumentalist with Sade and was living in the States. We met him the way many independent filmmakers meet their future collaborators, through a friend. Often the best people you will find for your team are connected to you by one or two degrees. There really isn't a stable of established film composers looking to work on a next-to-no-budget indie; sometimes a novice composer, just like a beginning filmmaker, needs a first break.

We decided the best way to ask Stuart to work with us was to write him a letter explaining that we were making a short film and that we would very much like him to score it. He rang us immediately to say he would absolutely do it, and his attitude was very generous: "You're first-time filmmakers and I am a first-time film composer. Let's see what we can do!" The problem was, even short films have some sort of budget and we were flat broke. We called up friends and friends of friends but couldn't raise the $5,000 (you may know the feeling). Three months went by when we received a call from Stuart asking us how the shoot was going. "Well," we said, "it's going rather slowly. In fact, we haven't started because we haven't been able to raise the dough." Stuart then asked us how much money we needed. "Five thousand dollars," we said, "to do it on location, the way we want." Without hesitation he said he'd wire the cash into our bank account that evening.

So there you go. You can read every book ever written about how to make a film, but sometimes you just need to get lucky and meet a benevolent rock star, if you will. So we went and made our short film, *Bajo del Perro,* with our composer's money. We had a small crew and paid everyone $50 a day. We shot for three days in Northern California, and when we got back to Los Angeles, we sent the footage to Stuart in New York, where he began writing the score. We put what remained of the budget into flying out to New York to witness Stuart score our film. He came up with some amazing music that fit seamlessly. It was the beginning of our relationship with him, which has spanned all of our movies.

Smelly hometowns must bring good luck, but perhaps your fortune may not be so blessed. In that case, another route you can take to find a talented composer is to inquire about the availability of known composers whose music you admire. While it will be difficult to attract experienced composers, it is not impossible. In some cases, their schedules can be in flux and they may be able to take on your project at a limited figure you can afford. Or in other cases, they may have an association with a gifted younger composer who can be hired based upon that acclaimed composer's recommendation.

If you have any reservations about any of the composers you are considering, make sure to sample their work. All composers, novice and professional, should have a demo for you to hear, showcasing something of their instrumental work. It is worth mentioning that a composer's demo may not be indicative of the type of music you envisage for your film. This does not mean he or she is incapable of achieving the sound you want. A talented composer should be able to work in many different styles, so what you ought to be listening for is general musicality.

Collaborating with a Composer

One of the best ways for a filmmaker to create synergy with a composer is to work with him or her early on in the project. Because we've built a unique relationship with Stuart, on our films the composer is the first and last crew member on the project. He is a key collaborator while we are writing. We have found that an original piece of music helps us get deeper into the subtext of story. In the case of *Northfork,* Stuart sent us funeral fugues sung by

Temp score: The best way to discourage your composer (who most certainly will have a limited budget) is to temp your movie with the music from a master composer such as Ennio Morricone. It's one thing to show an example of the feeling you want the composer to achieve, but by using an expensive temporary score, you will also be reminding him or her of your film's financial limitations and maybe the composer's talent limitations, too.

a Tuvan throat singer and obscure indigenous acoustical recordings that worked with the Montana landscape. Those recordings kept drifting in and out of our thoughts as we wrestled with the script.

Working early on with a composer also allows specific themes in a film to be fully fleshed out. On *Northfork* we knew it would be beneficial to the score to have Stuart see the landscape we planned on filming. Over a Christmas holiday, a good two years before we actually started production (read the finance chapter!), Stuart visited us in Montana. We took him east of Glacier National Park, up toward a town named Browning, to an expansive overlook of the northern Montana plains. We had written this location as the last scene in the film, where the Evacuation Committee looks out into a still-untouched panorama. Stuart was amazed at the landscape—frozen ground, frosted trees, jetting mountains, epic sky—and repeatedly said how incredible the environment looked: "I wouldn't even know where I was in the world if I was dropped off here, maybe Mongolia?" Stuart's comment sparked an idea: rather than limiting the score to instrumentation authentic of 1950s heartland America, other sounds of different cultures that related geographically or culturally could also be incorporated. An instrument like the banjo, which is very American, is actually the result of transcontinental migration. The banjo came to America via the slave trade; it is one of the spate of African drums stretched with a string. Stuart used the banjo throughout *Northfork* and also incorporated other African drum sounds in one of the climactic sequences with the ark. Taking this theme of a plucked drum a step further, Stuart used a harpsichord, which is the piano's equivalent to a banjo. All of these plucky tones gave the score a nice cohesion and a historical foothold.

During the gestation of *Twin Falls Idaho,* we again worked early on with Stuart. As we were developing our seed idea of isolation and interdependence, Stuart began to compose claustrophobic musical interpretations. We wanted to make musical reference to the twin Thai brothers Chang and Eng Bunker, whom the Western world termed *Siamese twins.* Stuart purchased music recorded by the Royal Court of Thailand and was inspired to infuse his theme with their unique vocal harmonizations. We found it haunting to hear a foreign voice fitting the dynamic of our American story. There was a traditionalism in the sound of the Thai choir that Stuart built upon to soften the freakish visual of the conjoined twins. Also early on in the discussion of *Twin Falls,* we told Stuart that we wanted to pay homage to Sergio Leone's *Once Upon a Time in America* and use one of the themes, "Amapola," brilliantly arranged by Ennio Morricone, which Leone repeated throughout the film.

Because we were able to work early on with Stuart, by the time the score for *Twin Falls* was done, Stuart had provided our movie with all types of music other than the score. He had written the songs for the Halloween party, provided us with a tabloid television theme, elevator music, diner music; whatever type of music we were looking for, Stuart composed. He took it upon himself to provide everything we needed, even in terms of supplying himself to be the DJ at the Halloween party.

> **OST rights:** One way to attract and secure a film composer is to offer him or her the rights to the original soundtrack (OST) that will be composed and recorded for your film. This may allow the composer to make some additional income once the film is released, and gives the composer some extra incentive to invest his or her own time and resources into the score.

Scoring the Mood

When a composer views a film for the first time, he or she is going to be look-ing for those scenes that would benefit from the addition of score, but this doesn't mean the composer's music should overtake an actor's dialogue or overwhelm a quiet moment. More often than not, the goal of a score should be to delicately enhance the audience's viewing experience. As our composer puts it, "Hopefully, no one really notices my music until it stops." We fully subscribe to the less-is-more philosophy of our composer. His music always seems to be serving the greater good of the film as a whole. This type of cre-ative selflessness is what a filmmaker should look for in a film composer. Writing a memorable score for a film and writing a memorable symphony are two separate endeavors. A film's score is more like one section of an or-chestra, whereas a symphony relies only on orchestration to achieve its aes-thetic effect. In a real way, a film composer's musicality is only as beneficial as his cinematic sensibilities.

There are times, however, when a score rightfully takes center stage in a film. Suspenseful scenes and transitional moments such as flashbacks and time lapses are often more powerful when coated generously with music. In *Northfork* (as we've discussed before), we transition in and out of the dying or-phan boy Irwin's dreamscape. Our composer would feature specific instru-ments every time we entered Irwin's dreamworld. An eerie harmonica and a timorous violin would rise in volume, cueing the audience that something was different in the world we were about to enter.

The Low-Budget Score

Scoring a low-budget independent film is entirely different from scoring a Hollywood picture. On most independents there will be no orchestra with a sixteen-piece string section; there will be no conductor cueing the percussionist or the brass section; there will be no engineer miking the acoustical hall; there will be no music editor ensuring that the picture and score are in sync. What there probably will be is one person working long hours in a home studio on an all-too-tight budget, occasionally calling in favors from studios and musicians.

Twin Falls woke us up to the fact that the independent film composer gets screwed when it comes to the budget. Of the half a million dollars we had allotted for production, the producers of *Twin Falls* had left just enough money in the music column to afford a Casio keyboard and a Japanese acoustic guitar. The producers had taken into account that we had a friend who was doing the score, a friend who would do the score for free if necessary. And, alas, that is what independent filmmaking is all about, pulling favors. But even if the budget had been double, at a million dollars, it still would have been too low for any kind of serious orchestral work. Like the rest of the film's production, only by working around the budgetary restrictions were there ways to create a memorably recorded film score.

Stuart was able to record lush strings on a super-low budget by hiring a four-piece string section from the New York Philharmonic, paying the musicians the union minimum for a four-hour spot. He then enhanced the recording by doubling, tripling, and even quadrupling the string parts on his keyboard using a string pad. Another trick Stuart has used to create fidelity in the score is to sample acoustical sounds and manipulate them with a synthesizer. On *Northfork* the music box needed a lush underscore to transcend both the dreamworld and reality. It was important not just to have a basic windup toy chime but to have a more complex melody come from a metal comb and a braille-like cylinder. By searching antique stores, we were able to find huge music boxes with intricate mechanics; Stuart was then able to write music that included these sounds and to also layer his own composition using the ideas behind music boxes.

Licensing Recorded Music

All three of our movies have had their share of country music, and all contemporary music needs to be properly licensed for use. From Lefty Frizzell and Webb Pierce playing from the dashboard radio of the 1948 Ford in *Northfork,* to Patsy Cline and George Jones crooning in *Jackpot.* In *Twin Falls* we saved ourselves the headache of licensing by recording an original country tune (we still get ASCAP checks for a few bucks every quarter). We felt it was important that the country songs in *Northfork* were the ones our father had heard while visiting his dad when he was working on the dam projects in Montana. The love of country music on the AM side of the radio inspired us to make *Jackpot,* a movie based around the song "Grand Tour" by George Jones. Most singers from that era lived what they were singing about. It was just as good to sing about drinking as it was to drink. *Jackpot* was also about a karaoke singer. We needed to assemble a list of songs that were affordable, but not so obscure that an audience wouldn't appreciate them.

Licensing popular music isn't cheap and is often a time-consuming journey through various publishing houses. The amount spent licensing music has grown exponentially over the years and often competes with the composer for dollars and dramatic impact on the finished film. When an independent film can afford to do so, a music supervisor is hired to help facilitate the licensing of music and the film's general musical needs. If one can't be afforded, the job usually falls into the line producer's lap. Having a music supervisor definitely makes a big difference; an experienced music supervisor will have a wide range of contacts in the music industry and can aid in the search and procurement of that special piece of source music that is right for your scene.

A music supervisor's job is part creative and part administrative. Creatively, the music supervisor will often play the filmmaker various record-

Penny and the twins/*Twin Falls Idaho*

ings of songs he or she feels would suit the film. A music supervisor with an extensive knowledge of recorded music is therefore a valuable resource for the filmmaker. Administratively, the music supervisor is in charge of licensing the agreed-upon songs from the publishing houses. As well, the music supervisor may work with the composer to arrange budgetary matters pertaining to the score, although on many independents the music supervisor and the composer work separately and from separate budgets. Of the three films we've made, we've had a music supervisor on two.

We enlisted the help of Jonathan Daniel to help deal with the rights issues of using multiple songs in *Jackpot*. Even though Jonathan Daniel wasn't a music supervisor, he had knowledge of the music publishing world and how to deal with record companies. His advice was to find a record label that had a catalog from which we could choose several artists. In some ways, making this a package deal is less of a headache when negotiating terms. Jonathan also compiled a list of songs that were easier to obtain because they were so often licensed. Having someone negotiate the prices of music licensing is a good way to go; there is a ton of phone time needed to make this happen. We needed the rights to the songs before we filmed *Jackpot* because the songs were sung by actors in the movie. This wasn't a postproduction issue where we could add the songs later and if they were unavailable we could change them. There was a lot of pressure to nail a song list before we shot the movie and only a few weeks to do so.

For a song to be used in a film, the film production needs to have both the **synchronization right,** which allows usage of the composition itself, and the **master use license,** which allows usage of the physical recording—usually controlled by the record company. Typically, the music supervisor negotiates these two licenses with the publisher and the record company.

The song "Grand Tour" was owned by a few different publishing houses. So we had to find all parties involved and get them to agree on the price. Trying to get George Jones to sign off on it is the stuff of a whole other book. We asked Mac Davis, who plays Sammy Bones, to help find Jones. He said he had been calling him for years with no luck. Funny enough, we asked Mac to sing his own song "Baby Don't Get Hooked on Me," and he stood in contemplation and then said jokingly, "I wrote it, but I don't know if I own that song." He may have given the song away, as is the case with the song "Lady" performed by Kenny Rogers and written by Lionel Richie. When we went to license "Lady," it was believed that Lionel Richie didn't own the song but his ex-wife did. Jon Gries, the actor in *Jackpot* who was supposed to sing "Lady" via karaoke didn't want to sing it. We said, "It's okay, your character does." A

Ben Foster as Cod/*Northfork*

few weeks went by and there was no way of attaining "Lady" for our movie, so we decided on the next best song, "Escape," aka "The Piña Colada Song" by Rupert Holmes. This song happened to work for our price and it was available; nevertheless, it was amazing to watch Jon try to get through his performance of "Escape," a song he hated more than "Lady."

The Evacuation Committee goes on record/*Northfork*

15 | Sound

Motion picture sound is a highly sophisticated team enterprise and, particularly on independent films, is often overlooked. Contrary to picture editing, where one or, at most, two people are designated editors of the visual component to the movie, a small arsenal of audio experts are required to fully render the sonic elements. On an independent's budget, sound is often left to inexperienced personnel, resulting in a noisy **dialogue track** and underdeveloped **audio design.** We have always made an effort to focus time and energy into the sound of our films. This is one of the reasons our independent films are often thought to be much more expensive to make than they actually are. Consider this: when an audience is watching a film, they are really using only two of their five senses. If your film's audio is weak, you've lost half of your film's sensory power.

Montana winds required the boom operator to cover his microphone with a windjammer/*Northfork*

Decisions that affect the sound of a film begin in preproduction. A film-maker, along with the producer, must decide who is going to do what on the audio front. The leader of the sound team is the **sound supervisor.** The sound supervisor isn't always chosen in preproduction, though it is most advantageous to do so. An early hiring allows the sound supervisor to be part of a film's maturation. In practice, the sound supervisor should be the first one in on the sound team and the last one out. He or she will oversee all sound components from design to coordination of the **mixer** and the **mix venue.**

A film's sonic journey begins with the **production recordist** (also known as the sound recordist) on the set. The production recordist is the person dedicated to recording the film's dialogue during production. The recordist must take into account the environment in which the actors will be speaking, choose which microphone works best, and work closely with the director to achieve clarity of dialogue and **backgrounds.** Most recordists will capture the dialogue on either a DAT recorder or a hard-disc recorder—the ¼ Nagra was once the recordist device of choice, but with digital's ease of use and cost-effectiveness, Nagra is no longer what it was. Some sound recordists fear the reliability of digital recordings and run both a Nagra and a digital format.

The sound supervisor is dependent on a passionate recordist who will fight for the clarity and control of the film's original recordings. There should be a sense of collaboration between these two key members of the sound team, even though it falls on the shoulders of the production recordist to capture a dynamic recording.

If you are fortunate enough to have your sound supervisor on your team early on, he or she should discuss some of the sound challenges and equipment choices with the recordist before production begins. The sound supervisor should also encourage the recordist to try to gather as much of the ambient sounds, **room tones, sync effects,** and **wild lines,** as possible during production. These organic sounds, in many instances, have far more resonance than canned effects pulled from a sound library. With respect to wild lines—non-sync dialogue usually delivered off-camera—the importance of capturing these on location can't be overemphasized. There is nothing that takes you out of a movie faster than a line of dialogue that was obviously

> **Sound supervisor:** The lead representative for all the artisans who work on a film's sound. The realm of the sound supervisor encompasses dialogue, sound design, backgrounds, footsteps—everything one hears in a film except for the musical score. Most crucially, the sound supervisor works with the director to ensure that his or her vision comes through sonically.

Open-range filmmaking/*Northfork*

recorded months later in the sterile confines of an ADR studio. The quality and performance on location can almost never be recaptured.

In the independent arena, the budget is often the enemy of this kind of creative process. Tight money is the norm and tight schedules the resulting reality. But when it is possible for the sound supervisor and the sound recordist to capture nature elements on location, it makes a great enhancement. These recording sessions can be invaluable if special vehicles or unusual props, for example, are made available for recording and can be added later to the final soundtrack. Within these constraints, great creativity can still be nurtured, though it requires a high degree of commitment and passion from the sound team.

Once a film has completed production, the schedule shifts over to post-production. For varying lengths of time, the picture editor is busy assembling the film and working intimately with the director. As the project moves toward a final cut, the sound supervisor is officially brought on to the project and meets with the director and editor for what is known as a **spotting session.** This meeting can last for a short day or stretch into several consecutive gatherings. The spotting session should be a very creative time in the filmmaking process where all the audio components to the movie are discussed and the crucial chemistry between director, picture editor, and sound supervisor is forged.

> **Spotting session:** A face-to-face meeting with the director, sound supervisor, and film editor where they watch each scene of the film and discuss necessary sound enhancements.

The following is a list of the essential elements that make up the sound of a film. Somewhat analogous to the sections of an orchestra, sound for motion picture is comprised of several interdependent parts. These are brief descriptions of the disciplines discussed during a typical spotting session:

ADR (AUTOMATED DIALOGUE REPLACEMENT) | While examining a film's dialogue track, the sound supervisor may deem that a scene (or a handful of scenes, in some cases) is too noisy. In that event, the sound supervisor will communicate the problem to the director. If the director is in agreement, an ADR session will be held at an ADR studio, where the actor or actors will rerecord the noisy dialogue, trying their best to match their former performance. Determining when ADR is necessary is very subjective, and a sound supervisor may be in a difficult position having to explain to the director that the dialogue of a scene needs to be rerecorded.

ADR may also be used to add additional off-screen lines to strengthen a performance or sonic texturing to the noted scenes. Sometimes this is a monologue delivered by the lead character. In other instances, the additional lines are simply background. In the case of group background lines and

Loop group: An ensemble of actors who have the specific skill of adding background voices and pieces of dialogue to further the story.

noises, a **loop group** is often hired. Most films enlist the services of a loop group, and most supervisors have suggestions on whom to use based on the nature of the film.

Finally, ADR may be employed to completely erase an actor's dialogue performance. Sometimes the actor's dialogue is replaced by another actor whom the director feels fits the piece better. There are various reasons for this choice, from the accent of the original actor not matching with the rest of the cast or to a performance being less than what the director had expected.

SOUND EFFECTS | Layering **sound effects** into a film is the nuts and bolts of the postproduction sound job. To get the job done right, a sound supervisor needs a quality **sound library** to cull from and, whenever possible, original location recordings. A well-placed sound effect adds character to a film, providing tension or release to a scene. The more original recording that can be done for the project, the more unique the final product will become.

SOUND DESIGN | **Sound design** pertains to the more stylized moments of the movie that often spring from the director and sound supervisor's attempt to achieve something sonically unique. The design elements of a movie are often, though not always, part of the sonic landscape offered in conjunction with the composer's work. Sound design should always be sensitive to the challenges of the composer. Subsequent to the spotting session, communication should be established between the music and sound departments to best achieve a clear vision of the filmmaker's imaginings.

BACKGROUNDS | The background sound effects are subtle enhancements to each scene. A movie's ambience has everything to do with sonic atmosphere. The backgrounds can be subliminal or boldly explosive, depending upon the dynamics of the canvas. During the spotting session, the director will often mention the need for a specific background here or there. But, often later, back in the sound shop, the sound supervisor will continue to add further elements to these categories to enrich the final product.

FOLEY | Simply put, **Foley** is when a film is played back while a **Foley artist,** along with the sound supervisor, records the sound of smaller props and footsteps to a given scene. Foley, to a certain extent, can become the fabric of the sound job. High-quality Foley, carefully performed and recorded, can weave all the elements of the sound department into a final product of exciting depth and subtlety. What and where Foley is needed is discussed during the spotting session but is usually left to the sound supervisor's discretion.

DIALOGUE | A skilled sound editor or two will meticulously polish the original production track once the picture editor has made the final cuts and turned the scenes over to the sound department. These dialogue editors can be the unsung heroes of the sound team with their highly honed abilities to clean up dirty recordings and sometimes avoid having to depend on ADR to save a scene.

On an independent film, this team of people is typically granted a four-week run (due to the exigencies of the budget) at cutting all the material and joining forces with the composer at the final mix. Sometimes this schedule can be extended, and a lot more textural additions can be achieved in a five- to six-week editorial schedule. Four weeks is the norm, though, and a good sound team must know how to move quickly and decisively to keep both the director and the business department satisfied.

THE FINAL MIX | This is the last part of the postproduction process. The sound supervisor becomes something of a conductor and works with the mixing crew to blend and polish each scene. The mixing schedule can range from days to weeks and should include several days of **predubbing.** This part of the mix schedule allows the lead mixer to polish the dialogue and review all the categories of sound before embarking on the **final mix.** This weave of music, dialogue, and sound effects (design, backgrounds, Foley, sync effects) can be a very exciting endeavor. The hopes and fears of the filmmaker all come to bear as the soundscape for the movie is decided upon, reel by reel. If the composer and sound supervisor have collaborated effectively during the editing schedule, all the components should have a contributing effect and the final mix should be more a blending than a painful process of eliminating or recutting.

Contemplating Sound

The sound design of *Twin Falls* was married to the sound of contemplation, of imagination, of film tracks running through the spokes of a projector. We really brought the set alive with not only the internal sounds of a water heater percolating and the rantings of a preacher next door, but also with the exterior sounds of city noises—ambulances, jackhammers. Because we couldn't afford to sound design the whole film, we focused on a few key characteristics. We wanted to not only see but also hear the twins' solitude. What is the sound of quiet sleeping? The sound of slicing cake? This is where we really learned of sound design's possibilities. For the main room, where the twins live, we created the sound of omnipresent breath atmospherically exhaling and inhaling throughout to accompany the dialogue.

Northfork was the first film where we had a comprehensive sound design for the entire movie. Supervising sound editor Christopher Sheldon worked with us to build a tapestry of original sonics that permeate the picture. The weathered old homes captured on film during production of *Northfork* later, in postproduction, became important sonic characters in the film's soundtrack. To sonically match the eerie visuals of a town soon to be abandoned, Christopher Sheldon went to Bodie, California, a historically preserved ghost town (once a mining town), to record footsteps and movements that were later matched to picture.

While most films, independent and Hollywood alike, rely on either prerecorded audio or the limited Foley surfaces to convey the sounds of the actors' movements, *Northfork* is unique in that all of its actors' movements were specifically recorded and edited from the Bodie **field recordings.** Literally thousands of footsteps were recorded in Bodie to match each scene in *Northfork.* The only other recent film that comes to mind that undertook this arduous sonic task is *The Green Mile,* where all the movements were recorded at a prison and later edited to the picture.

Recording organic sounds in an environment that matches picture is extremely time-consuming, and that is the principal reason sound companies rely on Foley artists in soundstages to capture the sound of actors' movements. But even masterful Foley will not match the organic recordings of a weather-beaten wood-frame house in a foreboding ghost town. Just like the

Field recordings: While the production recordist is busy capturing all the dialogue that is being spoken by the actors during production, the sound supervisor, if he is brought on the picture early enough, will visit either the locations of the film or visually similar locations to record specific backgrounds and props that will make the soundtrack unique. While most Hollywood sound companies offer an impressive array of library sounds, there is no substitute for field recordings, which convey sonically the uniqueness of the visual.

look of a film, the sound of a film, when it is organic, has a uniqueness that cannot be contrived.

Another unique design was the music box that plays in the gypsy sequences. We actually dismantled a music box in postproduction so that the tiny gears could be **close-miked.** Even the winds that flutter in and out of our Montana backdrop were original recordings that were then handcrafted to our specificity.

What we accomplished on *Northfork* was a layered, textural sound design to accompany our dense visuals. Since we come from a visual arts background, we undercoat the visuals in our early screenplays, adding more and more detail in subsequent drafts. By the time we actually shoot, we have a visual universe on the page. What we have learned since *Twin Falls* is to undercoat with sound and score, as well. This was the case when shooting one of the climax sequences in *Northfork,* where the silver Twin Beech plane flies away with Irwin and the gypsies. As we were shooting, the plane would fly toward our direction a few hundred feet in the air and the sound would almost be silent until the plane was just overhead and then it would grow intensely loud. There is a term for this: "buzzing." Wow, does it buzz when you are standing beneath a flying monster! So we wanted to create this "buzzing" sensation for the audience when the plane flew by them. When we did the final mix of *Northfork,* we had the mixer redline the plane engine just as it passes on-screen. It knocks people out of their seats and completely changes the somber mood.

The Dialogue Track

When the sound supervisor listens to a film for the first time, it will become immediately apparent how well the sound recordist recorded the dialogue on set. Our sound recordist has always done a masterful job recording clean

Nick Nolte stands at the podium and delivers his "peace" for the remaining citizens/*Northfork*

dialogue in challenging situations. We have been blessed to have had the same sound recordist, Matt Nicolay, on all three films. When you find someone who cares as much about the quality of the production sound as he does, it makes a dramatic difference when you move into postproduction. Wind, birds, planes—just about anything with a motor or wings— wreak havoc for the sound mixer. It takes a very inventive sort to maneuver through the conditions, someone who has the dedication to record the clearest sound possible, someone who has the courage to speak up when he or she is faced with obstructive noises. What you learn quickly in postproduction is that no matter how skillful your supervising sound editor is, if the dialogue is washed out, there is very little he or she can do. When the dialogue is unsalvageable, many films resort to ADR. The actor is put in an isolation room, and the sound editor cues the line or lines in question until it is a close match with the moving lips. But ADR often feels unnatural. We avoid it almost always and can afford to do so because our dialogue track is usually pristine.

On set we have built off-screen dialogue tracks to insert later in postproduction. We brought Garrett Morris to the side and handed him a Bible and said to him: "Start preaching." Matt Nicolay ran the sound and we captured many phrases that way. We did something similar with Patrick Bauchau. We were shooting *Jackpot* in a house with a shelf of philosophy books, and we had Patrick randomly choose and read some passages while we ran tape. Later in post we added Patrick's musings over the pink Cadillac's hypnotic travels. For *Northfork,* when Nick Nolte was getting ready to deliver his sermon to the clergy and the passing cows, we asked him to start off with an improv sermon to get into the part. Well, Nick starts telling this incredibly heavy story about his mother's passing and we were rolling tape, and all the extras and everyone in the crew was just riveted by his eulogizing. That off-the-cuff speech is what we decided to use as the closing narrative over a montage of Montana scenery.

Sound, as we have learned, is a whole other universe that complements the picture. So much time is usually spent on getting the picture perfect that all the possibilities of sound are often overlooked. Sound travels farther and deeper than most people think. Remember how your favorite songs made you feel, how they can even change your mood? It is worthwhile to think about this when contemplating the sound design for your film. When sound is thoughtfully employed in a movie, it can elevate the picture; it can enhance the tone and the feeling of a scene even if an actor hasn't given you a fully emotive performance.

And, finally, consider this: an audience will sit through a bad picture, shaky and out-of-focus camera work, in the name of artistic expression. Many 8 mm shorts and 16 mm films do well at film festivals. But few audience members will tolerate bad sound. It's just too irritating. Horrible sound will clear a theater faster than anything, except for, perhaps, an usher yelling "Fire!"

The distributors of American Standard soap, Les and Sunny/*Jackpot*

16 | Independent Distribution

We named her "Brittany." She's a thirty-five-foot motor home, fancy in her own trailer-trash way. We rented her for a whistle-stop press tour of America as our film *Northfork* opened from art house to megaplex across the country. When we promoted *Twin Falls,* flying from Seattle to Chicago to Boston, the publicist arranged a nice oversize love seat for us to sit in during our interviews. Later we found out the publicist actually thought we were conjoined twins. We must have either been really convincing or she hadn't finished watching the movie. Then, for *Jackpot*'s promotional tour, we jetted past the fly-over states, doing press only on the West and East Coasts. But this time we went by coach to travel the road less promoted. We wanted to see what independent film distribution looks like from the ground level.

Brittany, our motor ho, is actually the second motor home we rented. We dumped her mother, "Brenda," off in Los Angeles after our northern California press stops. Brenda's last moment in the sun came when we did an article for *Good Times,* a Santa Cruz weekly newspaper. She was featured by name in several photos with us as the article chronicled the beginning of our tour. But since we were heading across the country, she needed to be retired. A thing like a wobbly front dashboard is very hazardous. When we would hit a bump, the dashboard would bounce off the bottom frame, giving us a glimpse of her engine. On the winding Grapevine back from central California, we had to call in for a replacement. Brittany was fancier than her mother, but later, down the road, we found that the apple didn't fall far from the tree.

We have parked Brittany in Scottsdale, Arizona, outside an Anywhere, U.S.A., shopping mall on Highland Avenue. It is 7:00 P.M. and still above one hundred degrees. The AC on the new motor home has begun to shut down intermittently, which quickly turns our living space into a thirty-five-foot dry sauna. The fridge/freezer combo blew yesterday somewhere near Needles, California, and the generator is making a wheezing sound, which seems to be getting more acute by the hour. The local promotional rep named Ziggy, who looks more like a Zach, is telling us our press duties for the day. Each city we are traveling to has a promo rep; they come in all shapes and sizes. Each promotional rep is very beneficial to film in his or her market, arranging interviews with local newspapers, television shows, and radio stations.

We pop our heads out of our motor home and into the dense Scottsdale sunshine. A line of curious filmgoers, kept cool by overhead misters, has begun to wend around the theater. We will be speaking to them in a few minutes. The line of people is fairly long and is probably a direct result of the positive reviews *Northfork* received in two local papers. Unlike most big-budget movies with big advertising dollars, an indie can't overcome bad reviews by saturating the market with television commercials, print ads, or giveaway promotions—there's no money for it. If an indie gets a bad review in a smaller market, like Scottsdale, it can be quite detrimental because most people will learn about the film from the review. Sometimes it's the only advertising an independent movie receives.

If we were doing this tour fifty years ago, the Paramount that is distributing our film would also be the exhibitor that owned the theater. But in 1948 a Supreme Court decision in *U.S. v. Paramount Pictures, et al.*, changed the way Hollywood studios would do business from then forward. The Paramount Consent Decree put an end to a studio system that was not only controlling the films available to the public but the places in which they were seen. In a real way, an early form of the independent film business was involved in the coup. Newly emboldened independent producers successfully lobbied the government, claiming the Hollywood studios had become a de facto monopoly. The Federal Trade Commission agreed, calling "block bookings" anticompetitive and forcing the studios to sell off their interests in theater chains. A great dynasty was finished and the seeds of modern independent distribution sown.

Today an independent film can be distributed in a number of ways, but the most high-profile, and arguably preferable, way is to follow the Hollywood model but through an independent wing of a major distributorship, like

Review-proof: Unlike a Hollywood blockbuster, which can sustain and even overcome a blow from a bad review, an independent film usually cannot. Indies aren't review-proof because they rely heavily on good reviews to motivate their audience, which translates into strong word of mouth. A typical indie audience will choose whether to see a film based on its reviews, while members of the typical mainstream audience, who watch Hollywood star-driven movies, care little if a film received two or four stars.

One sheet: The movie poster that will be hung in movie theater showcase displays and used for most print advertisements, such as newspapers and billboards. The one sheet is the visual association potential audience members will make with your movie before they have seen it. Creating a one sheet is a concentrated effort by everyone selling the film to condense the movie's message into an image. Reviews and quotes will sometimes be added to a one sheet to add credence to the claim that the film is worth seeing.

Sony Pictures Classics. Most major studios now have a classics department that is part and parcel of the studio, although it has its own skeleton staff, offices, and operating expenses specifically for distributing and marketing independent films or (which is often the case) cheap mainstream films. Since the operating costs of a major film distribution company are so high and the infrastructure so enormous—from the payroll for a national staff and the piles of administrative duties to the coordination of ever-changing exhibitor demands—the classics divisions are able to interact with their parent company as an independent film grows while not having to keep the overhead of a full-fledged distribution company.

Inside the lobby of the Camel View Theater is a young girl wearing a homemade T-shirt with an ironed-on picture of Blake and Francis Falls (the Siamese twins from *Twin Falls*). It's nice to see that *Twin Falls* has reached the level of cult paraphernalia. Ziggy then introduces us to the assistant theater manager, a blond kid in his midtwenties. He knows a lot about film, a lot about our films, and even has an old *Twin Falls* poster that we gladly sign.

We follow the assistant manager through the dimly lit halls. We maneuver through a portly crowd as *Pirates of the Caribbean* is letting out. *Northfork* seems to be holding it's own against the summer blockbusters. Some distributors of independent films see a summer release for an indie as a death sentence, forcing it to compete with the year's biggest Hollywood movies. But there's also an advantage to coming out with an indie in the summer; not every moviegoer wants to see an explosive-laden, special-effects-heavy movie. Releasing a film that goes against the popular tide is called **counter-programming.** With the rise in the number of independent films since the early 1990s, independent movie distributors began releasing some of them earlier in the year rather than holding them for the fall. Counterprogramming has its risks and rewards. There truly isn't a formula for when it's best to release an independent film. A filmmaker has to find solace in the fact that his or her film is being released at all.

We turn left into a midsize theater past an encased *Northfork* poster. The assistant manager walks to front and center of the three-fourths-full theater. Our adrenaline is rising, as it always does; we've never gotten used to talking to a large group of people. We have done enough of these meet and greets to know the basics—who talks first, the all-important advice a theater owner gave us to "cuddle the mike"—but, still, there is always anxiety before the first few words. The assistant manager picks up a microphone that is connected to a little guitar amp. It's plenty loud and the kid's a pro. He warms up the audience, telling them what an honor it is to have the filmmakers speaking. Then it is our turn. We talk directly to the audience; we tell them a bit about the struggle and the joy of making *Northfork.* We thank them for supporting our film. We make a few jokes about Brittany, the motor home, then answer a few questions: "Nick Nolte gave everything we could have asked for." "Working with Jimmy Woods is as good as it gets." The audience seems a little disappointed about the truth, as if our stars were really refusing to come out of their trailers. The fact is, we didn't have any trailers. From the audience's questions, we see how major stars garner a lot of attention, how celebrity really helps a film's profile. Having Nick Nolte, James Woods, and Daryl Hannah in our movie has brought in

IFP: IFP (Independent Film Project) is a nonprofit organization that actively supports the making and viewing of independent films. Headquartered in New York, IFP has several chapters throughout the country, including in Chicago, Minneapolis/ St. Paul, and Seattle. Chapters currently in formation are set for Austin and Santa Fe. An IFP membership enables a filmmaker to participate in year-round activities ranging from popular screenings to indie film workshops and seminars. IFP programs help members make connections— who's buying, who's financing, and who's making what features, shorts, and documentaries. Check out www.ifp.org for more information.

a large part of the audience that otherwise wouldn't have come.

We finish talking and then the lights dim. For the first time Scottsdale, Arizona, is viewing our movie. At the same time our movie is playing in Scottsdale, it is also playing in twelve other cities around the country. That's the power of studio-driven distribution. And the following week, *Northfork* will open up in another eight markets, bringing the tally to twenty cities, and will expand to more from there.

Generally, the independent arm of a major studio will release an independent film in one of two ways. The first is a **platform release,** which opens a film in two to ten markets with a few theaters in each and builds to more as the film's campaign gains steam. This is what we are witnessing on this promotional tour. A film given a platform release will, in all likelihood, be committed to at least a hundred theaters in advance.

The other type of independent release is called a **limited release,** which has the film open in a few markets (usually L.A., New York, and Chicago) in one or two theaters in each market. A limited release is totally dependent on word of mouth and positive critical response because so little is put into a marketing campaign. By giving a film a limited release, a studio is covering its bet that the film has limited appeal. This is where a filmmaker's coordinated effort with the independent film community can make a huge difference. Plugs on public radio, at Independent Film Project events, in the local *Reader* all need to coalesce to raise a film out of a quick good-bye.

Although a platform release is much wider than a limited release, it is infinitesimally small compared to the **saturation release** given an expensive action film or a star-driven drama, where a picture opens in twenty-five hundred theaters or more. The studios can predict in the first weekend whether a movie is a hit. A saturation release can spell disaster when a film opens wide and doesn't perform, with the studio already committed to millions of dollars in marketing and advertisement. But when it works, a saturation release garners an incredible amount of money in the blink of an eye. A new trend is to open an anticipated film nationally with Europe, making the saturation that much more potent. For independent films, the saturation release isn't widely employed; however, if an independent begins to take off, a sort of delayed saturation release might be used, releasing the picture in up to an additional thousand theaters.

FIND: FIND (Film Independent) is essentially IFP-Los Angeles with a new name and complete autonomy from the other IFP chapters. The former IFP-Los Angeles was by far and away the biggest chapter of the IFP, with thousands of members and direct connections to the who's who of independent filmmaking, dwarfing, in resources and stature, even IFP-New York. FIND is now the dominant independent film organization in America, controlling the Independent Spirit Awards and the Los Angeles Film Festival. For indie filmmakers in the Los Angeles area, FIND should be a great repository of information. FIND will launch a new website for its members, separating itself from the joint website shared by the IFP chapters.

Outside the Camel View Theater, Ziggy suggests we go to P.F. Chang's for dinner. It is in an adjacent mall and we walk there, wondering if Scottsdale might have the most malls per capita. It is maybe two or three degrees cooler now that it is nightfall. Ziggy talks with the hostess: it's Friday and there's a long wait for a table. Ziggy turns around, asking us if we're willing to "pull rank." We look at each other. Our first thought is that maybe Ziggy is offering us some fine Scottsdale meth. We then realize Ziggy is asking us whether we should use our celebrity to attain a table. It's a million-to-one shot that the hostess has even heard of us or our films. But as luck would have it, the hostess has recently seen *Twin Falls Idaho* on cable. Once again we are reminded of the power of distribution as we are quickly seated at a center table. Cable television has been an enormous help to many independent films. It has allowed our film *Twin Falls,* which had a short theatrical stay, to have another life. More people have seen *Twin Falls* on cable than saw it in the theater.

After dinner Ziggy says we can park our motor home at his girlfriend's house and plug in our generator. That sounds like a good idea, a step up from the sketchy RV park we stayed at the night before.

It is now ten o'clock and still the mercury is pushing ninety. We pull Brittany up to Ziggy's girlfriend's house and then expand her midsection using the hydraulics, until we protrude over most of the shallow concrete front yard. Ziggy's girlfriend is hosting a party in her backyard. Everyone is friendly and somewhat inebriated, but we are tired. We excuse ourselves from the party and head back to the motor home.

Inside Brittany, the air conditioner is maxed out. We unfurl the fat yellow power cord and plug it into the garage wall. The generator needs a rest, as do we. The day of driving has caught up with us, and tomorrow is full with press, followed by more driving. We turn off the generator and then turn on the power—a giant flash and a large pop—Ziggy's girlfriend's house goes pitch-black. It's an odd moment: the music and the party noise quickly disappear into a still desert quiet. And then chaos is restored. Ziggy trips the fuse, and the house regains power. Because Brittany sucks way too much energy, we can't tap into the house. We stake out our beds and fall asleep in the heat; a long day of *Northfork* promotion lays ahead.

We wake up to the heat and Ziggy waiting outside. We have an appearance on *Good Morning Arizona* in an hour. We follow Ziggy in our motor home to a diner near KTVK Channel 3. We all order the house specialty, the Bacado—a bacon/avocado omelet. Inside the *Good Morning Arizona* building, there is a local band setting up to perform. During the next segment break, we take our seats. It's live television and suddenly hundreds of thousands of Arizonians are hearing us talk about *Northfork* and then watching a long clip of it. What's nice about smaller markets is that they aren't too precious with airtime.

We say good-bye to Ziggy and good-bye to Scottsdale as we head to New Mexico on our

Negative pickup:
For some indies with advance positive word of mouth and, usually, a strong cast, a distribution deal is struck before the film's completion. When the film is actually done, the distributor will receive the negative along with deliverable items, and is obligated to release the movie as stipulated in the negative pickup deal. This can be risky for the filmmaker and/or producer, because no overages will be covered by the distributor. The distributor requires the distribution rights for a set fee, and no more money will be forthcoming until the distributor has recouped its expenses and likely some sort of profit margin.

way to Texas, Tennessee, Kansas, Colorado, and finally Montana, where we will travel the entire Big Sky state, where *Northfork* was filmed.

When Paramount Classics acquired the rights to distribute *Northfork* in English-speaking territories, we hadn't actually completed the postproduction on the film. This type of distribution agreement is called a **negative pickup.** Essentially, the film is sold before it's a finished film. Commonly,

Deliverables: When a film is fortunate enough to secure distribution on even a modest level, the distributor will require the delivery of film-related items such as print materials, legal documents, and publicity materials, which altogether are called the deliverables. Creating and/or organizing the deliverables is a vast, costly, and consuming undertaking, and is wisest left in the hands of someone with previous deliverable experience, such as a veteran line producer. The costliest area will be the print materials required, which involve film labs, dupe costs, and the generating of film elements. Expenses quickly mount when such a thing as a color-corrected video version (which the distributor will use later to broadcast on television) is a required deliverable, paid for out of the film's budget. There will also be many legal

interested distributors will watch a first assembly or occasionally a few scenes of a picture and then judge whether they want to bid for it. If a deal is struck, upon the film's completion it will be delivered to the distributor along with what are termed the **deliverables,** which are a myriad of film elements such as digital transfers of film stock and an agreed-to number of on-set stills that will be used later for publicity. The deliverables are negotiable and can be very costly. It's wise to include the making and compiling of them in your budget. Many distributors attempt to put the expense of the deliverables into the film budget, forcing the filmmaker to pay out of pocket for them. The delivery of these elements to the distributor is what triggers payments from the negotiated distribution deal.

If your film is picked up by a classics division, chances are you may recoup your budget and perhaps even make a profit before the general public has seen your movie. How much a studio is willing to spend depends on many variables, such as the perceived marketability of your indie and how much heat or buzz your film has created on the festival circuit. If multiple companies are interested in acquiring your movie, this will likely raise its price tag. And just having your film picked up by a major distributor will raise your profile in the industry, allowing you to secure an agent, attorney, and all the things you probably didn't have when you began making your movie. We secured both before selling our film at Sundance. We felt choosing a proper distributor would be hard enough. Also, many more people will have a chance to see your movie if it's distributed through a major studio. Getting an independent film recouped and seen by as many people as possible, to our mind, are the top priorities.

There is still a downside to going with an independent wing of a major studio, and that is its rather capricious way of doing business. As we mentioned before, your film will live or die by how well it does at the box office during the first few weeks of release, regardless of what type of release your film is given. Despite strong reviews, if your film isn't filling seats, it will quickly be replaced by one that is. The competition for theater space has never been more fierce. While on the press tour with *Twin Falls Idaho,* Sony Pictures Classics had us meet the theater owners personally and have lunch with them. Having a rela-

deliverables, which, hopefully, a well-organized lawyer will foresee while doing the production legal work. The legal paperwork is standard and includes signed releases and contracts from the cast and crew, releases for each song played on the soundtrack, and copies of all licenses and deal memos pertaining to the movie. Lastly, there will be publicity deliverables such as on-set photos and slides, pressbooks, synopses, and biographies of key talent and creative crew. Generally, the best way to handle all of the deliverables is to plan ahead, stay organized, and seek help from someone experienced in the process.

tionship with the theaters is important and connects the filmmaker personally with his or her film. Every theater owner and theater manager we met truly loved independent films. They understood the marketplace and were willing to help our film succeed. A personal connection with a theater owner can make the difference when he or she chooses which films to continue to play. In smaller markets, sometimes a filmmaker's handshake is more binding than a distributor's ink.

P&A (prints and advertising): P&A is the amount of money a film distributor either has paid or is committed to pay for a film's distribution and promotion. From print copies to local and national advertisements, the P&A budget for a film can sometimes exceed the budget of the film itself, particularly if the film is an indie made on the cheap. The cost of prints and advertising for the opening of a midsize to large studio film in America is now upwards of $40 million. For indies, the P&A budgets vary wildly. Many indies have next to no P&A budget and are left to word of mouth and reviews to gain exposure.

Each of our films had a set print and advertising (P&A) budget. The **P&A** budget will increase if the distributor sees that they are going to make a profit, and the good news is they most likely won't cut the budget if the film isn't performing like they'd hoped for. They just won't sink any more money into it. The P&A budget is usually a contractual agreement that was made when you sold the film.

Alternate Distribution

Once upon a time, a counterpoint to independent film was going to be independent distribution, which would circumvent the major studios altogether. Well, things haven't really worked out that way in the theatrical world. For a film to be released across the country, it will almost always go through a studio. But there are alternative ways to get a film seen by theatergoers. One way is to **four-wall** an indie, by either contacting a theater owner and renting the space directly or finding a space, rolling in a projector, and collecting the door fees yourself. A typical deal has the filmmaker and/or producer pay a flat fee for the rental of the room, with the profits then going back to the production. It may sound like a headache, but one screening attended by a reviewer could change a film's destiny. Moving from one city to the next, films have been distributed around the whole country in this manner. It is the ultimate in self-empowered, independent-minded, grassroots film distribution. This route became popular in the early 1970s when a few tenacious independent directors and producers were given the cold shoulder by the studios. Such films as *Breezy* by Clint Eastwood, *Daisy Miller* by Peter Bogdanovich, and most famously *Billy Jack* by Tom Laughlin made their debut by renting the "four walls" of a theater. *Billy Jack* became a touchstone for the way films would be promoted in the future when writer/director/producer Tom Laughlin successfully sued Warner Brothers for undermarketing the movie. Warner Brothers was forced to buy television spots regionally as Tom Laughlin four-walled his film around the nation. *Billy Jack* went on to gross $22 million, a blockbuster for 1971. Unfortunately, the only thing the studios learned was the power of television advertising, which from then on became the backbone of marketing a film.

Another way to distribute a film independently is to use the Internet. Increased processing power combined with fast broadband connections allows more and more people to enjoy high-end video and audio on their laptops. These technological advances are really in the gestation phase but may very well end up challenging the classic film-distribution models. While digital distribution offers a quick and cheap way to view a film, piracy concerns are a major issue. It is estimated that there are as many as 700,000 digital movies being exchanged illegally over the Web. The goal will be for a format that allows the consumer to watch movies online while protecting the proprietary interests of the filmmaker and distributor.

The easiest and most affordable way to distribute a film is using your own two hands. Pressing and packaging your film in the DVD format requires only a DVD burner, which now comes included in many computers. We started to see this a lot while on the *Northfork* press tour. Young filmmakers were handing us their short films and features on DVD. Most had decent packaging with their contact information. Done right, an attractive package can get someone to watch your film who otherwise wouldn't. And DVDs can be popped into almost any computer. The bottom line is getting your film seen by as many important or influential people as possible, and the DVD format allows you to do just that.

Foreign Distribution

During the height of the independents in the 1990s, the foreign market was thriving. It helped fuel a lot of domestic films to get made and seen. It has since changed. The European film marketplace has become saturated, and, like the United States, theater space for independents is limited.

Not too long ago a filmmaker could attach even a well-known B actor to his or her movie and expect some foreign investment in exchange for distribution in that territory. Today the reality is quite different. Foreign markets look for proven box-office stars.

Selling Your Indie

After we had completed the postproduction on *Twin Falls Idaho* and had a finished film in our hands, one of the producers, a veteran sales representative, set up a few meetings for us with different film distributorships. The odd thing is that the companies we were meeting hadn't viewed our movie; they weren't allowed to, and so basically these were informal meet and greets. The idea, we were told, was to build a little buzz before Sundance, and then later when you see the distributor at your screening, the first date is already behind you.

We were in New York City just as the Christmas holiday break was moving toward full swing when we got the call to meet Sony Pictures Classics head of acquisitions, Dylan Leiner. It was Friday, the last possible day before everyone leaves town, and it was already four in the afternoon. Plus we were in the Village and the meeting was all the way uptown. Since we were about to screen our film at Sundance, the meeting seemed superfluous. Each distributorship we had met previously gave us the same friendly kind of smile, of course not knowing what the hell kind of picture we made, saying, "We can't wait to see your movie."

We were given the name and number of Dylan Leiner as our contact at Sony Classics, so we called him saying we couldn't make it uptown for at least an hour. But Dylan was very kind and persistent, saying how much he wanted to meet. After cab after cab flew by, we made our way to the foot of the Sony Building on Madison Avenue. It's a monolith with dark gray granite. There, we were given name tags and told to wait until Dylan was available. We waited for a long time, over half an hour, thinking that everyone had left for the holidays and forgot to tell the receptionist. She finally turned to us and said Dylan Leiner wasn't available and that we would be seeing Tom Bernard—at this point we didn't know who he was, but as we entered his office, there were team hockey photos lining his walls. Several things went through our minds; none of them prepared us for the verbal assault Tom Bernard had planned for us. As we took position in our chairs, there came a slap shot: "What the hell are you doing here!?"

One of us nervously replied, "We thought it would be a good idea if we met before Sundance."

"Do you have your film with you?"

"No."

"Can I see it?"

"I didn't bring it."

"Then why the hell are you here? All you filmmakers want is to hype your movie and make us overpay."

We were taking the brunt of him losing movies to bidding wars, something that was happening more at Sundance. Record numbers were making headlines and that had started to affect filmmakers' perception of independent distribution. Tom Bernard figured we were there to play into the hype machine and tell him how great *Twin Falls Idaho* was without him seeing it. We could feel how frustrated he was. Tom Bernard was part of a specialized market that was being popularized for its lottery-ticket mentality of small films selling for huge numbers. After our pep talk with Tom, we left the Sony Building and immediately decided we weren't going to sell our film to Sony even if they were interested. It was going to be anyone but them.

Sundance '99

We had set up a press screening of *Twin Falls Idaho* before the Sundance premiere, which was going to be held two days later. This would give the press a chance to see the movie and create a critical buzz if *Twin Falls Idaho* was well received. Most distributors seeking acquisitions sneak into this screening if they feel they need a jump on a particular movie; sometimes the press screening is after the premiere, and that is up to your discretion. Some producers feel that you can hurt your movie by showing it too early. You never know what people walking out of a screening may say. The only thing that travels faster than good word of mouth is bad worth of mouth.

The filmmakers aren't required to be at their press screening, but we felt as this was our very first screening we would like to get a sense of the reactions. We hung around the lobby and watched some distributors we had met earlier enter the theater. A movie about Siamese twins would be worth a laugh or satisfy their curiosity.

As *Twin Falls Idaho* finished and the empty lobby filled, we gravitated toward the farthest corner. The first person we saw was Tom Bernard, jetting across the lobby and leaving the crowd behind. Tom quickly disappeared; he appeared wounded, his eyes a bit red. We felt that we in some way kicked the bully where it counted. Later Tom told us he quickly got to a phone to call copresident Michael Barker. He told Michael, who was at the Golden Globe Awards, that he had just seen a gem of a movie and that he was going to make a bid.

The overall reaction was mellow. Since this was a press screening, the general audience reaction would have to wait. Our producer Rena Ronson came out of the screening and told us she had some interest from distributors and that we would wait to hear from all before we started fielding offers. Mark and I returned to our condo and waited. Our condo was filled with the cast and crew from *Twin Falls Idaho.* We kept the excitement to a minimum. The pressure was sort of relieved, but no deal was done and therefore we didn't sleep much. The next morning we got a call from Rena to be at the William Morris condo to start meeting the distributors that were interested in buying *Twin Falls Idaho.* We jumped into the SUV and headed down into Park City. Halfway there we ran out of gas. Metaphorically, we were and had been running on empty for some time. We knew if we didn't sell our film, we could close the door on any film career. We pushed ourselves into a gas station, where we filled up the tank.

We met nearly all the distributors, all wanting to do different things—from recutting the film to having us dress like Siamese twins to promote the film when it was released to the public. There was no way we were getting back into the suit—for reshoots or public appearances. The final meeting was with none other than Sony Pictures Classics. Dylan Leiner walked in with Michael Barker, whom we hadn't met at this point. Tom was coming; he had gotten sick and was laid up at their condo. Michael said something that made us sit up and smile. It wasn't the price he was going to pay and how he wanted to promote the film. He said, "I will buy *Twin Falls Idaho* as is." To us that meant everything. He validated our artistic choices and that meant he understood us as filmmakers. And that is what you want from a distributor. Someone who understands your film.

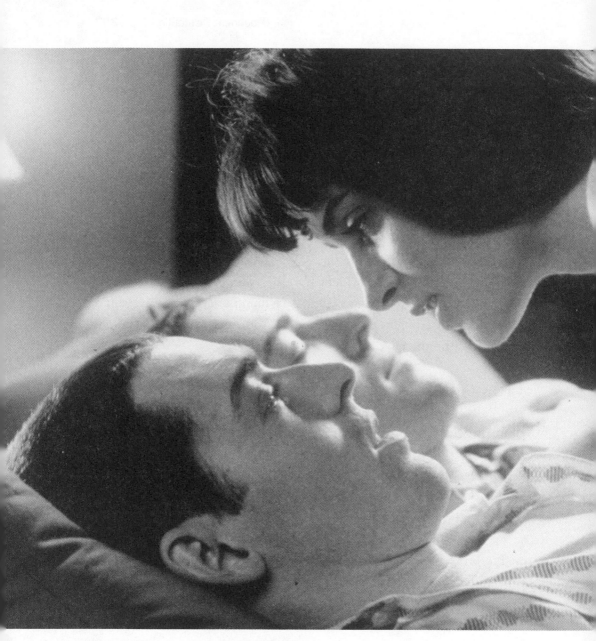

Penny and the twins, "Kiss and Tell"/*Twin Falls Idaho*

17 | Welcome to Hollywood

After we sold *Twin Falls Idaho* at Sundance to Sony Pictures Classics, we were accepted into the New Directors/New Films showcase. As Sony explained it to us, it was a very prestigious event at the Lincoln Center, showcasing a select few films each year. What we also learned from Sony was that Janet Maslin, the *New York Times* film critic, would be there to watch *Twin Falls* and write a review to be printed that Friday.

We ate at a French bistro; at our table was Michael Barker, copresident of Sony Classics. He told us that Janet had just seen the film and he had spoken with her briefly after she viewed it. "And?" we said.

"Well, she liked it," Michael replied, "but she has some reservations."

We looked at him for some more clarity. "Reservations?" we said.

"Well," he responded, "she is writing her review now and it will be in to-morrow's *New York Times.* So, no point in speculating."

We said good-bye to Michael at lunch's end and went over to Michele Hicks's apartment, telling her to be prepared, that our first review was to be in tomorrow's *New York Times;* it could be a quick end to all of our careers.

Restless that afternoon, we called up the *Times* and found out that to-morrow's edition would be printed in Queens and the first available copy would be dropped off at the distribution hub on the Upper West Side around 3:00 A.M.

We arrived at the hub at a quarter to three nervous and caffeinated. Ten minutes later we had the paper in hand. Sprawled out on the lobby floor with two copies, each of us rapidly scanned through the pages, finding the film section and then our review. "No matter how many films you see this year," the review read, "you haven't seen anything quite like *Twin Falls Idaho.*" We kept glancing up at each other from our respective papers, reading every few lines. "Have you read anything negative?" one of us would ask. "No!" the other would reply. The review went on to compliment the acting, directing, cinematography, and score, and closed with, "*Twin Falls Idaho* has style, grav-ity and originality to spare."

Our first review was everything we could have hoped it would be. We got home at five in the morning and slipped a copy of the *New York Times* under our composer's door. We fell asleep only to be woken two hours later by the buzzing of the phone. A driver was downstairs ready to pick us up and bring us to a photo shoot. In the midst of the excitement, we had forgotten about the pictures we were scheduled to take for *Filmmaker* magazine, an established zine for independent filmmakers that we read regularly. With only a few hours of sleep, we headed to the photography studio. The photographer was a pro and made the shoot painless. We had already taken so many photos promoting *Twin Falls* that we didn't care much about our appearance. We looked like hell but felt great from the review. We left the shoot thinking that no one was going to see these photos. Our tired faces ended up making the cover of *Filmmaker* for the summer 1999 issue.

Guns for Hire

After *Twin Falls* was released to critical acclaim, responses from people within the industry were also very positive. We had quite a few invitations to meet with top executives and influential people in Hollywood. Opening the door to Hollywood was, in a way, the true success of *Twin Falls Idaho:* we were going to be able to make another film, to work again in the industry we dreamed of as kids. As we stated earlier, we would have made all three of our films under the tent of a major studio provided they liked the screenplay. So once the doors opened, we welcomed every opportunity that was presented by the studios.

The first two opportunities that came our way were writing assignments for Touchstone and New Line Cinema. Both jobs paid us more money than we had ever seen before and got us into the Writers Guild of America (WGA).

We were hesitant at first to join a union. Up to that point, the WGA had been bashing heads with low-budget indies. But we didn't really have a choice; we had made no money on *Twin Falls Idaho*; in fact, we were in worse financial shape than when we had started.

Both writing assignments dealt with themes that were similar in ways to *Twin Falls.* One was about two close brothers conjoined not by flesh but by their spirit; and the other project dealt

Open writing assignment: Often a studio, or a producer, or a production company, has an idea, or a pitch, or a novel, that they intend to turn into a screenplay. What they need is a talented screenwriter to turn their water into wine.

Development: The process in which film studios develop film ideas with a producer and/or writer. The film idea is then developed into a screenplay with hopes of turning it into a feature film.

with finding the humanity in a person's mental illness. Both experiences were a great introduction into the world that Hollywood calls **development.** One of the two projects we were on had three executives and four producers. Round-table discussions about the story ideas were very fruitful, but later, when it came to script notes, with so many people involved it was overwhelming. Each person had their own set of notes, sometimes pages of changes, suggestions, and ideas. The hardest part was deciding whose notes to integrate. The producer who gave us the job? The executive who has the power to green-light the project? Unfortunately for us, the producer and head executive rarely had the same notes. What we began to see happening was that we were no longer writing for ourselves; we were making choices to appease the committee process. And the process wasn't making us happy—but miserable. It was like having a backseat driver telling you how to type through the Wite-Out. On one particular draft, we applied the notes from the executive verbatim. When we arrived at the next meeting to discuss the latest draft, we were told that the exec had moved on—resigned from the company.

We were left with the remaining executives and the producers who were collectively not very happy with the current draft. Seven different opinions coming at you was a little tough to take; it was hard not to bark back and let your one opinion be heard. It was difficult for us to think of screenwriting as a job removed from our personal passions. The whole "pleasing them" aspect of the writing assignment was something we wrestled with. It was a drastic change from independent filmmaking, where we had total control. Our new writing assignments were about having little control but, in exchange, a significant paycheck.

Once we completed our writing assignments, we had no control of the material. We weren't contractually bound as directors or producers. Our jobs were done; the studios had the screenplays and could do whatever they wanted with them.

Selling Out

People have asked us how we would feel about "selling out." We have been trying to sell out ever since we completed *Twin Falls Idaho*—sell out theaters, that is. If you're unfamiliar with the term *selling out*, it is when an artist forfeits his or her artistic integrity for a sum of money. It's a sort of payoff to suck it up when you are unhappy about what is happening to your creative career. Call it what you like, the transition into the studios is inevitable. Most every artist who is being honest wants his or her work to be viewed by the

Certificate of authenticity/*Northfork*

Open directing assignment: When a Hollywood studio, often in conjunction with a producer and/or production company, has a screenplay they plan to make, they will look for a director to attach to the project. What ensues is an interviewing process with potential directors. Because there are plenty of directors in Hollywood looking for their next assignment, how well a director's last film did will have a big impact on the studio's decision.

largest possible audience. It gets tiring being able to reach only a small audience; it's like preaching to the converted. We all grew up watching the studio films, because they had the power to reach the largest audience. Those films found us in a small town in northern California. And every independent filmmaker wants that. They want their voices to be heard.

For the past few years, we have flirted with going into the studio system as filmmakers. We have taken several interviews on open directing assignments. And like most job interviews, it can be painful while your qualifications are being checked.

We currently have a project at Warner Brothers, one that we wrote and will direct. We have been working on it for quite some time. It's a new process, but not entirely different from making an independent. More money, more problems. At this stage in the process, it's a waiting game. It takes weeks to get answers from the studios to the simplest questions. There is a high amount of volume getting shoved through these studios. For as many movies as a studio releases in a given year, there are five times as many more in varying stages—from development to production. The Hollywood studio system is a well-oiled machine—with a conveyer belt that slaps on San Fernando endings. You know that going into it. Studios are places that pump out product (as told to us by an executive). There is no kinder way to put it. They make movies for the masses. It's simple to understand their rules, but the question for any filmmaker is do you want to play by their rules? Our most recent screenplay,

The Astronaut Farmer, deals with a farmer who builds a homemade rocket and launches himself into orbit. Where he ends up landing once he reenters the atmosphere will determine our budget. Either he plops in the sea off New Guinea only to stare into the eyes of painted-faced villagers, or he lands near his home and reunites with his loving family. One ending will get us $2 million, the other, $20 million.

If we do eventually make a film within the studio system, that experience will be a book all unto itself. Before we call it a day, we will do a studio film. Some will say we are selling out. But then again, you aren't selling out unless someone is buying.

Forecast

It is difficult to predict the future of independent filmmaking. It's always changing. Every year someone comes out (mainly journalists) declaring the movement is dead. And yet every year a completely original independent film comes out of nowhere and has success. Sure, the definition is muddled, confusing, and mostly used as a marketing label. But there is a spirit that can be identified in true independents. Its pulse may be weaker at times, but independent film will always remain alive as long as there are original voices— and there always will be.

Swingers, the Brothers Polish/*Northfork*

Epilogue

"THE KING HAS DIED." That was the first headline we read. News of Stanley Kubrick's death was spreading at the speed of light over the Internet. We were in shock. Stanley Kubrick was a filmmaker whom we truly admired. Not just because of his films, but everything he was about, everything he stood for as an uncompromising visionary artist.

In November 1998 we were in the final days of postproduction on *Twin Falls Idaho*. Our composer, Stuart Matthewman, brought in a friend and fellow composer Abigail Mead, who had scored Stanley Kubrick's *Full Metal Jacket*. Abigail Mead is the professional name used by none other than Vivian Kubrick, Stanley's youngest daughter. From time to time, Vivian would pop in and out of our final mix. Her presence and encouragements gave us added confidence that *Twin Falls Idaho* wasn't all that bad, that all the hard work was worth it.

A couple of weeks later on a Saturday afternoon, we were attempting to transfer music files from Stuart's Macintosh G3 laptop. We wanted to spot the music to picture, and we just couldn't get the files into the Avid editing system. Vivian had stopped by our editing room—as she had been doing periodically—and we naturally asked if she knew how we could transfer our digital files. She didn't know, but she did know who would. She quickly got on the phone and called her dad, who was editing *Eyes Wide Shut* in London. Kubrick's editor was nice enough to get on the phone and take us through the file transfer. We could also hear Stanley in the background assisting with directions. That was the closest we ever got to the great one.

A few months later about seven thirty in the morning, we read the news of Stanley's passing online. We contemplated when or if we should call Vivian and give her our condolences. We had stayed in touch with Vivian. She had supported us in the final making of *Twin Falls.* We decided we would send some flowers with a note.

A few minutes later our phone rang. You know when you get a phone call very early in the morning that on the other end of the line is a pretty good chance of bad news. Once we moved out of our parents' house, our father told us whenever he heard his phone ring early in the morning, he would think something may have happened to one of us. He was a very early riser and would rarely receive a phone call before nine in the morning. We inherited this gene.

We picked up the phone; on the other end of the line was Vivian's older sister. She was desperately looking for Vivian and couldn't find her. She wanted to tell her the news of their dad's passing before she heard it from someone else. Our name and number had been written down by either

Stanley or his editor from before, when we had called about transferring the music files.

We didn't have a clue where Vivian was or really where she lived. We knew the general area because we once dropped her off near her apartment on the corner of a block in Hollywood. Without a second thought, we jumped in our car and drove to where we thought Vivian lived. On the way there, we were silent and Hollywood was eerily quiet—no one was outside. We didn't know how we were going to find her, and if we did, how we could possibly deliver that kind of news. Vivian loved her dad like no other.

We drove down a street that we vaguely remembered. Our car crept as we examined all the apartment buildings for any sign that would tell us where Vivian lived. In the middle of the block, we double-parked our car and started checking names on the mailboxes. After several minutes of searching, we came upon one that was marked VIV K. A wrought-iron security gate was protecting the entrance of this old Spanish villa building. It was a beautiful place. All of a sudden, the gate started to buzz and we pushed it open. We hadn't pressed the button or alerted anyone we were there.

We walked into the courtyard and looked around. A window to one of the apartments was open. A small breeze was blowing the sheer drapes. As we approached the apartment, we could see the silhouette of a girl. We immediately thought this must be Vivian. Nervousness mixed with grief hit us both. We had news to deliver. We took a moment to catch our breath. Then the phone rang inside the apartment, and we could see the silhouetted girl pick up. We knew it was Vivian because the girl said "hello" in an English accent. Within a second we could see Vivian wilt like a flower. Someone in her family was telling her the news. She let out a howl of grief that rattled the Hollywood sign.

Vivian had received the news, and she didn't need two knuckleheads to reinforce it. We retreated back to our car. Driving home, we had a sense of relief that we weren't the ones who had to tell her, but the sadness of Stanley's death was still overwhelming.

A few months later Vivian called, inviting us over to her same apartment for dinner. We told her our story of almost delivering her the news. She had no idea that we were ever outside her window. With a sense of humor and grace, she laughed at our predicament, how in a moment of tragedy something as absurd as a number written down by an editor would send us on a sad mission to find her. We then had a nice dinner and spent most of the time discussing her father and his work. After we were done eating, she left the room and returned with a small brown book. The cover read *Cinematographer's Handbook,* and on it a piece of white tape with black felt-tip writing said STANLEY KUBRICK. Vivian handed it to us, saying, "Keep it in a safe place." This was Stanley's personal book of notes he kept while filming. Inside were his handwritten notes on cameras, lenses, and lighting, a true treasure for any filmmaker.

We were shocked. Vivian was giving us a bible of sorts. We accepted the gift and left her apartment not knowing what to really think. The whole death to dinner was too strange to analyze. Maybe Vivian knew something we didn't. She knew *Twin Falls Idaho* was to be released in a couple of months. Being close to her father, she knew the rough road that lay ahead of us. She knew the hell her father went through. And she knew we were just about to get on that same road. And maybe that book would allow us to keep the faith and to keep going when we wanted to quit and give up.

In the spirit of Vivian's gift to us, we hope our *Declaration of Independent Filmmaking* will help you get on the path to making movies that will make you proud. We hope this book inspires you and keeps you focused on the journey to making your first feature.

Acknowledgments

Sade Adu • Len Amato • Rowena Arguelles • Michael Barker • Michael Barnes • Tom Bernard • CAA • Andrew Coffing • Dulce Con Huevos • Roy Fleischer Jr. • Daniel Glicker • Jon Gries • Kati Hesford • Lysa Hickey • Dawn Hudson • Jenna Johnson • Todd King • Alex Kohner • Dylan Leiner • Stuart Matthewman • Paul Mayersohn • Michelle Mitchell-Foust • Kevin Morris • Brigitte Mueller • M. David Mullen • Paramount Classics • Carmelo Pirrone • Adrianna Polish • Delbert Polish • Wendy Polish • David Pollack • Bingham Ray • Michael Reznick • Rena Ronson • Eden Rosenfelt • RSA • Alan Rudolph • Paul Schwartzman • Christopher Sheldon • Sony Pictures Classics • Jo Strettell • Paul Torok • Leo Trombetta • Warner Independent Pictures • Paula Weinstein

Glossary

above-the-line costs: The costs in the budget that are set aside for the creative team, usually the writer, director, actors, and producer.

act: A large section of a screenplay that invisibly divides a sequence of scenes into a major portion of the story. Screenplays are typically divided into three acts.

action: On a movie set, "action" is called after camera is rolling film to indicate the start of a current take.

ADR (automated dialogue replacement): When actors rerecord a noisy dialogue track, trying their best to match their former performances.

ambient sound: Tones layered into a film's audio tracks, usually by the sound supervisor, to create mood and heighten suspense.

anamorphic lens: A camera lens that compresses a wide-screen image to fit in a standard film frame. An anamorphic lens on a projector then decompresses the image to its normal width when shown on the screen.

answer print: The first full assembly of the edited film and mixed sound.

art director: An adjunct to the production designer, an art director helps the production designer's vision to be realized and assists the production designer in all facets of production design.

aspect ratio: A ratio between the width and the height of a picture frame, describing the shape of the rectangle formed.

associate producer: A discretionary credit given to someone who either has helped locate finances or deserves some further recognition for a job well done.

audio design: The digital manipulation of sound recordings to create original and unique audio components to the film.

audition: An in-person reading with an actor and either the director or casting director and sometimes the producer.

autochromes: A color photograph on a glass plate. The process was invented by the Lumière brothers in 1906. It was one of the first viable color processes.

Avid: A software/hardware digital editing program.

back-end: A negotiated percentage of a film's royalties that will pay out if the film is profitable.

backgrounds: Sound effects layered into the audio of a film to create ambience.

below-the-line costs: The costs in a film budget for everything other than the creative team, such as goods and services, including the production staff salaries.

bleach bath: The step in processing color film that converts developed silver back into silver halide so that it can be removed by the fixer and wash steps, leaving only color dyes.

breakdown service: A service that breaks a script down into available parts and then e-mails or faxes them to agencies that subscribe to its services.

breakdown sheet: Organizes all the various requirements in a shooting script, assigning to each scene a number and listing its required components. With a scheduling program such as Movie Magic, the assistant director divides up the script's contents.

breaking down a script: (1) For financial purposes, breaking down the script means reviewing it carefully and noting each item needed for filming, such as locations, equipment, costumes, etc. Each item needs to be included in the film's budget. (2) For casting purposes, breaking down the script means to separate the roles. See also **breakdown service.**

calendaring: To schedule the movie for various cast and crew members.

call sheet: A production paper that lists call times and locations for cast and crew. The call sheet is usually the responsibility of the second assistant director and is updated throughout the day and given to the cast and crew each night for the following day's schedule.

call time: The time at which an actor or crew member must arrive on set.

camera operator: The person who actually operates the camera during the shot, framing the action through the viewfinder and moving the camera on a tripod head as necessary. In some cases, the director of photography will also be the camera operator.

cast-contingent: Financing that depends on attaining bankable casting.

casting director: Typically a casting director sits with the director and they come up with a list of actors and actresses that they feel best complement the roles. After they complete the list from the most desired to the more realistic, it's then up to the casting director to contact the actor's representative—either an agent or a manager.

CGI (computer-generated imagery): A very expensive, time-consuming digital animation wherein each pixel in the affected area of the scene is re-drawn to create stunning visual imagery. A filmmaker can literally paint his celluloid canvas with whatever he or she imagines.

character arc: The distance—from point A of your story's premise to point B of your story's resolution—a character has traveled emotionally.

cheap mainstream: A mainstream Hollywood story with universal appeal made on an independent budget.

CinemaScope: A 1950s photographic and projection process in which an ana-morphic lens squeezes a picture onto the film so it can then be unsqueezed by an anamorphic projector lens and shown on a large curved screen.

cinematographer: Also referred to as the director of photography (DP), the person in charge of the photography of a motion picture. The visual im-ages created for a motion picture, from conception, preproduction, pro-duction through postproduction, and all processes that may affect those images, are the responsibility of the cinematographer, in creative collabo-ration with the director. This person directly oversees the work of three departments: camera, electric, and grip; supervises any additional camera crews and the photography of elements needed for visual effects work; and coordinates with other departments that will affect the visuals, par-ticularly editorial but also art, wardrobe, and makeup.

close-miked: A recording technique in which a microphone is placed very close to the sound source, which minimizes outside interference and am-plifies the sound source's subtleties.

close-up: A close camera angle, usually of an actor's face.

co-producer: A discretionary title that can be given to someone who either has contributed financially or has performed beyond expectation in a lesser position.

costume designer: The costume designer comes up with an overall look for the costumes, including palette, texture, and cultural, historical, or social references. When a look is decided, the costume designer presents the wardrobe concepts to the director, producer, and actors using research materials, fabrics, color samples, and sketches.

counterprogramming: Releasing a film at a time that is counter to seasonal expectations, for instance, releasing a horror movie on Christmas day or a cerebral indie during the summer blockbuster rush.

coverage: The coverage of a scene entails filming the action of a scene from different angles and shot sizes in order to have lots of editing choices. Often the action filmed overlaps that covered by a different angle. This allows flexibility in cutting.

cut: Sometimes referred to as the hard cut, where a scene immediately follows the previous scene without hesitation. A transition from one scene to the next.

dailies: The film footage from a day of production shooting.

deliverables: Postproduction film elements that are required to be delivered to the distribution company upon signing of a distribution deal.

desaturate: To reduce the intensity of colors in a shot, usually to a lower level than is normal, for an artistic effect.

development: The process in which film studios develop film ideas with a producer and/or writer. The film idea is then developed into a screenplay with hopes of turning it into a feature film.

dialogue: The written words in a screenplay to be spoken on camera by the characters in a film.

dialogue track: The spoken words of the actor recorded on set.

diffusion filtration: A camera filter that reduces definition for a softer effect, sometimes creating artifacts like halation (glowing around bright areas) and contrast reduction. Most commonly used for close-ups of actors' faces to hide imperfections in the skin.

digital intermediate: A process where film is scanned into a digital form, color-corrected electronically, and then recorded back to film.

director: On an independent film, the director has ultimate control over the making of the film. The director's responsibilities include choosing the cast and crew, overseeing the cast and crew during the film's production schedule, and overseeing the postproduction process.

director of photography: The director of photography (DP) (or cinematographer) is the one person besides the filmmaker who is most responsible for a film's look. The DP oversees a film's lighting, helps the director compose each shot, and technically directs the physical finished look of the celluloid.

dissolve: A slow fade-out from one scene while the next scene fades in, creating a momentary overlap.

dolly: A wheeled platform used to allow for smooth movement of a mounted camera.

dolly grip: The dolly grip operates and maintains the dolly equipment. On some independent films, the key grip doubles as the dolly grip.

dumb money: An investor who doesn't know the ins and outs of film finance. Investors who don't know what they are doing will eventually find someone who does—namely, a lawyer—and they will overcompensate for their lack of knowledge with a lovely lawsuit. See **smart money.**

dupe elements: A second-generation negative used for making copies of the film and transfers to other formats. "Dupe" is an abbreviation for "duplicate," a copy of another piece of film. Since the original negative of a movie is highly valuable and delicate, copies are made onto intermediate duplicating stocks, for archival protections and for making large numbers of release prints without risk to the original.

editor: An editor's job, in a broad sense, is to choose the best of the multiple-take performances and assemble all of the choices into one compelling narrative. If the filmmaker is the storyteller, the editor is the objective ear the storyteller relies on for input and guidance.

executive producer: Often an executive producer (EP) is someone who helped procure money for a film but creatively has nothing to do with its making. An EP may be involved with some of the logistics of location and cast, but the involvement is usually limited to financial matters.

exit strategy: Basically, how an investor plans on getting his or her return. As with all savvy investors, he or she will want to be the first money in and the first money out.

fade-in: Where a scene fades in from (typically) black, slowly overtaking the screen.

fade-out: Where a scene fades to black (or any color, but usually black) before the next scene enters the frame.

fade to black: An editing device where the picture dissolves to black.

fade to white: An editing device where the picture dissolves to white.

field recordings: Sound recordings made on location (or in a visually similar location) to record specific backgrounds and props to be added to a film's sound.

film loader: Loads film magazines, keeps reports of film, places film orders, and aids camera crew in storing equipment in the camera truck or camera room.

filter: A glass or gel placed before or after the camera lens to modify the light passing through it, to alter its color, contrast, intensity, or sharpness. Can also refer to the gels used on lighting units.

final mix: The final assembly of sound after picture editing is locked, sound editing is complete, and the score written and recorded, in which a mixer will combine all sound elements while watching the picture on playback.

final print: The last step in the filmmaking process where all the film elements are combined into their final state.

first assistant cameraman (1st AC): Responsible for maintaining all cameras and their accessories. Adjusts the focus during the shot (focus pulling), places filters into the camera, changes lenses, threads the film from the magazine into the movement, etc. Coordinates activities of other camera assistants and loaders, orders extra camera equipment as needed, arranges for replacements or repairs when needed.

first assistant director (1st AD): Responsible for keeping the film on schedule by coordinating with the director, the department heads, and the actors. The assistant director (AD) is also responsible for calendaring each scene to be shot and giving the actors their call times. The AD can be thought of as the chief communicator during preproduction and on set while filming. Contrary to what the title connotes, an AD doesn't creatively assist the director in directing the film. An AD orchestrates the mechanics of the set so that the director can better do his or her job, and makes sure the film is optimally scheduled, the actors are on set when needed, and each film department is coordinated. A talented AD frees up the filmmaker to focus on artistic concerns such as actors' performances and shot composition.

flashing the negative: When film stock is exposed to light either before or after the image is captured in the camera. The effect of flashing knocks down the overall contrast of the film, making the imagery more muted than it would naturally be.

focal length: The distance in millimeters between the optical center of the lens and the focal plane. Focal length, when combined with the size of the format, determines the field of view of the lens (how much of the scene it can see). The principal focal length of a lens is calculated by the radii of curvature of the surfaces, the index of refraction of the glass, and the medium in which the lens resides.

focus pulling: Adjusting a camera's focus during a shot.

Foley: Recorded sounds of smaller props and footsteps that will be added to the film.

Foley artist: A person who in postproduction matches footsteps and prop sounds to the characters and props in a film's picture. A Foley artist must walk in stride with the characters, move as they move, and convincingly create sounds to follow the picture.

foreign film sales agent: A person who sells domestic films to foreign distributors for release in foreign territories around the world.

foreign presales: Refers to the acquisition of a film, prior to its completion, by a foreign distributor for exhibition in a foreign territory or territories. Often some or all of the foreign rights to an independent film are sold in advance to help finance the film. The sales agent will want to leverage the star power of the cast against the film's proposed budget.

four-wall: To show a film by either contacting a theater owner and renting the space directly or finding a space, rolling in a projector, and collecting the door fees yourself. A typical deal has the filmmaker and/or producer pay a flat fee for the rental of the room, with the profits then going back to the production.

four-wall drama: A term to describe an independent film that uses one location heavily.

gaffer: The chief electrician who works with the director of photography to execute the lighting of each scene.

green-lit: A script is green-lit when it has received approval to be made into a movie.

grips: Shapes the lighting of a shot by taking light away using set nets, setting flags, or silks to soften the light, or by using mirrors and reflectors to "bounce" the light in an optimal way. Responsible for any rigging needed to achieve a shot. See also **dolly grip; key grip.**

hard cut: An editing device where a scene immediately follows the previous scene without hesitation.

headshot: A photo of an actor used for submission in the casting of film and television. The photo usually includes agency representation information, whether the actor is a member of SAG, basic measurements, and often a brief résumé.

high-definition video: Video that is higher in resolution than standard-definition video (NTSC, PAL, etc.). This brings it up to the resolution level of the super 16 and 35 mm film formats. The "24P" version (twenty-four frames per second, progressive scan) emulates the motion reproduction of film normally shot at twenty-four frames per second.

Hollywood production companies: Either as a separate entity or an adjunct to a Hollywood studio, a Hollywood production company often acquires book rights, develops screenplays, and sometimes funds film production.

Hollywood studios: The Big Seven are Disney, MGM, Paramount, Sony, 20th Century Fox, Universal, and Warner Brothers. These make mostly expensive commercial films that are produced for mass entertainment and maximum profit. Like most big businesses, these are public companies with shareholders. Most of the films made through the studio system are expensive star-driven vehicles.

IATSE (International Alliance of Theatrical Stage Employees): A labor union that represents most crew members working on a film set and in postproduction in technical areas. Almost all studio features and some of the larger indie productions are made under an agreement with various unions, including IATSE.

incident light meter: A device that measures the amount of light falling on the subject. The alternative is a reflective meter (such as a spot meter), which measures the amount of light reflected off a subject.

insert shots: Additional film shots other than scenes filmed with actors, such as landscapes and backgrounds, to be inserted into the film during editing.

intercut: An editing device that splices together various camera angles from a scene.

International Brotherhood of Teamsters: A large labor union representing millions of workers in transportation, freight-related jobs, and other industries. Transportation on a union movie set requires Teamster involvement, and a contract must be negotiated with them prior to production.

internegative: An internegative (IN) is a duplicate copy of the original negative, used for making release prints. Also known as a dupe negative.

interpositive: An interpositive (IP) is a positive version of the negative. Made on intermediate duplicating stock off the original negative, the IP is then used to make an internegative. It is also commonly used as a protection master and for the final transfer of a theatrical movie to home video.

jump cut: A tense shift in the narrative of the film from one scene to the next.

key grip: The key grip works with the gaffer during lighting procedures, and maneuvers the camera during moving shots. Technically, the gaffer lights the shot and the grip "shapes" the light, using set nets, setting flags, or silks to soften the light, or using mirrors and reflectors to "bounce" the light in an optimal way. Usually several grips work for the key grip. They also build, rig, and safety-rig lighting and camera and grip equipment, as well as lay dolly track and operate small cranes (if there is no crane operator).

limited release: A type of distribution in which a film is opened in a few markets (usually L.A., New York, and Chicago) in one or two theaters in each market.

line producer: The line producer is in charge of planning and then running the business side of the shoot. This includes making sure all guild contracts are filed and creating the budget.

location manager: Responsibilities include scouting sites, talking to their owners, and coming up with rental bids. During the shoot, the location manager is responsible for arranging crew parking, making maps to locations, acting as a liaison between the property owner and production company, securing all necessary government permits, and dealing with any neighbors who may be affected by the shooting of the film.

locked picture: The point in the postproduction process when the editing of the visual is complete and the film, sans completed sound, can be viewed in its final running order. When a picture is said to be "locked," the length and chronology is determined and will be altered only in the case of an emergency.

loop group: An ensemble of actors who have the specific skill of adding background voices and pieces of dialogue to further the story.

magazine: The detachable container on a film camera that holds the film stock.

master use license: Allows usage of a song's physical recording, which is usually controlled by the record company.

match cut: A hard cut that connects a scene with the previous scene through a visual reference point.

micro-studio: Usually a smaller film company within a larger one, charged with acquiring and sometimes producing commercially viable independents and broadly appealing foreign films. An example of a micro-studio is Sony Pictures Classics, which is a division of Sony Pictures.

mid-shot: Also known as a medium shot, a shot between a full shot (head-to-toe) and a close-up (head and shoulders or tighter).

mix venue: The facility that houses you while you are performing the final mix on your film. A mix room will likely have a large mix board, a projection screen, and mounted speakers to simulate the theater-going experience.

mixer: The person who mixes all of the sound components of a film to its picture.

mixing facility: See **mix venue.**

ND gel: A gel is a sheet of dyed plastic, and ND stands for neutral density filter, which is gray in color and affects all colors equally by reducing the amount of light. See also **filter.**

negative film: The photochemical process naturally produces a negative image of what is being photographed, because light striking the film, followed by processing, causes formation of silver (on black-and-white film) and dye (on color film). Therefore, the brightest areas of the frame produce the greatest density of silver or dye, and the darkest areas of the frame produce very little or no density. To make a positive image off this negative, you simply rephotograph it onto another type of "negative" stock (usually called a print stock). A negative image of a negative is a positive. There are special stocks and processes that can turn a negative into a positive image in the original film, called reversal stocks (also known as slide films).

negative pickup: When a distributor purchases the rights to distribute a picture after it has already been made and paid for.

optical effects: An editorial term to describe certain types of effects like fades, dissolves, freeze-frames, etc. Often created in an optical printer and then cut into the rest of the edited negative for printing. A postproduction manipulation of picture that includes the title sequence at the beginning and end of a film. When you see a scene dissolve into another, or watch credits scroll across the frame, you are witnessing an optical.

optical house: The laboratory where the optical effects for a film are created.

optical printer: A machine used for rephotographing one piece of film into a new piece of film, somewhat resembling a film projector pointed into a camera. This allows for various effects to be created, including composites (multiple film elements combined onto one film element) and editorial devices like fades and dissolves.

option: *X* amount of dollars paid to you for the exclusive rights to your screenplay for *y* period of time. The amount and period vary depending on the financial standing of the person or company optioning the material, the perceived commercial viability of the project, and the talent of the lawyer or agent negotiating the deal.

overdubbed: The rerecording of previously spoken dialogue for either performance enhancement or for a language change.

P&A: The amount of money a film distributor will pay for a film's distribution and promotion (prints and advertising).

personal guaranteed loan: A loan from a bank or investor to the film production, made with the personal guarantee of an individual (usually the filmmaker) that the money will be repaid. If the money isn't repaid, the filmmaker's personal assets are at risk.

platform release: Opening a film in two to ten markets with a few theaters in each, and building to more as the film's campaign gains steam.

playback: The playing of recorded audio and/or visual film.

plumbing: To attain strong water pressure, the rule is to go from the street to the house with as few ninety-degree turns as possible, reducing the pressure by turns only when absolutely needed. A thoughtful plumber surveys the surroundings and works with the land to negotiate a straight path. It's very simple, really.

postproduction: The process that begins once principal photography has finished. In postproduction all elements of the film are edited together, polished, and finally printed.

postproduction supervisor: The postproduction supervisor (PPS) oversees all of the tasks left after principal photography has wrapped. When postproduction is complete, the PPS will help deliver the film to the distributor. The PPS has a slew of decisions to make in post, all impacting the creative and financial needs of the film, such as where to mix the film, the length of the final mix, and who the mixer will be. The post supervisor will help control the costs and keep the creative engine running smoothly during this final stretch. The post supervisor must sift through all of the project's editorial needs and demands and create realistic solutions to satisfy the financial parameters of the project.

predubbing: A modern movie soundtrack is made up of thousands of individual sounds. These elements are far too numerous to mix in one session. Therefore, predubbing is the method used in modern film mixing in which tracks are organized into categories and premixed by one or two members of the mixing team and later blended together into a final soundtrack.

preproducing: Finding out the true cost of making your film by researching all the major elements and pricing them out.

preproduction: The span of time before you shoot (usually around six weeks for an independent film) where all the logistics are thought through and organized.

producer: The one on and off set making the big decisions of finance and logistics. The plain "producer," without a prefix, is the one most in charge of the business of making a film; his or her word is usually final, and crew decisions are all subordinate to the producer's.

production boards: Paper strips listing each scene to be shot so that the shooting schedule can be changed around easily and adjusted as needed. This allows the cast and crew to see the big picture of shooting day by day, week by week.

production coordinator: Gives administrative support to the production manager. The production coordinator works hand in hand with the PM to make sure all the administrative details are being executed. They often come to the job with a ready list of contacts in crew, tech department, and craft service. The job can be thought of as a catchall for the needs of the production manager.

production design: The overall aesthetic conceit of a film; its look, its sense, its style.

production designer: In a strict sense, the production designer is the head of the art department and oversees everything from set design and costuming to makeup and hair. However, on an independent, the production designer, if the production is fortunate enough to have one, is mostly concerned with the design and decoration of the locations and sets.

production manager: The production manager's responsibilities include tending and managing the budget (a responsibility sometimes shared with the line producer), hiring the crew, and actively supporting the needs of the film. Also known as the unit production manager (UPM).

production recordist: The person dedicated to recording the film's dialogue on set. The recordist must take into account the environment in which the actors will be speaking, choose which microphone works best, and work closely with the director to achieve clarity of dialogue and backgrounds.

prop master: The prop master reads the script and breaks down all the needed props. The prop master and the set decorator have very different jobs: the prop master deals with any object an actor uses (like a cane or umbrella) while the set decorator works with intransigents like a couch or a bedframe.

protagonist: A protagonist is the center of the story's solar system, around which all other characters and their subplots revolve.

rack focus: The changing of focus within a shot from one subject to another.

raw: Film that has been neither developed nor removed from its packaging.

recans: Unused film stock that has been left over from another shoot.

recouped: When one's investment in an independent film has been paid back in full.

room tones: Each interior location used in a film contains an inherent ambient quality. Whether it's a small apartment or a train station, each room has its own acoustical properties that should be recorded independent of the actual filming. The dialogue in a scene can be greatly enhanced by adding room tones, recorded separately and later blended into the final mix. Room tones are recorded when absolute quiet is ensured so that only the ambient tone of the location is captured. It is often advantageous for the sound supervisor to visit the locations after production, using specific stereo-microphone positioning to record several minutes of undisturbed room tones for the final mix.

SAG: The Screen Actors Guild of America is the premier union representing American actors. Established in 1933 during the American labor movement, SAG fights aggressively for actor compensation. For an independent film of whatever budget, SAG offers an applicable contract for the casting of SAG members.

San Fernando ending: What becomes of a film after it has been test-marketed in the San Fernando Valley by a mixed crowd of supposedly average Americans. Following the screening, a new ending is edited in at the studio's request. More likely than not, a sad ending becomes happy.

saturation or wide release: A film that opens in hundreds to thousands of theaters. The studios can predict in the first weekend whether a film is a hit.

scene: A screenplay is a series of scenes that combine to tell a cohesive story.

scene description: The necessary visual information included in each scene of a screenplay.

scene heading: In a screenplay, the beginning of a scene is marked by a scene heading. The scene's location and whether it is day or night will be written in capital letters and underlined, informing the reader of a new scene and its basic setting.

scope: See **CinemaScope.**

scouting and tech scouting: When the key crew members, from director of photography to set designer, visit different locations to determine the ideal places to shoot the movie.

script coverage: At film studios, big and small, people are hired solely to read scripts and write critiques of them. The higher-ups are too busy to read a pile of scripts weekly, so they employ people to weed out the pap. If a screenplay doesn't condense conveniently for the reader, a script may be dismissed regardless of its potential.

script supervisor: The script supervisor is in charge of making sure the continuity of the film is being tended to. Typically a script supervisor will do a continuity breakdown, noting all elements of the story from props to hair color that must maintain continuity throughout the shoot. The continuity breakdown is given to each crew department. On set, the script supervisor is there to oversee all those little details of continuity.

second assistant cameraman (2nd AC): Assists the first AC, especially during lens changes and film reloading, places marks, runs the tape measure out, keeps photographic logs and camera reports, handles the slate, and loads film magazines.

second unit: A stand-alone mini film crew with its own cinematographer and director, with all the necessary film equipment to shoot independently. A second unit often films insert shots of landscape and background, which frees the first unit to focus on the actors' performances.

set costumer: Crew member who keeps the actors' clothing in perfect order during filming to ensure continuity throughout the shoot. Often this is done by the **wardrobe assistant.**

set decorator: The set decorator is in charge of dressing the sets with whatever is necessary to make the scene visually pleasing. Everything that should reside in each scene (other than those items being used by the actors), including floor mats, lampshades, framed pictures, flowers, and furniture, is the set decorator's job to note after reading the screenplay. As filmmakers, we tend to work directly with set decorators because so much of what we want to see in a given scene is already noted in the script.

set designer: On an indie, the set designer is helping the production manager in whatever way he or she can. On a Hollywood film, a set designer is essentially an architect dealing with specificity of big builds. For independent purposes, finding a set designer who can integrate with your production manager is all that matters. When the production designer has conferred with the filmmaker and a general sense of how the sets will look is established, a set designer will draft the general architectural plans for the builds.

setup: The configuration of crew, lights, and equipment for each scene.

shot composition: The various visual elements that are inside the frame of a given shot.

show print: See **answer print.**

sides: A reduced version of the script containing only the pages of the day's shoot. These are particularly useful to the actors, who want to be able to eyeball the day's dialogue without skimming through an entire script.

skip-bleach process: A film development process in which the film skips its usual bleach bath, leaving silver that normally is removed.

slate: A hinged piece of wood, the size of a clipboard, struck together before a take to create a loud "clap" sound. The slate (sometimes referred to as the clapper or sticks) creates a visual and aural marker used later to match picture and sound.

smart money: Smart money can be expensive, too, because the investors know what they are doing. They understand the risk versus the reward. But the terms are laid out on the table for all parties to see. See **dumb money.**

SMPTE time code: A time code standard for media. In 1967, the U.S. Society of Motion Picture and Television Engineers introduced the SMPTE ("simpty") time code, which makes it possible for all media players and recorders to use the same technique for reading and writing time codes.

sound design: The art of manipulating and layering sound effects into the film's soundtrack.

sound effects: The added sounds to the audio track of a film.

sound effects supervisor: See **sound supervisor.**

sound library: A digital library of sound effects that a sound supervisor culls from to create the sound elements of a movie. Usually stored in digital on a computer hard drive.

sound mixer: The person who combines all the sonic accompaniments to picture at the close of postproduction.

sound supervisor: The sound supervisor is the lead representative for all the artisans who work on a film's sound. The realm of the sound supervisor encompasses dialogue, sound design, backgrounds, footsteps—everything one hears in a film except for the musical score.

soundstages: Where movie sets are designed and built. Soundstages are usually large spaces the size of a warehouse. Some are prebuilt to popular settings like a police or fire station. Soundstages are built to prevent extraneous environmental sounds—such as freeway noise, dogs barking, traffic—from affecting the sound production, and they often have open ceilings, allowing more flexible camera setups.

splinter unit: Similar to a **second unit** but without its own director and equipment.

split-screen: An editing device that splits the projectable frame in half with two images.

spotting session: A face-to-face meeting with the director, sound supervisor, and film editor where they watch each scene of the film and discuss necessary sound enhancements.

standard-definition interlaced-scan video: Standard definition is regular video, such as NTSC and PAL. It is below HDTV in resolution. Traditionally video has been interlaced scan, meaning that each frame of video is made up of two "fields" containing alternate lines of picture information. When the two fields are interlaced, an entire frame is created. Most TV monitors are interlaced scan, with one field being scanned line by line, followed by the next field. Most computer monitors are progressive scan, with an entire frame being displayed at once. Film is more like a progressive-scan process—entire frames are captured and displayed. Therefore, progressive-scan video more closely resembles film.

storyboards: The sketched rendering of each scene from the camera's point of view. Gives the filmmaker and cinematographer a starting point for each setup.

superimposition: A superimposition is when two or more images appear on top of each other simultaneously. In a dissolve, one image fades in, replacing another image that fades out (in other words, one image dissolves into another).

sync effects: A term used to describe the multitude of on-camera sounds that must synchronize perfectly to the picture. Seamlessly mating sound to picture is one of the sound department's most important jobs, and sync effects create cohesion with the visual. What sync effects go where is discussed at the spotting session with the director. The sound supervisor will draw on his own personal library or establish a field recording schedule to supply the sound team with these essential sounds.

synchronization right: Allows usage of the composition rights to a recorded song.

temp track: Temporary music and sound effects added to the soundtrack of a work in progress to create an atmosphere and convey a sense of what the finished movie might sound like.

test marketing: Where a studio rents a theater, gives away tickets to a target audience, and then has the audience fill out a scorecard that rates various elements, from an actor's performance to the film's ending.

torque motor: A rotating sectional electric motor often found in film cameras.

transition: A screenwriting device that defines a specific kind of cut from one scene to the next.

transportation coordinator: Renting shuttles and vans, finding classic automobiles, hauling trailers for the cast—anything and everything on wheels is the transportation coordinator's responsibility. A small independent film may or may not employ a transportation coordinator depending on the demands of the shoot. If your budget can afford one, a transportation coordinator takes care of many of the time-consuming and logistically challenging elements of preproduction.

24P: Twenty-four frames per second, progressive-scan video. Often refers to a camera that captures reality twenty-four times per second as entire frames, just as a film camera does running at the standard twenty-four frames per second rate. Playback devices, storage media, display devices, etc., can also be 24P. 24P video can be either high definition or standard definition. Traditional video has usually been 60i/50i (60 or 50 fields per second), interlaced scan.

unit production manager: See **production manager**.

wardrobe assistant: Crew member who helps the actors get dressed, maintains the wardrobe, and keeps track of the money spent. See also **set costumer.**

wardrobe supervisor: Responsible for the continuity, maintenance, and cleaning of clothing.

wide shot: A wide camera angle that usually includes several cast members or the exterior of a building.

wild lines: Background conversations in a film that are used for ambience.

wrapped: When principal photography has been completed. This period is usually the initiation into postproduction.

written offer: A formal offer for a part in a film. Includes the name of the role you are offering to the actor, how much you are willing to pay for the actor's time, and a general start date and approximate time commitment.

Movie Synopses

Twin Falls Idaho

1999

The minute he wakes up and the minute before sleep—for two minutes each day, Blake Falls feels alone. He tries to grab those minutes before they vanish. They are enough to remind him who he is.

Francis Falls understands that if it weren't for Blake, he wouldn't be able to make it. His conjoined twin's heart is very strong. Blake, he knows, could live without him.

The brothers live quietly in an eccentric hotel peopled with odd characters, talking in a shorthand formed over twenty-five years. They dress impeccably in a custom-tailored suit, adjusting each other's ties; they dine on cotton candy, and on their birthday their only meal is their trademark chocolate cake; they blow out two candles, one at a time. They can keep straight faces while telling outrageous tales from their earlier days in show business. When Francis becomes ill, Blake holds him through the night, the way he always has. Together, they feel complete.

When Penny (Michele Hicks), a beautiful young woman, enters their lives, for the first time someone sees the brothers' world from the inside. She makes them think of possibilities when they're certain there aren't any. They start to wonder how it would be to feel complete in new ways.

They imagine living not as medical anomalies but as individuals who can breathe, walk, and dream on their own.

Jackpot

2001

Jackpot is part road trip, part buddy movie, as we follow the travails of starry-eyed karaoke singer Sunny Holiday (Jon Gries) and his equally deluded manager, Lester (Garrett Morris), as they hit the road to compete in a string of karaoke contests. Convinced that fame and fortune are right around the bend, the duo heads west to Jackpot, Nevada, hitting every saloon and bar along the way. Each stop means a new contest that will potentially take Sunny Holiday closer to his dream. Unfortunately for Sunny, destiny has other plans for him, as he must cope with the wife and child he left behind, and the growing burden for him and his manager living hand-to-mouth.

Northfork

2003

In the next two days, the town of Northfork will cease to exist.

The year is 1955 and Northfork is literally about to be "dammed," flooded to make way for a new hydroelectric project. The town's rugged plains are going to drown, its heartland houses will be swept away, and its citizens are heading for higher ground. With the exception of a few stoic resisters.

Now a team of six trench-coated men has been charged with removing the last few stragglers before it is too late. As the Evacuation Committee spreads out across Northfork, they encounter a group of people not quite ready or willing to leave. They are each in limbo. Some are looking for a sign. Others are hoping for a miracle. Yet, one way or another, they will all have to say good-bye.

Among these tenacious individuals are a lustful young couple, a man who has built an ark (complete with a pair of wives), and a frail orphan whose fevered visions have led him to believe he's the lost member of an ancient herd of roaming angels calling him home.

Northfork is a beguiling story of loss and resurrection, about adjusting to the strange new places toward which we sometimes find ourselves heading. Blending surreality and history, the film is spun in the manner of an American fairy tale that tackles such themes as land, life, faith, death, the afterlife, and the power of dreams with a distinctively playful touch.

Index

above-the-line costs, 93
accountant, film, 98
accredited investors, 78–79
action, 23–24
actors
  ADR (automated dialogue replacement) and,
    231–32
  auditions and, 115, 116–17
  determining costs of hiring, 107–8
  directing, 182–90
  experienced, 182–88, 245–46
  first-time, 189
  headshots of, 115
  listening to, 190–91
  losing your lines and, 190
  readings and, 117–18
  scheduling, 112, 119–21
  sidelines and, 189
  unions and, 98–99, 169
  see also cast and casting
acts, 47–48
ADR (automated dialogue replacement),
    231–32, 236–37
Agfa, 197
alternate distribution, 252–54
ambient sound, 207
American Express, 87, 121
anamorphic lenses, 158
Andrews, Chris, 112–13, 118
answer prints, 196–98

Arriflex 16S, 144–46, 147
art director, 124
ASCAP, 222
aspect ratio (CinemaScope), 157
associate producer, 164
Astronaut Farmer, The (screenplay), 264–65
attorney, film, 85–86, 97, 250–51
audio design, 227
auditions, 115, 116–17
autochromes, 157
Avid system, 198, 205, 268

"Baby Don't Get Hooked on Me" (song), 224
backgrounds, 229, 233
Bajo del Perro (film)
    camera work for, 147–49
    financing of, 67–68, 72, 216–17
bank loans, 80–81
Barker, Michael, 256, 257, 259–60
Bauchau, Patrick, 110–12, 182–83, 238
Bauer super 8, 144–48
Beckel, Graham, 119
Bell, Marshall, 119
below-the-line costs, 93
Bernard, Tom, 255–56
best boys, 25
Beta SP, 204–5
Billy Jack (film), 253
block bookings, 243
Blue Sky laws, 78–79
Bogdanovich, Peter, 253
breakdown sheets, 99–102, 115–16
breaking down the script, 99–102, 115–16
Breezy (film), 253
Brittany (motor home), 241–46, 248–50
Brooks Standard Rate Book, 97
budget
    above-the-line costs in, 93
    below-the-line costs in, 93
    crew size and, 94–95

developing, 56–60
distribution and, 250–54
first-draft, 93
for *Jackpot,* 12
for *Northfork,* 33, 56–57, 106, 168–71
preproduction, 93
screenplay considerations for, 32–33
for sound, 230
for *Twin Falls Idaho,* 10, 20, 24–25, 33, 55–56, 74, 110
Bunker, Chang and Eng, 28, 219
business affairs, 75

CAA, 110
calendaring, 100–101
call sheet, 15
    defined, 16
    sample, 18–19
call time, 172
camera package, 59
camera speed, 24
camera work, 143–59
    with Arriflex 16S, 144–46, 147
    for *Bajo del Perro,* 147–49
    camera directions in screenplay, 46
    high-definition video in, 77, 152–56, 184
    for *Jackpot,* 152–56, 184
    learning to shoot, 146–48
    for *Northfork,* 148, 157–59
    second unit in, 158–59
    setups in, 148, 156, 184
    with 16 mm, 146–47, 239
    storyboards and, 46, 58, 148–49, 182
    with super 8 handheld, 144–48, 152, 207, 239
    with 35 mm, 146–47, 157–58, 197, 207
    with 24P high-definition video, 77, 152–56, 184
    for *Twin Falls Idaho,* 149–52
Canada, location rebates and, 169
Canal+, 75–76
Canonero, Milena, 94

Cassavetes, John, 66
cast and casting, 105–21
 auditions in, 115, 116–17
 breaking down the script for, 99–102, 115–16
 casting directors in, 108–9
 determining actor's worth in, 107–8
 for *Jackpot*, 12, 77, 115, 183–85
 meeting at talent agency in, 117–18
 for *Northfork*, 84, 105–7, 108–9, 112–15, 118–21, 185–88, 189
 SAG (Screen Actors Guild) contracts for, 98–99, 169
 scheduling actors in, 112, 119–21
 talent agencies in, 12, 110, 112–13, 115, 117–18
 for *Twin Falls Idaho*, 15, 17, 20, 25, 73, 106, 107–8, 110–12, 118, 182–83
 written offers in, 108–9
cast-contingent productions, 105
casting director, 108–9
Casualties (film), 68
catering, 100, 161, 170–71
CGI (computer-generated imagery), 20, 58, 59, 139, 199–200
character arc, 49–50
character development
 methods of, 36–37
 in screenplay, 44–46
cheap mainstream, 9–10
Chelsea Girls (film), 208
Chinatown (film), 4
CinemaScope, 157
cinematographer, 15–16, 94, 147–52
Cirque du Soleil, 72
Cline, Patsy, 222
close-miked, 236
close-up shots, 206–7
Coffing, Andrew, 17, 22, 24, 120–21, 167
collaboration
 with composers, 217–19
 between sound supervisor and production recordist, 229

color, 125–29
 for *Jackpot*, 128–29
 for *Northfork*, 126, 128, 134–41, 157–59, 176–77, 178
 for *Twin Falls Idaho*, 126, 127–28, 149–52
color grading, 196–98
color saturation, 151–52, 157–58, 197
color timing, 196–98
composer, 217–19, 233
composite print, 196
computers
 CGI (computer-generated imagery), 20, 58, 59, 139, 199–200
 for design, 62–63
 for scheduling, 99–101
 for screenwriting, 40–42
 in sound recording, 229
 see also software
construction, for *Northfork*, 131–33
co-producer, 163–64
costume design, 134–37
 for *Jackpot*, 137
 for *Northfork*, 138–41
 for *Twin Falls Idaho*, 137
costume designer, 21, 94, 135–41
counterprogramming, 245
coverage
 scene, 180–81
 script, 57–58
creative control
 in independent films, 7–13
 and *Jackpot*, 12–13
 and *Twin Falls Idaho*, 10–11, 12–13, 25, 73
credit-card financing, 87, 121, 166
credits, producing, 121, 162–65
crew
 catering and, 100, 161, 170–71
 listening to, 190–91
 for *Northfork*, 75–76
 pay for, 95–97, 172–73
 in preproduction, 93–98

size of, 94–95
for *Twin Falls Idaho* (film), 15–16, 17, 21–24,
    61–62
unions and, 95–97
cut, 46, 206–7
cut film, 198

dailies, 195, 204–5
Daisy Miller (film), 253
Daniel, Jonathan, 223–24
DAT recorder, 229
Davis, Mac, 224
Day Out of Days report, 99–102
Deauville Film Festival, 75
Declaration of Independence, U.S., ix–x
Dedolights, 154–56
deliverables, 250–51
Deluxe Laboratories, 195
desaturation, 150–52, 158
details, in screenplay, 51
development, 262
dialogue
    dialogue track, 227, 231–32, 233–34, 236–39
    method for developing, 35
    in screenplay, 35, 44–46
diffusion filtration, 158
digital intermediate, 196–97, 198
directing, 175–91
    of actors, 182–89
    coverage of scene in, 180–81
    dream shot in, 176
    final take in, 189–90
    first-time directors and, 180–82
    of *Jackpot*, 183–85
    listening in, 190–91
    of *Northfork*, 176–77, 178, 186–90
    open directing assignment, 264
    of *Twin Falls Idaho*, 178, 179, 181–83
    vision in, 176–80
director of photography (DP), 21–22, 95,
    147–49

director's cut, 207–8
Directors Guild of America, 67, 97
Disney, 8
dissolve, 46, 206–7, 211
distribution, 241–57
    alternate, 252–54
    deliverables in, 250–51
    end of studio system in, 243
    festivals and, 8–11, 67, 70, 75, 114, 208, 247,
        250–51, 254–57, 259–60
    foreign, 74, 82, 254
    for *Jackpot*, 77–78, 241
    negative pickup, 80–81, 249–52
    for *Northfork*, 241–46, 248–50, 253–54
    power of, 248
    press tours in, 241–46, 248–50, 253–54
    release types in, 246–47
    selling independent films, 254–56
    television advertising in, 253
    for *Twin Falls Idaho*, 139, 241, 251, 254–57
distributor's advance, 80
dream shots, 176
DreamWorks, 8, 145–46
dumb money, 81–83
dupe elements, 157–58
dupe negative, 197
DVD distribution, 253–54

early assembly, 206
Eastwood, Clint, 253
edgy, 35
editing. *see* film editing
editor
    role of, 204
    routine for, 204–8
    sound, 204, 207, 237–38
    see also film editing
Edwards, Anthony, 84, 117–18
EFILM, 153
8 1/2 (film), 47–48
ENR process, 198

"Escape" (song), 225
executive producers, 81–87, 121, 163
exit strategy, 86
Eyes Wide Shut (film), 268

fade-in, 47
fade-out, 47
Farnes, Duel, 189
Federal Trade Commission (FTC), 243
Fellini, Federico, 47–48
festivals, 8–11, 250–51
    Deauville Film Festival, 75
    Directors Guild of America, 67
    Los Angeles Film Festival, 247
    New Directors/New Films, 259–60
    Seattle International Film Festival, 114
    Sundance Film Festival, 8, 11, 70, 208, 210, 251, 254–57
field recordings, 235–36
film editing, 203–13
    dailies in, 195, 204–5
    first cut in, 205
    in independent film, 210–13
    for *Jackpot*, 211–12
    for *Northfork*, 212–13
    pre-editing, 180–81, 203–4
    reel breaks, 209–10
    routine for editor, 204–8
    sound and, 204–7, 237–38
    temp track in, 207
    for *Twin Falls Idaho*, 10–11, 203–4, 206–9
    types of shots and, 206–7
film labs, 195–96
Filmmaker magazine, 260–61
film stock, 20, 59
filter, 154, 158
Final Cut, 205
final mix, 234
final print, 195
final take, 189–90

financing, 65–87
    accredited investors and, 78–79
    of *Bajo del Perro*, 67–68, 72, 216–17
    bank loans in, 80–81
    Blue Sky laws and, 78–79
    for cast-contingent productions, 105
    credit cards in, 87, 121, 166
    dumb money in, 81–83
    exit strategy in, 86
    foreign financiers and, 107–8
    friends and, 72–78, 216
    of *Jackpot*, 77–78
    limited liability companies (LLCs) in, 78–80
    limited partnerships (LPs) in, 78
    local contacts and, 67–74
    of *Northfork*, 67–68, 75–76, 81–87, 121
    persistence and, 65–67
    personal guaranteed loans in, 162
    preproduction and, 90–91
    recouped investment, 80
    smart money in, 83–87
    of *Twin Falls Idaho*, 65–67, 71–74
    verbal versus written agreements in, 70–72
Fincher, David, 150
FIND (Film Independent), 247
first assistant cameraman (AC), 21
first assistant director, 17, 100–102
first cut, 205
first-time actors, 189
first-time directors, 180–82
flashing the negatives, 150–51, 158
focal length, 147
focus puller, 21
Foley, 233, 235–36
Foley artist, 233
foreign distribution, 74, 82, 254
foreign film sales agent, 73
foreign financiers, 107–8
foreign presales, 74
Fort Peck Dam (Montana), 128, 187
Foster, Ben, 139, 167

FotoKem, 195
four-wall distribution, 252–53
four-wall drama, 125
FOX, 171–72
framing, 179
Frank, Robert, 157
French New Wave, 10, 182, 211
friends, financing and, 72–78, 216
Frizell, Lefty, 222
Fujifilm, 59, 197
Full Metal Jacket (film), 267

gaffer, 16, 20
Geffen, David, 145–46
general partner (GP), 78–79
Ghosts of Mississippi (film), 113
Glicker, Daniel, 94–95, 109, 138–39
Good Morning Airzona (TV program), 249
Good Thief, The (film), 113
"Grand Tour" (song), 212, 222, 224
green-lit, 48–49
Green Mile, The (film), 235
Gries, Jon, 12, 67–68, 77, 110, 154, 166, 171,
    183–85, 224–25
grip, 16

hairstyling, 133–34
Hannah, Daryl, 84, 85, 105, 138–39, 245
hard cut, 46
hard-disc recorder, 229
Harrison, Jay, 110
headshots, 115
Hicks, Michele, 15, 208, 260
high-definition video, 77, 152–56, 184
HMI PARs, 154–56
Hollywood production companies, 7, 8
Hollywood studios, 7
    beginning of studio system, 94
    business affairs, 75
    defined, 8
    editing process in, 211
    end of studio system, 243
    independent film distribution versus, 243–44
    list of studios, 8
    protagonist and, 48–49
    test marketing and, 7–9, 211
    three-act standard in, 47–48
Holmes, Rupert, 225
Hopper, Edward, 149
Hulk (film), 119–21
Hungry Horse Dam (Montana), 32

IATSE (International Alliance of Theatrical Stage
    Employees), 96
icing, 187
ICM, 110, 112–13
IFP (Independent Film Project), 246
incident light meter, 144
independent films
    as brands, 9–10
    characteristics of, 7–13
    cheap mainstream and, 9–10
    creative control and, 7–13
    editors of, 210–13
    festivals for, 8–11, 67, 70, 75, 114, 208, 210, 247,
        250–51, 254–57, 259–60
    future of, 265
    Hollywood studio model versus, 243–44
    micro-studios and, 7, 8, 11–13
    as movement, 7–9, 66
    private equity and, 8
    and San Fernando ending, 13
    transition into studios and, 263–65
Independent Spirit Awards, 210, 247
insert shots, 159
intercut, 208
International Brotherhood of Teamsters,
    96–97
internegative (IN), 197
Internet
    distribution via, 253
    research and, 38

interpositive (IP), 197
Investigating Sex (film), 114

Jackpot (film)
  budget for, 12
  camera work for, 152–56, 184
  cast and casting for, 12, 77, 115, 183–85
  characters in, 50
  color palette for, 128–29
  costume design for, 137
  creative control and, 12–13
  dialogue in, 44
  directing, 183–85
  distribution, 77–78, 241
  editing, 211–12
  equipment decisions in, 95
  financing of, 77–78
  music for, 77, 211–12, 222, 223–24
  New American Cinema Award, 114
  postproduction for, 194, 195, 199
  preproduction for, 95, 223–24
  press tour, 241
  production design for, 128–29, 137
  production schedule for, 77–78
  protagonist in, 49
  release of, 77–78
  screenings of, 113
  screenplay, 42, 44, 49, 50
  sound for, 238
  title sequences for, 199
Jaws (film), 37
Jones, George, 212, 222, 224
Jordan, Neil, 113
jump cuts, 211–12

Katzenberg, Jeffrey, 145–46, 208–9
Kilmer, Val, 67–68
King, Todd, 194
Kino Flos, 154–56
Knievel, Evel, 89–90
Kodachrome 64, 152
Kodak, 59, 197

Kubrick, Stanley, 267–70
Kubrick, Vivian, 267–70

Lacy Stages, 15–16
"Lady" (song), 224–25
Lakeshore, 71–72
Laughlin, Tom, 253
Legends of the Fall (film), 169
Leibovitz, Annie, 143–46
Leiner, Dylan, 254–56, 257
Leone, Sergio, 219
Life magazine, cover story on dams, 38, 128
lighting package, 154–56
light meters, 144
limited liability company (LLC), 78–80
limited partnership (LP), 78
limited release, 246–47
line producer, 17, 57, 90–97, 164, 222
loans
  bank, 80–81
  credit cards and, 87, 121, 166
  personal guaranteed, 162
location manager, 97
location rebates, 169
locked picture, 11, 208
loop group, 231–32
Los Angeles Film Festival, 247
losing your lines, 190
Lucas, George, 77

magazines, 21
makeup, 133–34
makeup artist, 133–34
Maslin, Janet, 259–60
master use license, 224
match cut, 47
Matthewman, Stuart, 210, 215–21, 267–68
Mayersohn, Paul, 85–86
Mead, Abigail (Vivian Kubrick), 267–70
medium shots, 206–7
MGM, 8

micro-studio, 7
  defined, 8
  independent film and, 11–13
Miles, Henry, 94
Miramax, 8
mixer, 228
mixing facility, 201
mix venue, 228
Morricone, Ennio, 218, 219
Morris, Garrett, 12, 77, 110, 183–85, 238
Movie Magic Scheduling, 99–100, 101
Mullen, David, 15–16, 22, 58, 94, 147–48, 149–57
Munch, Edvard, 149
music, 215–25
  adjusting score length, 205–6
  collaborating with composers, 217–19
  for *Jackpot*, 77, 211–12, 222, 223–24
  less-is-more philosophy for, 220
  licensing recorded, 77, 212, 219, 222–25
  low-budget scores, 218, 220–21
  for *Northfork*, 217–19, 220, 221, 222
  with reel breaks, 210
  for *Twin Falls Idaho*, 219, 221, 222
  see also sound
music supervisor, 222–23

Nagra, 229
NBC, 171–72
ND gel, 155–56
negative film, 21
negative pickup, 80–81, 249–52
New American Cinema Award, for *Jackpot*, 114
New Directors/New Films (New York City), 259–60
New Line Cinema, 261–63
Newman, Paul, 106
New Wave, 10, 182, 211
New York Philharmonic, 221
New York Times, 259–60
Nicolay, Matt, 236–39
Nolte, Nick, 105, 109, 113–15, 119–21, 190, 238, 245–46

Northfork (film)
  budget for, 33, 56–57, 106, 168–71
  camera work for, 148, 157–59
  cast and casting for, 84, 105–7, 108–9, 112–15, 118–21, 185–88, 189
  characters in, 50
  color palette for, 126, 128, 134–41, 157–59, 176–77, 178
  construction for, 131–33
  costume design for, 138–41
  crew for, 75–76
  directing, 176–77, 178, 186–90
  distribution, 241–46, 248–50, 253–54
  editing, 212–13
  equipment decisions in, 95
  financial difficulties of, 161–62, 165–73, 194
  financing of, 67–68, 75–76, 81–87, 121
  idea for, 31–32
  location decision for, 168–71
  music for, 217–19, 220, 221, 222
  postproduction for, 81, 194, 195, 198–200
  preproduction for, 94–95, 168–71
  press tour, 241–46, 248–50, 253–54
  production design for, 126, 128, 131–33, 134, 138–41
  protagonist in, 48
  research for, 38–39
  scene description in, 43–44
  scene heading from, 42–43
  screenplay, 2, 31–33, 38–39, 40, 42–43, 47, 48, 50, 51–52, 68, 114
  sets for, 131–33, 172
  sound for, 235–36, 238
  story structure of, 40
  title sequences for, 198–99
  transitions in, 47
  vision for, 176–77

Oldman, Gary, 108–9
Once Upon a Time in America (film), 186, 219
one light printing, 197
one sheet, 244

one take (oner), 178

open directing assignment, 264

open writing assignment, 261–63

optical effects, 208

optical printer, 157

opticals, 198–99

options, 70–72

OST (original soundtrack) rights, 219

overdubbing, 208

Overton, Rick, 115

Owen, Bic, 137

Panaflasher, 150–51, 158

Panavision, 59, 158

P&A (prints and advertising), 251–52

Paramount Classics, 81, 249–52

Paramount Consent Decree, 243

Paramount Studios, 8, 153, 243

Pearl Arts & Crafts, 62

Peck, Gregory, 106–7

personal guaranteed loans, 162

Pierce, Webb, 222

pitching, 31

platform release, 246

playback, 208

plumbing project, and *Twin Falls Idaho*, 2–4

Polanski, Roman, 4

postproduction, 77, 193–201

  answer prints in, 196–98

  CGI (computer-generated imagery) in, 199–200

  importance of, 193–94

  for *Jackpot*, 194, 195, 199

  length of, 193

  for *Northfork*, 81, 194, 195, 198–200

  opticals in, 198–99

  raising funds for, 81

  schedule for, 201

  sound in, 196, 200–201, 204–7, 230–34, 235, 238

  for *Twin Falls Idaho*, 194, 195–96, 198–99, 200, 267–68

postproduction supervisor (PPS), 194–96

  role of, 194–95

  schedule for postproduction, 201

  selecting, 195

predubbing, 234

pre-editing, 180–81, 203–4

preproduction, 89–103

  breaking down the script, 99–102, 115–16

  budget in, 93

  costume design in, 135–36

  crew in, 93–98

  defined, 90

  for *Jackpot*, 95, 223–24

  line producer in, 90–97

  music in, 224

  for *Northfork*, 94–95, 168–71

  production boards in, 100, 102–3

  production manager in, 91–98

  research in, 58–60

  SAG contracts in, 98–99, 169

  shooting schedule in, 90, 102

  sound in, 228

  steps in, 92–93

  for *Twin Falls Idaho*, 58–60

  vision in, 177–78

preselling foreign, 74

presentation, screenplay, 31–32, 60–63

press tours

  Jackpot, 241

  Northfork, 241–46, 248–50, 253–54

  Twin Falls Idaho, 139, 241, 251

Pretender, The (TV program), 171

private equity, 8

producer's agreement, 81–87

producing, 161–73

  financial problems during, 161–62, 165–73

  giving credit for, 121, 162–65

  role of producer in, 162

  titles in, 162–65

production boards, 100, 101, 103

production coordinator, 91, 92

production design, 123–41
    art director in, 124
    color in, 125–29
    construction in, 131–33
    costume design in, 21, 94, 134–41
    defined, 123–24
    for *Jackpot*, 128–29, 137
    makeup and hair in, 133–34
    makeup artist in, 133–34
    for *Northfork*, 126, 128, 130–33, 134, 138–41
    production designer and, 95, 123–25,
        131–33
    prop master in, 125
    research and, 124
    script supervisor in, 136
    set decorator in, 125
    set designer in, 124–25
    show versus tell and, 130–31
    for *Twin Falls Idaho*, 126, 127–28, 129–30, 133–34,
        137, 139
    visual screenplay and, 129–30
production manager, 57, 91
    described, 91–92
    in preproduction, 91–98
production recordist, 228–30, 235–39
ProMist diffusion filtration, 158
prop master, 125
protagonist, 48–49
Psycho (film), 37

rack focus, 21
raw stock film, 20
readings, 117–18
Real Genius (film), 67–68
recans, 20
recouped investment, 80
reel breaks, 209–10
Regulation D, 78
research
    importance of, 29, 37–39
    Internet and, 38

for *Northfork*, 38–39
preproduction, 58–60
for production design, 124
for screenplay, 17, 20, 29, 37–39
for *Twin Falls Idaho*, 17, 20, 39
review-proof films, 243
rewriting, 50–53
Richie, Lionel, 224
Rogers, Kenny, 224
Ronson, Rena, 68–72, 73–74, 257
room tones, 229–30
rough assembly, 205
Royal Court of Thailand, 219
Rudolph, Alan, 114

Sachs, Robin, 109, 138
SAG (Screen Actors Guild) contracts, 98, 169
San Fernando ending, 13, 264–65
saturation release, 247
scene
    acts in, 47–48
    coverage of, 180–81
    pre-editing, 180–81
    in screenplay, 42
scene description, in screenplay, 43–44
scene heading, in screenplay, 42–43
scheduling
    of actors, 112, 119–21
    computers in, 99–102
    postproduction, 201
    production, 15, 24–25, 77–78, 182
    shooting schedule, 17, 24–25, 91, 99–102
Schwartzman, Paul, 51, 208
Schweickert, Joyce, 74
scope, 157
scouting, 20
screenplay, 27–53
    books on writing, 30–31
    budget considerations in, 32–33
    character development in, 36–37
    commitment to writing, 28–30

screenplay (*continued*)
  detail in, 51
  dialogue in, 35, 44–46
  elements of, 42–50
  ideas for, 30–32
  interpreting, 177
  for *Jackpot*, 42, 44, 49, 50
  length of, 34–35
  for *Northfork*, 31–33, 38–39, 40, 42–43, 47, 48, 50, 51–52, 68, 114
  open writing assignment, 261–63
  pitching, 31
  presentation of, 31–32, 60–63
  research and, 17, 20, 29, 37–39
  rewriting, 50–53
  software for writing, 40–42
  storyboarding, 46, 58, 148–49, 182
  story structure of, 39–40
  style and, 34–35
  time needed to write, 29
  for *Twin Falls Idaho*, 2, 28, 33, 35, 36–37, 39, 40, 48, 50, 52–53, 57–58, 68–71, 236
  visual, 129–30
script
  breaking down the script, 99–102, 115–16
  in screenplay presentation, 60–63
  script coverage, 57–58
script supervision, 136
Seattle International Film Festival, 114
second assistant cameraman, 21
second assistant director, 17
seconds, 25
second unit, 158–59
Securities and Exchange Commission (SEC), 78
sequencing, 205–6
set costumer, 137
set decorator, 125
set designer, 124–26
sets
  constructing, 131–33
  for *Northfork*, 131–33, 170

soundstages and, 15–16
  for *Twin Falls Idaho*, 16, 17, 33, 126, 127–28, 179–80
setups, 148, 156, 184
Seven (film), 150
sharing storyboards, 182
Sheldon, Christopher, 235
Sheldon, Jonathan, 112
shooting schedule, 17, 24–25, 91, 99–102
shot sequences, 205–6
show prints, 197
sidelines, 189
sides, 16, 17
Sim Video, 153
16 mm filmmaking, 146–47, 239
skip-bleach process, 149–50, 196
slate, 21, 22, 23–24
Sling Blade (film), 48
smart money, 83–87
SMPTE time code, 205
software
  design, 62–63
  editing, 205
  movie scheduling, 99–102
  screenwriting, 40–42
song licensing, 77, 212, 219, 222–25
Sony, 8
Sony Pictures Classics, 75, 77–78, 243–44, 251, 254–56
sound, 227–39
  audio design, 227
  budget for, 230
  in composite print, 196
  dialogue track, 227, 231–32, 233–34, 236–39
  elements of, 231–34
  for *Jackpot*, 238
  for *Northfork*, 235–36, 238
  in postproduction, 196, 200–201, 204–7, 230–34, 235, 238
  in preproduction, 228
  production recordist and, 228–30, 235–39
  with reel breaks, 210

sound supervisor and, 228–33, 237–38
temp track, 207
for *Twin Falls Idaho,* 234, 236
see also music
sound design, 232, 234
sound editor, 204, 207, 237–38
sound effects, 232, 233
sound effects supervisor, 201
sound houses, 200
sound library, 232
sound mixer, 24, 201, 237
sound recordist, 228–30, 235–39
sound speed, 23–24
soundstage, 15–16
Sound Storm, 200
sound supervisor, 228–33, 237–38
Spielberg, Steven, 145–46
splinter unit, 159
split screen, 206–7, 208
spotting session, 231, 233
standard-definition interlaced-scan video, 153
Staples, 62
Star Wars: Episode II (film), 77
Stewart, Potter, 9
storyboards, 46, 58, 148–49, 182
story structure, 39–40
Strettell, Jo, 133–34
style, writing, 34–35
Sundance Film Festival, 8, 11, 70, 208, 210, 251,
    254–57
super 8 filmmaking, 144–48, 152, 207, 239
superimposition, 206–7, 212
sync effects, 229–30
synchronization right, 224
synthesizers, 221

talent agencies, 12, 110, 112–13, 115, 117–18
Technicolor, 195
tech scouting, 20
television advertising, 253
temp score, 218

temp track, 207
test marketing
    defined, 9
    studio use of, 7–9, 211
    for *Twin Falls Idaho,* 10–11
35 mm filmmaking, 146–47, 157–58, 197, 207
Thornton, Billy Bob, 48
three-act standard, 47–48
title sequences, 198–99
Torok, Paul, 72–74
torque motor, 145
Touchstone, 261–63
Transatlantic, 68, 70–71
transitions, in screenplay, 46–47
transportation coordinator, 97
trimming, 205
Tromans, Matt, 113–14, 114–15, 119–21
Trombetta, Leo, 204, 206–9
Tunnicliffe, Gary, 109, 139–41
20th Century Fox, 8
24P high-definition video, 77, 152–56, 184
Twin Falls Idaho (film)
    budget for, 10, 20, 24–25, 33, 55–56, 74, 110
    camera work for, 149–52
    cast and casting for, 15, 17, 20, 25, 73, 106,
        107–8, 110–12, 118, 182–83
    characters in, 50
    color palette for, 126, 127–28, 149–52
    costume design for, 137
    creative control and, 10–11, 12–13, 25, 73
    crew for, 15–16, 17, 21–24, 61–62
    cult following for, 244
    decision to make, 1–5
    directing, 178, 179, 181–83
    distribution, 241, 251, 254–57
    editing, 10–11, 203–4, 206–9
    financing of, 65–67, 71–74
    inspiration for, 36–37
    music for, 219, 221, 222
    at New Directors/New Films (New York City),
        259–60

Twin Falls Idaho (film) (*continued*)
  New York Times review of, 259–60
  plumbing project and, 2–4
  positive responses to, 75
  postproduction for, 194, 195–96, 198–99, 200,
    267–68
  premise of, 28, 35
  preproduction for, 58–60
  press tour, 241, 251
  production design for, 126, 127–28, 129–30,
    133–34, 137, 139
  production schedule for, 15, 24–25, 182
  protagonist in, 48
  release of, 75, 259–60
  research for, 17, 20, 39
  rewriting, 52–53
  sale to Sony Pictures Classics, 254–56
  screenings of, 10–11, 208–9
  screenplay, 2, 28, 33, 35, 36–37, 39, 40, 48, 50,
    52–53, 57–58, 68–71, 236
  screenplay presentation for, 60–63
  script coverage and, 57–58
  sets for, 16, 17, 33, 126, 127–28, 179–80
  shooting, 4, 15–25, 183
  Siamese twin illusion in, 20–21, 23–25, 37,
    58–59
  sound for, 234, 236
  soundstage for, 15–16
  story structure of, 40
  studio pricing of, 4, 58
  test marketing for, 10–11
  title sequences for, 198–99
  vision for, 178–79

unions
  actor, 98–99, 169
  crew, 95–97
  director, 97
  writer, 97, 261–63

unit production manager (UPM), 57, 91
  described, 91–92
  in preproduction, 91–98
Universal, 8
U.S. v. Paramount Pictures et al., 243

Vermeer, 127–28, 149
videotape
  dailies on, 195, 204–5
  high-definition, 77, 152–56, 184
  standard-definition interlaced-scan, 153
View-Master, 199
vision, 176–80
  communicating, 178–79
  importance of, 176–79
  interpreting screenplay in, 177
  losing, 179–80
visual screenplay, 129–30

wardrobe assistant, 137
wardrobe supervisor, 136–37
Warhol, Andy, 128–30, 208
Warner Brothers, 8, 253, 264–65
Warren, Leslie Ann, 183
"What if?" questions, 30
wide shots, 206–7
wild lines, 229–30
William Morris, 110, 257
Willow Creek Reservoir, 132
Woodlawn, Holly, 208
Woods, James, 84, 105, 109, 112–13, 118–21, 130,
    132, 165–66, 185–88, 190, 245–46
wrapping, 151–52
Writers Guild of America (WGA), 97, 261–63
writing. *see* screenplay
written offers
  in casting process, 108–9
  in financing process, 70–72
Wyeth, Andrew, 157

Photo Credits

pages ii, 110, 223, 258: Sébastien Raymond; pages viii, 26, 54, 61, 64, 69, 76, 90, 96, 104, 116, 127, 132, 138, 139, 140, 142, 145, 151, 160, 174, 186, 192, 199, 202, 212, 225, 226, 228, 237, 263, 266: Andre Blaise; pages xiv, 6: David Mullen; page 14: Paul Torok; pages 22, 230: Maury Duchamp; pages 24, 45, 128, 155, 214: Jo Strettell; page 88: Adam Rehmeier; pages 101, 184, 211, 240: Michael Polish; page 122: Delbert Polish; page 168: Mark Polish; page 181: Eli Akira Kaufman